THE DISRUPTER

Gautam Chikermane is a writer, tracking the unholy trinity of money, power and faith. He is currently working on a subaltern trilogy based on the Mahabharata. As a journalist, he has held leadership positions in some of India's largest newspapers and magazines, including *Hindustan Times*, *The Indian Express* and Outlook Group. A keen participant in non-profits, he is a director at CARE India and has served three terms as director (and once as vice-chairman) at Financial Planning Standards Board India. His body lives in Delhi, his soul in Pondicherry. You may follow him on Twitter at @gchikermane.

Soma Banerjee, in her first innings of twenty-three years, worked as a journalist for *The Economic Times*, and chronicled politics and the energy sector. While she still feels the tug of that profession, she recently embarked on a second innings, heading the energy vertical of the Confederation of Indian Industry. Here, she participates in public policy by engaging with key stakeholders and trying to make energy a part of coffee-shop conversation. When she's not dealing with such weighty matters, she immerses herself in music and threatens to become serious about Hindustani classical practice.

THE DISRUPTER

ARVIND KEJRIWAL AND THE AUDACIOUS RISE OF THE AAM AADMI

Gautam Chikermane
with Soma Banerjee

RUPA

Published by
Rupa Publications India Pvt. Ltd 2014
7/16, Ansari Road, Daryaganj
New Delhi 110002

Sales centres:
Allahabad Bengaluru Chennai
Hyderabad Jaipur Kathmandu
Kolkata Mumbai

Copyright © Gautam Chikermane

All rights reserved.
No part of this publication may be reproduced, transmitted,
or stored in a retrieval system, in any form or by any means,
electronic, mechanical, photocopying, recording or otherwise,
without the prior permission of the publisher.

The views and opinions expressed in this book are the author's own and
the facts are as reported by him/her which have been verified to the extent
possible, and the publishers are not in any way liable for the same.

ISBN: 978-81-291-3133-1

First impression 2014

10 9 8 7 6 5 4 3 2 1

The moral right of the authors has been asserted.

Printed and bound at Thomson Press India Ltd., Faridabad

This book is sold subject to the condition that it shall not,
by way of trade or otherwise, be lent, resold, hired out, or otherwise
circulated, without the publisher's prior consent, in any form of binding or
cover other than that in which it is published.

For the aam aadmi—your time is now.

CONTENTS

Introduction:
Battle of Varanasi ix

Prologue:
Rise of Audacity xiii

1
Streets of Disruption 1

2
Breakdown of Governance 27

3
Alchemy of Power 44

4
Corruption of Freedom 65

5
Politics of Entrepreneurship 90

6
Challenge of Party 113

7
Anatomy of Success 135

8
Broom of Ambition 164

9
Currencies of Change 193

10
Hand of God 212

Epilogue:
Consolidation of Audacity 222

INTRODUCTION: BATTLE OF VARANASI

On Monday, 12 May 2014, Varanasi will choose. And forty-nine days before the world's oldest living city, in India's most populated state of Uttar Pradesh, elects its Member of Parliament, its 36,82,194 people—approximately the number of citizens in Bosnia—are preparing for a never-seen-before battle. Stretched across 1,535 square kilometres, this holy city of Hindus—referred to as the 'seat of learning' in the *Rig Veda* some four thousand years ago or as the 'city of Shiva' in the *Skanda Purana*—is going to be drawn into a clash of opposing ideological identities. The stakes are high.

Standing before the voters are two faces, holding two different philosophical and political positions, seeking votes from an area steeped in history, an area viewed as the soul of the land. On one side, travelling 1,407 kilometres from Ahmedabad, stands Gujarat Chief Minister and Bharatiya Janata Party's (BJP) prime ministerial candidate Narendra Modi. As a challenger to incumbent Congress Vice-President Rahul Gandhi, he draws his legitimacy here from his roots in the Hindu right-wing Rashtriya Swayamsevak Sangh (RSS). With this crutch, Modi hopes to establish first himself and then his party in this constituency. With his Hindu moorings clear and secure, the message on display is governance and growth—ideas that a slowing economy, suffering from political and bureaucratic somnolence, desperately needs.

But it is the second face that will be especially visible in this book. In a brazen and audacious bid to challenge the challenger, India's most disruptive leader, Arvind Kejriwal has travelled 816 kilometres from Delhi to Varanasi—a David standing before a Goliath. Even though this will be the first general election he will fight, the former forty-nine-day chief minister of Delhi remains his accusing, noisy best. No religious symbolism for him, no experience in governance, no promises of economic growth. With his renowned anti-corruption stance, that he says will deliver everything any citizen could want or need, political entrepreneur Arvind Kejriwal is wreaking disruption in the traditional playground of politics, changing the system, moulding it and forcing his opponents to follow.

Irrespective of who wins Elections 2014, in Varanasi in particular and in India in general, the real story lies beyond incumbent Rahul Gandhi, challenger Narendra Modi and disrupter Arvind Kejriwal. It lies in the hopes and aspirations of a new player—the aam aadmi, the common man, who is here to stay and steer the country's political destiny. Whichever political coalition comes to power, the aam aadmi's voice will reverberate within and outside the walls of Parliament. Whosoever becomes the prime minister, it will be impossible for him to ignore the manifesto of change, now bubbling over with confidence and self-assurance. For a long time, politics has been conventional; now, disruption is the new narrative. The aam aadmi will steer the ideas of all three political players—he will propel them to make promises; he will force them to realign their politics; he will push them to reassess their governance models, so these meet modern-day aspirations; he will force a transformation that will do justice to India in the twenty-first century.

This disruption—in the way politics is perceived, governance is dispensed and privileges are secured—has a new face, Arvind Kejriwal, and his sixteen-month-old Aam Aadmi Party (AAP).

As is evident from the success of AAP in the December 2013 Delhi state elections, there is simmering anger among Indians, now being expressed in the polling booth. AAP has articulated these rumblings and made anger a force that it calls 'alternative politics'. The two large and traditional parties, the governing coalition at the Centre, incumbent Congress, and challenger BJP, are introspecting and adapting, so they can confront this rising new and audacious force.

Nobody expected AAP to win twenty-eight out of the seventy assembly seats in the Delhi elections, the second-highest after BJP's thirty-two; this all but decimated Congress that had been governing the capital of India for the past fifteen years, and that secured merely eight seats. The hugely-successful, three-time chief minister Sheila Dikshit, one of the most popular leaders the city has seen ever since it became a state in 1992, lost her prized seat. But more surprising was the unsolicited support Congress gave AAP, almost dragging it, kicking and screaming, to power. Overnight, former Income Tax Commissioner Arvind Kejriwal, who had turned into an anti-corruption activist and had fought a long battle to bring an anti-corruption law, became the chief minister of Delhi. Only to resign in forty-nine days.

In these forty-nine tumultuous days, the AAP government changed the way the Indian electorate looked at governance. On one side was Arvind Kejriwal and his six-member cabinet, who carried protest politics into the government. On the other side was the traditional establishment, comprising the governing coalition Congress as well as the principal opposition party BJP, who were perplexed by the street antics of this political newbie. But outer manifestations aside, this babe in the vicious political woods has brought an irreversible change, by focusing unflinchingly on one issue: corruption. While anti-corruption remains its core, its other two fundamental ideas—decentralisation of decision-making and devolution of power, and the right to recall and reject candidates—fester, waiting for the right time to create their own disruption. In the process, Arvind Kejriwal has bound a large number of ordinary people, made them a cohesive force, given them a political voice, and unleashed them.

Chasing this phenomenon has not been easy. How, after all, do you keep track of a moving target? How do you evaluate and re-evaluate a change agent, who shifts from one disruptive tactic to another in a matter of days, if not hours? How do you sit back and analyse an event unfolding around you? How do you observe shifting shadows? How do you hold flowing water?

It is a challenge, but this book attempts to do just that. In the short space of five weeks, it has tried to first follow, then understand and analyse, and finally contextualise three ideas—one, Arvind Kejriwal and his unique brand of political entrepreneurship; two, the audacious rise of the aam aadmi on whose back this disrupter and his party rides; three, the new and unique phenomenon called disruption that's spreading its roots. Each of these ideas can be explored, layer by layer, and can offer intellectual challenges to the best of political analysts.

Moreover, each of these three ideas is changing, growing, getting more complex. This book, therefore, is only the first, not the last, word. The disruption we see will create new writers, new thinkers, new analysts who will dissect the changing political landscape. It will offer huge opportunities, and indeed encouragement, to future authors, who will widen the boundaries of thought, dig deeper than their predecessors. From Varanasi to Delhi, and beyond, they will trace the new, disruptive world order.

PROLOGUE: RISE OF AUDACITY

It wasn't audacity to begin with, says Ashutosh Dikshit, sipping coffee, as we assembled in his Alaknanda home in South Delhi after a Sunday meeting of Citizens' Alliance, a non-political, local neighbourhood movement, whose birth chart is linked to the rise of the biggest political phenomenon known to Indian politics since Independence—the Aam Aadmi Party (AAP). Chief Minister Arvind Kejriwal had formed the Delhi government thirteen days ago with the support of Congress. 'It just got built into an audacious force,' Ashutosh Dikshit says. 'When we started, the intention was not to be audacious, not to fight. We just wanted to…know.'

Around the same time that former civil servant and activist Arvind Kejriwal was building the foundations of what is now seen as an 'alternative politics' to Congress and Bhartiya Janata Party (BJP), this middle class neighbourhood was raising questions about how it was being misgoverned. The story of how Alaknanda's residents are fighting the government is not very different from other similar fights dotting India's corrupt landscape and whose cause AAP has taken up politically.

What makes the Alaknanda story stand out is that perhaps for the first time in recent history, a handful of educated and affluent urban citizens have felt so angry about an issue impacting their neighbourhood that they've attempted to uncover what's really going on. In the process, they've transformed into a community audacious enough to challenge the might of the Delhi government and India's largest company, Reliance Industries Ltd. What puts this fight in context is the coincidence that both the aam aadmi's fight with the Delhi government in Alaknanda and AAP's fight with the central government have pivoted around the same person—India's wealthiest man, Mukesh Ambani.

In less than a month from now, Arvind Kejriwal will file an audacious FIR (First Information Report) against Mukesh Ambani for allegedly conspiring with two central government ministers and a senior bureaucrat—former and current Petroleum Ministers Murli Deora and Veerappa Moily, and former Director General of Hydrocarbons V.K. Sibal—to inflate gas prices from the Krishna-Godavari basin, off the coast of Andhra Pradesh. Three days after filing the FIR, Arvind Kejriwal will go on to resign as chief minister and do what he does best: return to the streets to disrupt existing structures, adopt a moral highground, align himself with an anti-corruption mission, and offer an alternative politics to Indian voters for the forthcoming Lok Sabha polls, less than two months away.

The audacity of Citizens' Alliance, obviously, has been smaller, almost statistically insignificant compared to this larger political discourse happening in the capital. The foundations of its audacity were built around a 3.3-hectare tract of land in Alaknanda (about the size of four football fields) that had allegedly been earmarked for a 'community centre' and was instead being turned into a mega mall. The group of citizens, led by entrepreneur Ashutosh Dikshit, economist Laveesh Bhandari and lawyer Vivek Sharma, did their research and asked basic questions—why was a mall coming up here, why were permissions given, who gave the permissions?

'As we went along, more and more people from the neighbourhood began to join,' Ashutosh Dikshit says. 'The sheer size of the mall, the consumption that it would have, the amount of solid waste it would generate, the number of footfalls it would require to break even, the number of cars that would come in...all these would have turned our neighbourhood into a nightmare.' Small, insignificant issues, irrelevant to the larger politics of India, not worth reporting? Perhaps in the smooth, predictable, stable world of yesterday, issues like these got no hearing in the corridors of power, no mind-space in the larger administration, no place in public consciousness, definitely none in traditional media.

Today, one man is changing all that and, with it, shaking the edifices of extant power structures, its decaying institutions, in a system that's so closely intertwined that if you pull out one strand, the entire network collapses. For right or wrong, Arvind Kejriwal needs to be credited with being the focal point, the face that's driving disruption in almost every aspect of governance today. Whether disruption is the way forward or not is a debate we explore later in the book.

Behind Arvind Kejriwal and AAP though, there is a larger force in whose hands the two are little more than instruments of change. This is the ongoing transformation of the timid common man to an audacious aam aadmi. Alaknanda, a cluster of upscale residential societies and seven schools, within a 1.5 square kilometre area, adjoining two other residential neighbourhoods, Chittaranjan Park and Greater Kailash II, is one such tiny force.

Like its size, Alaknanda's issues too are tiny. 'When the movement started, people around us said it did not concern them,' says Madhulika Chatterjee, a resident of Chittaranjan Park. 'But there are only two roads leading into Alaknanda, one from Chittaranjan Park and the other from Greater Kailash II. Every day, during office and school hours, we have a tremendous traffic problem. This will only increase once the mall comes up.' Compared to the larger problems of India such as poverty, inequality, gender rights, justice and so on, Alaknanda's concerns pale into insignificance. But the spirit driving the neighbourhood's political initiative binds it to other audacious aam aadmis, to those who are victims of class and caste barriers.

Like all things big, it takes something very small to ignite the fire. In the case of Alaknanda, it was a simple observation. The land that had been left open for years together got barricaded overnight. 'We thought it belonged to the government and the government was trying to safeguard its own property,' says Ashutosh Dikshit. Later, when the first hints of information began to flow in, residents realised that it was indeed a mega mall that was going to come up in the middle of the neighbourhood. When this information began to go public, reactions started trickling in and propelled the aam aadmi into becoming a cohesive force.

Unlike most movements of audacity and struggle that begin with a trigger—usually violent—the Alaknanda initiative settled on the community by chance and has been remarkably peaceful. 'Somebody said, "A mall is coming up". I didn't believe it. Then I went online and checked. And there was one article saying that a mega mall was going to be built in Alaknanda,' says Ashutosh Dikshit. 'Reliance Industries plans to build a flagship shopping mall in South Delhi—a part of a plan to invest heavily in real estate to complement its retail business,' a 29 August 2012 story in *The Economic Times* stated.

On the same day, Arvind Kejriwal raised the question of corruption in both Congress and BJP. 'There is no difference between Congress and BJP as far as corruption is concerned, and the two are playing out a charade these days in Parliament on the Coalgate issue,' Arvind Kejriwal told reporters. Two days earlier, along with hundreds of supporters, he had marched to the residences of Prime Minister Manmohan Singh, Congress President Sonia Gandhi and BJP President Rajnath Singh, protesting against the allegedly wrongful allocations of coal mines.

Around fourteen kilometres away, in Alaknanda, a group of shocked residents began to investigate the threat of the mega mall. They went to the ministry, the state-level impact assessment authority, and finally found the document granting permission to the mega mall on the pollution control site. But walking the streets and surfing the net can only get you so far. They needed another form of protest, something more effective, something legally tenable, something far more tangible than a news report or an off-the-record discussion with officials.

They gravitated towards a tool now rearing its head and empowering India's citizens like no other tool has so far—the Right to Information (RTI), a law that entitles a citizen to seek and get information from the government. Along with Aruna Roy and other social activists, Arvind Kejriwal had campaigned to get Parliament to pass this law in 2005, for which he won the Ramon Magsaysay Award. The law mandates a timely response to citizen requests for government information, just the kind of tool activists from Alaknanda needed to fuel their cause.

They sought information about the project from the various bodies that oversee urban development in Delhi and that were involved in giving this mega mall the go-ahead: Delhi Development Authority (DDA), Department of Environment, State Level Environmental Impact Assessment Authority, Delhi Jal Board, Delhi Traffic Police, Delhi Urban Art Commission. The fact that so many bodies were involved in giving clearances to a single project highlighted the impediments stalling the smooth functioning of businesses. It also highlighted the hurdles that citizens routinely encountered while questioning projects and seeking information. In the case of the residents, however, it seems that the presence of multiple bodies helped—the several arms of the government could not keep tabs on what each arm was doing and, hence, some of the information the citizens were seeking slipped through.

On its part, although the RTI is a straightforward tool of information, it can, and often does, hurt public officials. So, fear stalked members of Citizens' Alliance while they were on their quest. 'We never attacked anybody,' Ashutosh Dikshit says 'There were times when we would get scared because people would tell us that we had taken on something huge and powerful interests could hurt us. And I completely admit, without a shadow of doubt, that there were times when we were scared.' Fortunately, he says, nobody said anything, much less harm the members in any way whatsoever.

'Someone told me that what I'm doing could be dangerous,' says Meena Gangahar, a doting grandmother living in M-Block, Greater Kailash II, who served two terms as its residents' association representative. 'I was asked, "Do you want to be Indira Gandhi?" But I'm a born fighter. My father taught me to always stand up and fight for what's right.' There is the courage of conviction underlying her seemingly casual tone.

Nobody was hurt, leave alone directly threatened. A lot of fears are impressions, not truths, the movement discovered. 'It is wrong to say that officials don't listen,' says Madhulika Chatterjee, also an active participant of Citizens' Alliance, who organised meetings and awareness campaigns through pamphlets and hoardings for residents. 'If you are persistent, officials do come around.'

The magnitude of the problem was large. But once the residents collected and began circulating the information they received on a neighbourhood-focussed Internet e-group, anger spread like wildfire. 'This wasn't a structured movement with an organisation and all that,' Ashutosh Dikshit says. 'We were about six to eight people, who said, "Let's take it up". We drafted a petition. Then the petition had to be circulated in the colony. So we had to talk to a lot of people, explain to them what we were referring to. And a lot of people were aghast.'

Not every resident was against the mall, though. 'There were some people who said, "No, it's great to have a mall". They were friends. They thought it was great. We didn't think so and provided them with information on why a mall in the neighbourhood was not a good idea. Funny questions came up, like "Don't you go to malls?" We said, we go to the airport, does it mean we must have it next to our house?' In the politically-charged atmosphere outside Alaknanda, questions regarding motives came up. The petitioners were asked if they were politically aligned, and if so, to which party. This was a loaded issue that presumed politics is bad, self-centred, and that surely those seeking to stop the mega mall had vested interests.

The other internal problem the petitioners came up against revolved around property prices. The mall, its proponents within the community argued, would double property prices. 'We then gave them data to show that it would do no such thing. Property prices in Delhi are growing everywhere. Growth is not the issue. It is the rate of growth that is the point.' The rate of growth in Chittaranjan Park and Greater Kailash II is higher than that in Saket, another upscale neighbourhood stretched out about four kilometres west of Alaknanda, with a series of mega malls in it.

Against an 86 per cent rise in property prices in Saket, the growth in Alaknanda was 102 per cent between the first quarter of 2009 and 2013, according to MagicBricks, a website that tracks property prices. The reason is simple. 'When you commercialise an entire area and choke it with traffic, the rate of growth of prices will drop,' Ashutosh Dikshit says. 'We tried to explain that to people. We said, even if the price of your property increases, and you're living here, how does it help you? Unless you want to sell it and run.'

There was also a great degree of surprise that the DDA had allowed a mega mall to come up right next to seven schools. 'Increase in traffic (due to the mega mall) threatens us with impending danger of road accidents, delay in plying of school buses and much more,' a 30 March 2013 letter, with the subject line 'Requisition to check/evade the construction of a mall in Alaknanda', to Delhi's lieutenant governor, by Kalka Public School Principal Anju Mehrotra, stated. 'The level of pollution will multiply. It startles me when I wonder how and why this happened. Why did the authorities choose to ignore all this?' The school and the proposed mall are separated by just a twenty-four-metre wide road.

What's shocking is the authorities' contention that they weren't even aware that there are schools in the vicinity of the upcoming mega mall for which permission had been given. 'Is it correct that just 50-100 metres away from the construction site of the mall, there are two senior secondary level schools operation (sic) and another three senior secondary schools functioning in close proximity of the construction site,' an RTI query from Citizens' Alliance asked. The March 2013 terse answer: 'No information available.' For the government to give permission to build a mega mall, without knowing this crucial piece of information that stares anyone visiting the place, is rather strange.

Such indifference from the government, despite a law mandating that accurate information be given to citizens, is not surprising. If push comes to shove, the bureaucracy has enough ammunition to turn the best of laws ineffective. And that's the system Arvind Kejriwal wants to disrupt. While schools were writing letters to the government, protesting against the mega mall in South Delhi, he was on the seventh day of his fast at Sunder Nagri, a Northeast Delhi neighbourhood, protesting against inflated power bills in the city. The atmosphere of protest was thick in the capital.

As the issue began to escalate within Alaknanda, conspiracy theories began to circulate about corruption in societies, in government, how people were getting paid off and so on. About forty-five days later, when the residents had their first meeting on the issue, 150 denizens landed up. 'Ours is a very educated area. There are doctors, government officers, teachers, chartered accountants, architects, economists, journalists and businessmen who live here,' says Meena Gangahar. 'This is not a crowd you can sway by relying on rhetoric,' says Ashutosh Dikshit. 'None of these people would accept purely emotional statements. So, we presented facts and gave them the sources of those facts.'

A lot of back-breaking work went into making clear and coherent arguments. If a similar mall in Saket breaks even only after attracting a huge number of people, for instance, it would be unlikely that the one in Alaknanda would survive with fewer footfalls. Such data was procured, rearranged and presented to the community. Except for a few, eventually most residents realised that the mall was going to make life difficult for them.

RTI papers gave power to Citizens' Alliance. 'Once we placed the RTI information before the community, things began to change faster,' Ashutosh Dikshit says. 'For example, when the environment ministry says it is not aware of any school in the neighbourhood, it is not something people take kindly to. They asked, "You have given sanction for a mega mall in this neighbourhood without knowing there are schools here?" The bitter truth of that information made people feel they had been taken for a ride.'

For an affluent community that has always borne the unfortunate reputation of being primarily concerned with the pursuit of material ambitions, taking the government on was a large step. But Ashutosh Dikshit argues it differently. 'These are stereotypes. It is not true that all these professionals are a smug lot who don't even go out to vote. They are all concerned in some way. They watch TV, they have opinions. Of course, there are people who really don't give a damn. But that's a minority. The truth is that most people are so busy attending to day-to-day worries that they cannot invest in politics beyond a point.'

The thousands of people who went to the various dharnas of Anna Hazare or Arvind Kejriwal during the Jan Lokpal agitation were people like these, citizens who don't usually engage with 'the system', who keep to themselves and their jobs, their hobbies and their holidays, steering absolutely clear of politics. What brought even more of the aloof elite to the streets was the brutal gang-rape of a young woman in the heart of Delhi. That incident brought the entire city to a standstill and forced the government to use water cannons in the cold of winter to disperse crowds. Films like *Rang De Basanti*, with their revolutionary spirit, further emphasised that the common man was ready to take on the system.

In any organisation, whether it is a political party or business enterprise, the start-up stage witnesses the heroic getting together of people for a vision; they're bound by the impulse for change. 'I think the instinct for initiating change existed within the community,' Ashutosh Dikshit says. 'I think it exists in human beings. I realised that when the alliance began to form, people started getting together. Even to begin with there were about thirty to forty people who were more inclined towards the neighbourhood, giving time to these causes. They had the streak in them. They were motivated.'

Petitioners tapped into the minds of the old and the young, alike. In a 6 July 2013 meeting with teenagers, for instance, they were able to convince this varied group about why the mall didn't fit into the community. 'Teenagers understand atmospheric pollution, they understand hydrocarbons,' Ashutosh Dikshit says. 'They have begun to realise that not everything the government does is well planned.' Even within the tiny segment of adolescents, there is a huge gap between a thirteen-year-old and a nineteen-year-old. 'Some of the thirteen-year-olds hadn't even thought about these subjects, but the eighteen- to twenty-one-year-olds saw the issue differently.'

The other tool that Citizens' Alliance used effectively was technology and communication. 'Our tools,' Ashutosh Dikshit says, 'have largely been Facebook, email and social media, that's it. Facts get disseminated quickly.' But he insists that the movement is not a social media creation. 'The Arab uprisings may have been a Twitter or a Facebook phenomenon, but our movement is not. Ours revolved around meeting people, going to them, explaining things to them, answering questions. Social media may have aided the process. It's a myth that you can run these movements on Facebook.'

This experience is not very different from AAP's. Across Twitter and Facebook, Arvind Kejriwal's social media team has actively supported the on-ground work done by party workers and enlarged the ideas of AAP in cyberspace. The party has 1.6 million 'likes' on its Facebook page, while Arvind Kejriwal himself has 4.3 million. On Twitter, AAP has half-a-million followers, Arvind Kejriwal has 1.3 million. While AAP's workers were using social media and other tools to reach out to citizens, many of whom had given up on political engagement, there was another force working simultaneously—the middle class was waking up and grabbing the political space once again.

Information in place, and with the Alaknanda community having reached a common platform, the next step was to effect change, which in this case was to stop the mega mall from coming up. To do that, political engagement was necessary. The community wrote to then Member of Parliament and Cabinet Minister in the Centre, Ajay Maken from Congress. They got no response. They also wrote to their then Member of Legislative Assembly Vijay Kumar Malhotra of BJP, who handed them a 20 February 2013 letter he had written to the lieutenant governor of Delhi.

The letter stated that the slum cluster on the contentious land that had been cleared was to be replaced with gardens and playgrounds. He said he was shocked to learn that the government had given permission to build a large mall there. He emphasised that the area was already under pressure from existing markets, which resulted in traffic jams. This would worsen with the mall. It would, he said, also be in breach of the city's masterplan.

Wasn't it just politics—a BJP MLA trying to score over a Congress MP and embarrass the Delhi government? 'The letter is far too factual to be purely political,' Ashutosh Dikshit says. 'As far as we were concerned, we were not in the business of wondering if it was politics or not politics. For us, it was a statement given by a former MP and a letter written to the lieutenant governor. But people did think it was political.'

On the day Vijay Kumar Malhotra wrote that letter, a different kind of politics was playing out in the city. Arvind Kejriwal and AAP were seeking interns to work on increasing enrolments for the Delhi elections later in the year. The success of this initiative that reached out to engage citizens who, so far, had been outsiders, surprised AAP. In twenty-four hours, they got five hundred applications from colleges across the globe, including far-away Texas and Boston.

Politics has a circular life and for the residents of Alaknanda, that circle ended when Ajay Maken came to the neighbourhood for an inauguration. That's when another Citizens' Alliance member, Laveesh Bhandari, who heads economic research firm Indicus Analytics and is now part of the committee drafting the economic blueprint of AAP, asked him what he proposed to do about the mega mall. 'It's not a good thing,' Ajay Maken said. Good or bad was not the issue here anymore. The issue was what he planned to do about it. The residents got no straight answer. In the AAP-led whirlwind of changing politics, evasion was simply not acceptable anymore.

The questions raised were many. In the masterplan, DDA classifies the mega mall's 3.3 hectares as commercial land. If so, why can't the mall come up—surely, a mall is 'commercial'? 'Our argument is not with how it is classified because that's there in the masterplan,' Ashutosh Dikshit says. 'Our argument is with the nature of commercial use.' According to Citizens' Alliance, the permissions that had been given to the developer were not in accordance with law. 'There are parts of it that are illegal,' Dikshit says. For instance, the law says you need to submit a site picture. The picture submitted was taken from inside the barricade, not showing any area of the neighbourhood—a fact that the Delhi Urban Arts Commission (DUAC) also accepted.

Just when it seemed as though the government's impudence could not get worse, it did. In a Kafkaesque twist, the map accompanying a 28 October 2005 sub-committee report of DUAC shows a wide, 428-metre long road and reasons that traffic to and from the mega mall will be manageable. There is just one problem—the road does not exist. A Google Maps check, as well as a physical walk to the spot, shows that there is no such road. When Engineering and Planning Consultants, the firm that gave this report, was confronted with this question by angry Citizens' Alliance members, its owner Jeewan Mittu said a 'modified transport impact assessment' needed to be conducted.

All through, members of Citizens' Alliance have maintained

that their problem was never with Mukesh Ambani, Reliance Industries Ltd or any other company. 'Our anger was purely, absolutely, totally and completely directed at the government. At the DDA, at the DUAC, at the environment ministry for its utter callousness and for what we thought was a complete lack of public interest,' says Ashutosh Dikshit.

If the anger within Alaknanda was coalescing into a concentrated force, outside it was gathering a never-seen-before momentum. Arvind Kejriwal was tapping into an angry citizenry, offering them an outlet to express their angst. The anger that had often dissipated when confronted with humdrum middle class worries or else turned violent when pushed to the extreme (as in the case of Naxalism), now could be nurtured, organised and turned into a potent political voice that would govern India's capital city, Delhi, if only for forty-nine charged days.

That political victory of AAP in Delhi was not yet visible—it was still three months away. So, the Alaknanda residents turned to the judiciary. In its 348-page-long, 4 October 2013 petition in the Delhi High Court, Citizens' Alliance sought to prevent the mega mall from coming up. The only charge in the petition was that the authorities did not follow their own processes. In terms of prescription, the petition suggested that authorities could speak to RWAs (Resident Welfare Associations) before making any changes—many RWAs have stated in their resolutions that they were not consulted. 'The house felt that the construction of the mall is not in the interest of the residents of Alaknanda area,' a 30 March 2013 resolution of Aravali Residents Welfare Association stated.

This struggle of Citizens' Alliance to prevent a mega mall from coming up is a case study in the changing nature of the neighbourhood-government relationship. Much before AAP brought in the concept of decentralisation of power through mohalla sabhas in urban centres in its manifesto, Citizens' Alliance had already planted the idea, suggesting that before any change was made to land use in their neighbourhood, the government had to publicise the change within the community and invite RWAs for official consultations.

You would expect that an angry residents' movement that fights the money-power nexus would face a backlash from all power structures. That may be the plot of films, but not so for Citizens' Alliance. The roadblocks that came their way were internal, mostly and only initially posed by RWAs. 'Among RWAs too, it came from executive committees, which are largely made up of senior citizens,' says Ashutosh Dikshit. 'Because they have to get a lot of work done from the political class, they don't want to upset them in any way.'

Once again the simultaneous functioning of two political movements—AAP's and that of Alaknanda's—came into focus, illustrating a coalescence of ideas. This time it barely seemed coincidental. Around the time this small fight was gathering in momentum, protest movements were gaining legitimacy. The mascot of Maharashtra, Anna Hazare, was definitely a reason for the success of Citizens' Alliance, Ashutosh Dikshit says. 'These things don't happen in isolation. I'm quite certain that the prevailing mood of the citizens to question the system, the growing courage of society as a whole played a part. And when I see the middle classes and the educated come out and try to save their neighbourhoods or challenge anything that's wrong, the mood becomes infectious.'

The protest of Citizens' Alliance is underlined by audacity; it is a change in consciousness of a small group of people—but one that reflects the overall mood of the land. What AAP under Arvind Kejriwal is doing at the state or national level echoes this change of consciousness.

Such movements are not exceptions to the rule. Similar is the struggle between tribals and Anil Agarwal's Vedanta for the control of bauxite in the Niyamgiri hills in Odisha in 2010; between the farmers of Bhatta Parsaul and the Uttar Pradesh government in 2009; between the villagers of Nandigram and the West Bengal government in 2007...the list is long and growing.

These islands of audacity provide political fodder to Arvind Kejriwal, who has worked at capturing the essence of such aspirations and packaging them into a political identity under AAP. But both Citizens' Alliance and AAP are in their early stages of growth, are works-in-progress. Citizens' Alliance has been able to put together an armoury of information and turn it into a writ petition, true. But the threat of the mall coming up still remains. Arvind Kejriwal has been able to gather escalating political momentum in Delhi, but has had to let go of that momentum when Congress and BJP joined hands and prevented the Jan Lokpal bill from being tabled in the Assembly; taking the moral high ground, he resigned. In different ways both movements pivot around the business interests of Mukesh Ambani. Both movements began around the same time, with the same spirit. And both dangle today at the edge of uncertainty—Citizens' Alliance in the court of justice, AAP in the court of the people.

1
STREETS OF DISRUPTION

At her Noida residence, a second- and third-floor duplex home, utilitarian in spirit, a cotton mattress lies on the floor, surrounded by two plastic chairs and a small table. Two large, brown eyes flit from a wristwatch to a BlackBerry, trying to accommodate an 11.00 a.m. interview. The smell of coffee fills the air, as Atishi Marlena gathers her muddy-brown phiran that ends in hand-knitted socks (from a Himachal Pradesh NGO). 'It's my mother's 70th birthday today and I haven't been able to call her yet,' she says, walking back from the adjoining room, where she had gone to take a telephone call out of earshot. It was Yogendra Yadav, wanting to discuss media strategy with her and a few others on a conference call. This, after missing his call thrice in the space of an hour.

In Aam Aadmi Party, Atishi Marlena is the policymaker, who coordinates, drafts and assembles the party's stance on various issues ranging from women's safety to economic policy. Yogendra Yadav is the party ideologue, the genteel voice of liberal reason that emerges triumphant in many arguments. Being two of the more articulate and persuasive voices in a party that is scripting a beginning and is short on leaders, they are often seen serving as important talking heads for their party on prime-time.

Suddenly, on 21 January 2014, the imperative for both Atishi Marlena and Yogendra Yadav to face the nation had acquired greater numerical urgency. The reason was linked to a basic tenet of economics: demand and supply. Demand was soaring, for every news channel wanted to hear from a member of AAP, whose leader, the chief minister of Delhi, Arvind Kejriwal, had brought the city to a standstill with an act it had never seen before—protesting on the street for thirty-three hours. But this time, though AAP was the focus of conversation, even the normal supply of AAP members willing to talk about the issue could not be found. Several AAP leaders did not want to go on television; they shyed away from defending what they felt was indefensible.

The genesis of this imbalance—the act of a constitutional authority taking to the streets, Atishi Marlena's inability to spare a few minutes of time and mind-space to wish her mother, against general cries that AAP was imploding under its own brand of protest politics—was a late-night action by the party's legislator in Khirki Extension about a week back. Acting on multiple representations by residents of this South Delhi neighbourhood that foreign nationals were allegedly peddling drugs and running a sex racket, Somnath Bharti, the legislator for the area and also the law minister in the Arvind Kejriwal government, landed there with a few of his supporters and a team from the Delhi Police. This was after three written complaints to the police did not lead to any action.

That night, when the inspector leading the Delhi Police team did not display the proactiveness that Somnath Bharti was seeking, the legislator and AAP activists allegedly took matters in their own hands. On 19 January 2014, the Delhi Police registered a case in the Malviya Nagar police station against the 'local MLA and his supporters'—implying Somnath Bharti—for rioting, molestation, wrongful restraint, criminal intimidation, outraging a woman's modesty and promoting enmity between two groups or religions.

The complaint, on the basis of which Delhi Police registered a case, said that four African women were forcibly detained, they were assaulted by the group that barged into their house and abused them with racist taunts, asked to urinate in public and forced to undergo medical tests. From trying to uphold the law, Arvind Kejriwal's law minister was being accused of breaking the law. He and his party denied all charges. But the fire had been lit.

Within a day of that FIR being filed, a local issue expanded into a state issue—and subsequently a national outcry. Khirki Extension became Delhi. The social, gender and race prisms, through which the issue was initially being seen, ceded to administrative and political ones. Activists from across India handed certificates of condemnation to AAP, as did some of its supporters. 'I am definitely one of those who found Somnath Bharti's midnight raid on women, and the forcible narco-tests he got conducted on them, utterly distasteful and despicable,' a donor to the party, called 'Nm' wrote in response to a blog-post on the AAP site. 'I was intending to continue my donations to the party through the entire election season. As long as Bharti stays in the cabinet, and AAP leaders continue to defend his actions, that is not going to happen.'

The disappointment was not restricted to outsiders; the crisis singed members alike. 'What was exhibited in Khirki Extension by Somnath Bharti and his mob, was a mentality that is based on dominant prejudice and hatred of the "other". It was followed by a disturbing statement by Arvind Kejriwal that "prostitution and drugs lead to rape",' wrote former diplomat and founding member of AAP Madhu Bhandari in an 8 March 2014 article in *Economic and Political Weekly*. 'This sort of catering to prejudices of the majority may be convenient for electoral gains. Others might find collecting funds illegally equally convenient for electoral gains.' She quit the party soon after the incident.

Not to be left behind, political parties cashed in on the

opportunity. The principal opposition party BJP as well as AAP government's supporter Congress trooped into the Delhi assembly and demanded Somnath Bharti's resignation when the House reconvened on 13 February 2014. When Delhi Commission for Women chairperson Barkha Singh summoned Somnath Bharti, he refused to come. 'They (Kejriwal, his ministers) have become dictators,' she told reporters on 30 January 2014, when AAP took steps to remove her from office, alleging that she was politicising the commission.

On the one hand, a section of the polity saw the Khirki Extension incident as a microcosm of the fundamental problem with the politics and worldview of AAP—a disdain for institutional structures and a self-indulgent belief that they were always right and everyone else always wrong. This public stance had got created during the 2012 agitation for a stern anti-corruption law; AAP was born from this movement. It consolidated during subsequent negotiations with the government. It got fossilised during pre-election campaigns. And now, its ugly face stood before all.

On the other hand, AAP leaders saw the same incident as yet another example of weak policing in Delhi and the inherent contradiction riddling the governance of the state—the Delhi government has, at best, dotted-line control over the Delhi police and hence when the police refused to act on Somnath Bharti's suggestion in Khirki Extension, it was symptomatic of a larger administrative issue. Unlike the case in every other state, the Delhi police does not report to the state government, but to the Union home ministry. The explanation given is that Delhi is the seat of power, it is where the Union government operates from, it is where the ministers and parliamentarians reside, it is where India's important state institutions are located, and the policing dispensation needs to service that. That is how it has been since Delhi became a state in 1992.

Every party has opposed this split arrangement—some though with greater meaning and force than others. So great has been the demand for ending this arrangement, that the three leading parties, Congress, BJP and AAP, put it down in their manifestos. Each said the Delhi police should report to the state government, that the current arrangement was not effective as it created an accountability gap in policing Delhi. 'Central and Lutyens' Delhi have all the police and the rest of Delhi hardly has any policing,' says Atishi Marlena. 'Look at the number of chowkies (police stations). They are so much lower in other parts of the city.'

Yogendra Yadav calls the political bluff of Congress and BJP. He points out that Congress governed Delhi, at both the state and the Central levels, for ten years, and still had the cheek to put its objection to the split arrangement in its manifesto. His contention was that it was AAP that had made policing a central issue in its manifesto and was willing to fight for it, in ways that have now become characteristic—through disruption. 'There was, sooner or later, bound to be this struggle for control over the police,' says Atishi Marlena. 'We had mentioned in our manifesto that we would struggle to get full statehood. And something like this would not come by simply writing letters.' This was a confrontation preordained.

But when the confrontation finally began, Arvind Kejriwal did not pitch it as an issue about whom the Delhi police reports to. The pitch was that the Delhi police had failed abjectly in its policing responsibility in three cases in the preceding eight days—besides the Khirki Extension incident, AAP took issue with the Delhi Police over the gang-rape of a fifty-one-year-old Danish woman tourist near Connaught Place, and the death by burning of the former landlady of an AAP MLA, allegedly by her in-laws.

On Sunday, 19 January 2014, Arvind Kejriwal demanded the suspension, or at least the transfer, of three SHOs (Station House Officer, the person in charge of a police station) and two ACPs (Assistant Commissioner of Police) involved in these three cases. When the Union home ministry did not take that action, Arvind Kejriwal announced a token protest the next day, 'for the sake of women's security', with his ministers and MLAs outside the office of Sushilkumar Shinde, the Union home minister, at North Block. In a tweet, he urged supporters and the public not to come for the dharna because preparations for the Republic Day Parade, scheduled for 26 January 2014, were happening in the vicinity.

The following Monday morning, all hell broke loose, with a series of advances and retreats, and looming flashpoints. First, Arvind Kejriwal set an 11.00 a.m. deadline for the home ministry to take action, following which he and his MLAs would start moving towards North Block. With the Central government not bending, Arvind Kejriwal began his promised march. He was stopped by the Delhi police on the way, near Rail Bhawan, which houses the Ministry of Railways. Arvind Kejriwal, along with his fellow AAP legislators and ministers, squatted on the Rail Bhawan lawns. And it was now that he urged people to join them there in large numbers.

Till that point, it was still widely expected to be a token, short-lived protest. After all, Arvind Kejriwal was the chief minister of Delhi, a constitutional authority. He was expected to run a government, not sit on the streets against another government. Worse, he was jeopardising preparations for India's sixty-fourth Republic Day—an occasion that carried nationalistic overtones—scheduled for six days later, less than five hundred metres away, on Rajpath. Meanwhile, outside Rail Bhawan, Arvind Kejriwal raised the stakes even higher—he announced an indefinite protest and his demand now was nothing less than the Delhi police being placed under the Delhi government.

'It wasn't scripted,' says an AAP leader, of Arvind Kejriwal's decision to turn what was meant to be a token protest into a standoff with the Union home ministry. This leader, who did not want to be identified because of the sensitivity of the issue, says the discussion among AAP's own leaders was that it would just be a symbolic protest: 'I don't know if you heard Arvind's speech, he said, "meri atma nahin maani" (my conscience didn't agree), and that is factually the case. He felt that if people were so agitated, then it had to be reflected.'

In a rousing speech delivered in Hindi, standing atop an electric transformer, Arvind Kejriwal gave a call to action. 'Some say I am an anarchist, I am spreading disorder. I admit I am an anarchist and I am spreading disorder,' he said. 'There is lawlessness in every home in the city. There is so much inflation, women are being molested. I have come here to spread disorder in the home minister's house. We want to spread the anarchy that is there in every Delhi house to theirs.'

He also asked upright police officials to take leave and join him in his protest. 'I promise, in case the commissioner harasses you because of this, main unhe dekh loonga (I will deal with him),' he said. And with that, Arvind Kejriwal, along with about two thousand supporters, prepared himself resolutely for the long haul, in the heart of the establishment, while a city was caught unawares.

But the Union government wasn't. Behind the scenes of what detractors called 'anarchy', there was constant and steady coordination between the Prime Minister's Office, Ministry of Home Affairs and the Delhi police on how to tackle this evolving situation. 'We are standing firm,' a senior official said. 'Let them self-destruct.' What the establishment was clear about was that it would not arrest Arvind Kejriwal. 'We learnt our lesson in the Anna Hazare agitation.'

Traditionally, the politics of agitation has always worked best when an outsider protests in order to bring about change within the government. According to J.W. Bowers and D.J. Ochs, agitation can be defined in two ways. One, the persistent, long-term advocacy for social change, where resistance to the change is also persisting and long term. And two, as a style of persuasion characterised by a highly emotional argument based on the criterion of grievances and alleged violation of moral principles. The definition evolved over time, and in their 1980 book, *The Rhetoric of Agitation and Control*, it had been sharpened to this: 'Agitation exists when (1) people outside the normal decision-making establishment (2) advocate significant social change and (3) encounter a degree of resistance within the establishment such as to require more than the normal discursive means of persuasion.'

The definition fits Arvind Kejriwal's brand of disruptive politics almost like a glove. He is an outsider, who has just about stepped into a system of governance, and carries an attitude of protest already inside him. He seeks significant social change—in this specific case by wanting to make the Delhi police more accountable to the people of Delhi, primarily by bringing it under the control of the Delhi government. And in order to do this, he faces resistance from the Central government. This asks for strategies that go beyond writing letters; hitting the streets, therefore, is one tool that he uses to usher change in.

Disruption seems to be the order of the day. Yet when Arvind Kejriwal is quizzed about his stance on disruptive politics, he throws back rhetoric-laced, politically-sharp counter-questions. 'That depends on what you call disruptive,' he says. 'We would say that what we are doing is a shake-up of present day politics.

And disruptive politics is what Congress and BJP are doing. If you allocate natural resources like coal blocks free of cost to a handful of people, then isn't that disruptive politics—or is protesting against such an action at Jantar Mantar to be branded protest politics? What is disruptive: Giving away the 2G spectrum or protesting against it and going on a hunger strike?' He bears the stance of a victim, speaks the language of the voiceless and marginalised.

Kenneth E. Boulding in his 1969 paper, 'Towards a Theory of Protest' states: 'Protest arises when there is strongly felt dissatisfaction with existing programs and policies of government or other organisations, on the part of those who feel themselves affected by these policies but who are unable to express their discontent through regular and legitimate channels, and who feel unable to exercise the weight to which they think they are entitled in the decision-making process. When nobody is listening to us and we feel we have something to say, then comes the urge to shout. The protester is the man in the advertisement who does not read the *Philadelphia Bulletin*, but who has something very important to say that clearly isn't in it. Furthermore, as he apparently has no access to the Bulletin, all he can do is to stand in the middle of its complacent readers and scream.'

A lot of protests we see around us—from the Narmada Bachao Andolan against the Sardar Sarovar Dam, and the Niyamgiri tribals against Vedanta and the Odisha government, to the agitation against Tata Motors and the West Bengal government in Singur by the farmers, all the way to Anna Hazare's Jan Lokpal agitation in Jantar Mantar against corruption—stem from this smothering of voices. If in one case it is the government and companies taking land away, in the other it is the institutionalisation of corruption that these agitations have highlighted.

Further, Kenneth E. Boulding writes: 'Protest is most likely to be successful where it represents a view which is in fact widespread in the society, but which has somehow not been called to people's attention. Societies, like solutions, get supersaturated or supercooled; that is, they reach a situation in which their present state is intrinsically unstable, but does not change because of the absence of some kind of nucleus around which change can grow. Under these circumstances, protest is like the seed crystal or the silver iodide in the cloud. It precipitates the whole system toward a position which it really ought to be in anyway.'

If Mamata Banerjee provided the nucleus for the Singur agitation and Medha Patkar became the voice of the Narmada Bachao Andolan, Arvind Kejriwal is the nucleus around which the new politics of disruption is forming, bringing voices from varied sections of society together to get rid of corruption—a ubiquitous phenomenon across modern India, eating into the vitals of every household. The pervasiveness of corruption has been highlighted, many times over, through smaller movements that eventually get suppressed by the 'system'. With AAP, the movement has attained a critical mass, if not in Parliament or state assemblies, definitely in the political discourse sweeping across India.

Enthusiastic protestors face a big risk while playing their part in politics. Kenneth E Boulding concludes: 'The form of a protest should be closely related to the object of protest. This is why, for instance, on the whole, the sit-ins have been very successful, whereas marches and parades are usually less so. It can be particularly disastrous to the protest movement if the protest takes a form which arouses a counter-protest over the form itself, and not over the object of protest. Any object of protest can easily be lost in argument and counter-argument over the question as to whether the form of the protest is legitimate or appropriate.'

This helps us place the Somnath Bharti episode at Khirki Extension in context. The entire debate has shifted to one of form—what Somnath Bharti did, how he allegedly barged into homes and harassed residents, how he and his supporters allegedly made a woman urinate in public and so on, and how these actions are illegal, even though he lists out laws that back his actions. His language made matters worse. Lost in translation was the objective of his drive—to get the police to act on alleged drug peddlers and sex racketeers. In the quest to deliver and to be seen delivering results, the practice of disruptive politics can, and as in this case, does, backfire. To think that detractors in Congress and BJP would let this go calmly is expecting too much. To expect media to act as cheerleaders for such acts is immaturity.

The allegations of anarchy and a breach of dignity of a Constitutional position by Arvind Kejriwal, according to political opponents and the media, are allegations of form, not object—a dharna by a serving chief minister at Rail Bhawan, detractors allege, denigrates the office. To say that all actions can be justified, once political objectives are met, is incorrect. 'The means may be likened to a seed, the end to a tree,' Mahatma Gandhi, from whom Arvind Kejriwal has borrowed his protest politics, wrote in his 1910 book, *Hind Swaraj or Indian Home Rule*. 'And there is just the same inviolable connection between the means and the end as there is between the seed and the tree.'

The right means must be adopted to pursue the right ends, Mahatma Gandhi wrote. 'If I want to deprive you of your watch, I shall certainly have to fight for it; if I want to buy your watch, I shall have to pay you for it; and if I want a gift, I shall have to plead for it, and, according to the means I employ, the watch is stolen property, my own property, or a donation. Thus we see three different results from three different means. Will you still say that means do not matter?'

To Russian Marxist revolutionary, politician, and the founder and first leader of the Red Army, Leon Trotsky, they didn't. In a June 1938 essay, 'Their Morals and Ours', Trotsky wrote: 'The ruling class forces its ends upon society and habituates it into considering all those means which contradict its ends as immoral. That is the chief function of official morality. It pursues the idea of the "greatest possible happiness" not for the majority but for a small and ever diminishing minority. The mixing of this cement constitutes the profession of the petty-bourgeois theoreticians, and moralists. They dabble in all colours of the rainbow but in the final instance remain apostles of slavery and submission.'

Which of these two intellectual platforms of the past is the aam aadmi going to choose to launch the India of tomorrow?

The Agitator's Handbook: Eight Strategies

From a bystander's view, it seems the aam aadmi hasn't made up her mind on whether the ends justify the means just yet. There are strong proponents on both sides. But irrespective of the choice, the expression will be one of protest. And when Somnath Bharti in particular, Arvind Kejriwal and AAP volunteers and leaders in general, and those who propose to pursue disruptive politics as a full-time career on a more universal canvass, use the tool of agitation as a means of change, they must consider the eight strategies that Kenneth E. Boulding listed.

Strategy 1: Petition. Here, the agitators present their case to the authorities, build arguments, try to persuade them through engagement and debate. This is important because if the agitators jump this step, the authorities can discredit the agitators, saying they are irresponsible, and to use the word thrown at Arvind

Kejriwal, 'anarchic'. The road to societal support, then, becomes a little steep, as we saw in the Rail Bhawan protest, when even staunch supporters of AAP paused to rethink.

Strategy 2: Promulgation. With this strategy, the agitators go public. Usually, the media is soft and leans towards them, if only to get a new story. But in this age of technology-led and hugely democratised media, going public doesn't have to follow the beaten path. Disruptive media like Facebook, Twitter and blogs can get the message across directly. If powerful enough, the message will go viral, and the traditional media will be forced to take note.

Strategy 3: Solidification. This is a reinforcing strategy. It uses tools like slogans, art, song, books, posters and bumper stickers. Until the 1990s, street theatre in India was a common tool used by agitators, largely left-leaning, to convey and consolidate their ideas in smaller groups—a tool that AAP uses to address focus groups even today. With fora like YouTube, the same play can potentially reach out to millions more. Protest songs are yet to catch the popular fancy of India, but two songwriters-singers-musicians, Bob Marley of Jamaica and Bob Dylan of the US, stand as worthy global benchmarks. On a separate note, the field is open for Indian musicians to experiment with protest songs.

Strategy 4: Polarisation. For this strategy to work, the movement needs a following. In essence, it creates an impression that anyone who does not support the movement supports the establishment. Effectively, it says, 'If you're not with us, you're against us'. A convenient whipping boy for AAP has been the media—as long as it delivers positive coverage, the media is a friend; the moment it changes stances, allegations begin to fly that media owners are influencing decisions. What AAP is effectively saying is that not applauding the party means you're part of the status-quo, want the corrupt system to continue and are, therefore, against AAP—a ridiculous stand.

Strategy 5: Nonviolent Resistance. The Jan Lokpal agitation in Jantar Mantar, under Anna Hazare, was a spectacular example of successful nonviolent resistance. This strategy, a favourite of Arvind Kejriwal's, has two arms—physical presence and boycott—to create tension that leads to negotiation. The most effective user of this strategy was Mahatma Gandhi. Do it once, it works. Do it twice, or even thrice, it may work. But if this becomes the permanent medium of discourse, it could fail.

Strategy 6: Escalation and Confrontation. The key here is to raise the stakes of the agitation so high that the establishment is compelled to use force. The water cannons used during the cold December winter of 2012 to scatter the agitations around the Delhi gang-rape is a prime example of the successful use of this strategy. AAP tried to use this strategy during the Rail Bhawan agitation, but a government that had learnt its lesson did not respond. The strategy failed. The lesson: Use with discretion.

Strategy 7: Gandhi and Guerrilla. With this strategy, agitators use the symbolism of nonviolent resistance along with the aggressive force of the guerrilla war force. Perhaps, this was the strategy AAP was planning to use in the Rail Bhawan agitation, when at first Arvind Kejriwal asked supporters not to come and later invited them. A handful of protestors did get hurt, when they broke barriers and the police was forced to lathi charge. This happened even as Arvind Kejriwal, his cabinet and AAP leaders protested nonviolently.

Strategy 8: Revolution. 'The strategy of revolution is not symbolic,' writes Kenneth E. Boulding. 'It is war.' Thankfully, so far, AAP has steered clear of this. In the rare chance that it takes even one step towards a violent revolution, the party will self-destruct. Not even the most loyal supporter of Arvind Kejriwal will pick up a gun and shoot her own fellow-citizens. This is outside the pale of politics.

'They (AAP) will have to raise questions and must consider their accountability to the electorate,' says former Comptroller and Auditor General of India Vinod Rai, over coffee at the Delhi Gymkhana Club. 'But if you adopt agitation politics from inside, positions harden. It's a matter of tactfully doing it. There are issues that have to be sorted out, some by brain, the rest with brawn. And you have to select which issue deserves what, you cannot substitute one for another.'

The error Somnath Bharti made was adopting the strategy of confrontation as the starting point. Its failure showed that such a stance can, and in this case, did, backfire. But Somanth Bharti is a small cog in the larger disruptive wheel of AAP. When the organisational DNA is one of confrontation, aggressive leaders like Somnath Bharti are bound to follow through. That is the danger in institutionalising aggressive disruption. Somnath Bharti has become an incident now. The question is, will he be the first of many such 'incidents' ahead? If yes, at some point voter fatigue will set in to offset the looming sense of instability. A country can't be kept on the edge for too long.

On the other side, those complaining about the inconvenience caused to them because of the Rail Bhawan protest, and their consequent disappointment with AAP, are probably approaching the incident as they would a film, within the comfortable confines of a theatre, munching popcorn. They seek change but are unwilling to make the small adjustments needed to usher it in. Electricity costs, for instance, must fall—but the interim disruption in power is not acceptable; let the power utilities and the government thrash the issue out. The moment the whiff of protest enters the stable lives of citizens, their discomfort soon turns into contempt for those fighting their battles.

But as all students of political science know, protests are a legitimate means a democracy provides for expression of dissatisfaction, even discontentment. A democracy without protest infrastructure like rallying grounds, or administrative props like permission to walk the roads, is an incomplete, a shallow democracy.

Protest politics is well-entrenched in India's DNA. With a rich history and tradition of protest movements during the freedom struggle, imparted to every Indian as part of her school curriculum, the legitimacy of protest within a democratic setup is widely accepted. And yet, for a lot of Indians, it was precisely when protests became ubiquitous that the AAP magic began to wear off.

'We are shaking up the politics,' Arvind Kerjiwal says, still walking. 'Protest is basic to our Constitution. Since when have protests become disruptive?' He pauses to catch his breath as he takes the discussion towards the abstract. 'If protests are disruptive then the Constitution collapses. The Supreme Court has said that democracy is alive only because of protests in the mohalla sabhas and at the blocks and various parts of the country.' You may argue that as chief minister, there is a Constitutional position he needs to be sensitive about, that it is ridiculous to be disruptive when in power. But you can't ignore the clarity of thought that backs his faith in disruptive action.

There are those, however, who would hope for a more nuanced approach. 'Agitation politics is a part of democracy, it should be there and this should be allowed and there should be space for it,' says social activist Nikhil Dey of Mazdoor Kisan

Shakti Sangathan, the organisation that worked with Arvind Kejriwal to bring the Right to Information law to India. 'But I do think that if you take the oath as a chief minister you have a duty, an executive duty, to fulfil and you cannot, at the cost of that, do agitation politics. That is unethical. Otherwise you don't stand for elections.'

Sociologist Dipankar Gupta, Director, Centre of Political Affairs and Critical Theory, deepens the discussion by segregating law enforcement from law making. 'Arvind Kejriwal as of now is only agitating against the fact that rules are not being abided by. And this is one part of the agitation. The other aspect of the agitation is to do with the Lokpal Bill, which is something new that is being inserted into the system. So he is playing on both sides and one is supposed to reinforce the other. But these issues will have to be dealt with separately and there are occasions when one should be stressed over the other. And not always can you push both together.'

Retreat of the Agitators

In order to prevent crowd mobilisation, four metro stations in Central Delhi had been closed throughout the morning of 20 January 2014. The Delhi police had enforced Section 144—a law that bans the gathering of five or more people—in the area, but AAP supporters kept streaming in. As the police blocked several roads leading to Rail Bhawan, traffic was thrown out of gear. The Delhi police had to summon backups. From an initial 1,000, the number of police personnel deployed in the area jumped four-fold to 4,000. By noon, paramilitary troops and the Rapid Action Force had also been called in to flank the Delhi police personnel.

As the day progressed, the crowds swelled. The tea and food vendors in the vicinity of Rail Bhawan did roaring business. But if for vendors it was business as usual, for the government the Rail Bhawan had turned into unusual business. Arvind Kejriwal converted the small space he had appropriated into a street secretariat. Carted by government officials, piles of files landed at Kejriwal's strike station for his signature. Cabinet ministers sat in Kejriwal's blue WagonR, from whose rear-view mirror hang two white-coloured dice, while a twin tri-colour stands proudly on the dashboard, a miniature replica of what government officials hold in their high-offices.

The atmosphere around was heavily charged. The roundabout near Rail Bhawan turned into a sea of AAP supporters singing patriotic songs and shouting slogans against the Delhi police and the Centre. Information and Broadcasting Minister Manish Tewari, who was crossing the venue, was heckled. The odd skirmishes between AAP supporters and the Delhi police further charged the atmosphere.

After the Khirki Extension incident, the debate moved to the politics of protest by those in power. 'Did the AAP form a government to wreck the system from within?' tweeted BJP leader Arun Jaitley. 'He (Arvind Kejriwal) remains a protestor, has failed to be an administrator,' tweeted former accomplice Kiran Bedi, once a contender for the top job in the Delhi police. Yogendra Yadav defended the means adopted, asserting that protests such as these were the only way of finding a solution to certain issues. 'This game will continue infinitely,' he said. 'To my mind, and I say this with a complete sense of responsibility, the only way of shaking these structures was to take it to the street. All major decisions in democracies are through contestations, most of which happen on the street.'

In other words, disruption remains AAP's primary tool of change.

On the news channels that were broadcasting this drama to

the nation, several AAP members stayed away from defending Somnath Bharti, both for what he did that night in Khirki Extension and how he did it. 'My sense is that he (Somnath Bharti) should have done it differently,' says an AAP leader on the condition of anonymity. 'The first attempt should have been a dialogue within the community if there was a problem. Going to arrest people like that may not have been the best first step given the fact that it could be misconstrued as racial prejudice.'

As the question of colour infected the debate, the nature of discourse turned ugly, challenging a party that claimed it was neutral to caste, gender and religion. That day, under the spotlight of the media, Yogendra Yadav was a lone man standing for AAP, clarifying and spelling out the absurdity of Delhi's law and order structure.

Buoyed by Yogendra Yadav's genteel defence, backroom party functionaries cobbled together through the day and late into the night, devising strategies on how to deal with the situation. While some argued that the protest and the growing support it was receiving from the public would be good for the electoral fortunes of the party, others disagreed as the events of the recent past had hinged on issues of great sensitivity. The questions and dilemmas were many. Could this trigger a Constitutional crisis? What if the skirmishes between AAP supporters and the police degenerated and turned violent?

As multiple conversations happened, news trickled in that there was a chance of violence breaking out in Khirki Extension. So, AAP pushed supporters from constituencies neighbouring Khirki Extension, like Greater Kailash, to maintain vigil and monitor the ground situation. Any violence, and AAP would be blamed—something the party could hardly afford or even handle. For all its disruptive rhetoric, violence was not an option.

Even as these events unfolded, commentators wondered:

Would this create a crack within the newly-born party?

On its part, the Union government believed so. 'They are imploding,' a senior government official said, unable to mask his glee. 'Look at the media headlines: "Bawaal (chaos) aadmi party" on Hindi TV channels.' There was no question of giving in to AAP's demands. Apart from tactics such as ignoring—the first step in the strategy of control—the government was banking on an ally from the skies: bitter cold.

As temperature in the city fell to 13 degree Celsius, with wind chills that made it colder, the night of 20 January 2014 was body-numbing. While Yogendra Yadav was seen walking purposefully with a toothbrush in hand, Arvind Kejriwal slept on the ground, by the side of the freezing road, his head about three feet from the rear left wheel of his blue WagonR. The chief minister of Delhi lay huddled on a sheet and a light mattress, his hand serving as a pillow. Underneath the light blue quilt with a floral pattern, he slept in the same clothes he had worn all day, his signature muffler wrapped in its trademark style, his well-worn sandals waiting at the edge of the makeshift bed to begin a new day. The night temperature dropped to 6 degree Celsius.

Delhi was in a state of unrest. And AAP in a state of unease.

Tuesday morning was drearier. The skies were grey, rain fell intermittently. Arvind Kejriwal woke up, dazed but stubbornly unflinching. The giant 'human banners', which AAP had used as a guerrilla tactic while campaigning for Delhi, came out and sheltered groups of supporters from the fury of the skies. The supporters huddled under blankets. They squatted on the wet streets. They drank milky tea in white plastic cups. They protested and had skirmishes with the police. Their bodies were cold, but their eyes spewed fire.

With neither side willing to relent from their stated positions, matters seemed to be reaching a point of stalemate. The clock was ticking. The following day the army would secure the venue for the Republic Day Parade, and there was a good chance that authorities would forcibly evict protesters. On ground zero, support for AAP had not grown in the preceding twenty-four hours, despite Arvind Kejriwal's call to the people to join the dharna, and his demonstration of resolve by sleeping in the open on a cold winter night.

Arvind Kejriwal, whose already weak health had turned worse from the cold, spent most of Tuesday inside his car, conducting government business and meeting people. Through the day, he also went in and out of Rail Bhawan, where he had been allotted a room till his entry into the complex was reportedly banned and he returned to the roundabout outside. He was not his usual picture of measured outrage. Soon began a spate of media bashing. He attacked the media for 'being sold' to either Congress or BJP. He threatened the Centre that if his demands were not met, he would take over Rajpath on 26 January with 'lakhs of people from across the country'.

Every move, every statement was being watched. A battle of perception was on, and in the mass media, AAP was losing political capital. Somnath Bharti was not helping his party's cause, either. 'I want to spit at the faces of BJP leader Arun Jaitley and senior lawyer Harish Salve to tell them to mend their ways,' he said, his expression matching the crudity of his words. 'I warn you, the public is going to hound you and beat you.'

Agitation fatigue was setting in, sapping the spirit of the supporters out in the cold rain. But there was a section in the party that wanted to persist. They cited information pouring in from other states, suggesting that the poor and the marginalised sympathised with Arvind Kejriwal and saw something heroic in his politics of protest. Imagine, they said, how the footage of a chief minister and his cabinet colleagues being hauled away by

Delhi Police—a possibility the next day—would strike a chord with the people? Despite physical limitations, the political advantages were clear.

The party brass—including Arvind Kejriwal, Yogendra Yadav, Manish Sisodia, Rakhi Birla and Sanjay Singh—moved to the neighbouring Press Club for an hour-long meeting. All afternoon, AAP supporters had been pushing at the two police barricades that barred their entry to the roundabout. At around 3.50 p.m., while the meeting was on, a sudden surge in momentum resulted in AAP supporters breaking through. The police resorted to the only tool at hand: a lathi charge. As AAP supporters took on the police, about thirty people were injured. It took Manish Sisodia and Sanjay Singh half-an-hour to step out and address the gathered supporters.

As abruptly as it had begun, in the midst of the prevailing chaos, at around 7.45 p.m., Arvind Kejriwal called off the agitation. Najeeb Jung, the lieutenant governor of Delhi, had cobbled together a compromise and AAP leaders had decided to make a dignified exit. Two of the five cops, whose suspension or transfer AAP had been seeking, had been sent on leave, one of whom had sought it earlier. As for the other three, Arvind Kejriwal said no action against them was required as all those accused in the alleged dowry case had been arrested. 'He is on leave already,' said a senior government official. 'This is a face saver to them (AAP). His (Arvind Kejriwal's) people met the L-G and said he was unwell.'

Declaring it a 'great victory' for the people of Delhi, Arvind Kejriwal said, 'The L-G has appealed to us to maintain the sanctity of Republic Day. He has agreed partially to our demands. We respect him and see this as a solid first step in making Delhi police answerable to the people of Delhi. We will keep protesting, but as of now, we are calling off the dharna.' The crowd cheered, but there was neither a feeling of victory nor a sense of closure. The fire of protest had once burnt high, but now that it was stamped out, 'victory' carried the taste of ashes.

About an hour later, in TV studios, Yogendra Yadav was not alone anymore. Atishi Marlena too had joined him on that circuit, to defend their outspoken minister, to defend their agitating chief minister, to defend the politics of agitation their party had practised while being in power. While he had spent the last evening steering the debate towards the anomaly of Delhi police's reporting relationship, Yogendra Yadav spent the next evening apologising on behalf of Somnath Bharti and reaching out to 'his African friends, people from the land of Nelson Mandela'.

But Yogendra Yadav does not think that either the actions of Somnath Bharti in Khirki Extension or Arvind Kejrwal's dharna at Rail Bhawan were out of line. Somnath Bharti, he says, was acting on a complaint from the people he represents, and there was a genuine issue of drug peddling and sex trade in Khirki Extension; further, he adds, the footage does not show Bharti over-reaching or misbehaving or uttering racial slurs.

A fortnight later, Yogendra Yadav and AAP got a shot in the arm when three Ugandan women residents of Khirki Extension registered a complaint with the Delhi Police on how they were lured to the city with the promise of jobs, but were held hostage with their passports taken away by people they have reportedly described as the 'drug mafia'. They also alleged that they were forced into prostitution, which they resisted. Acting on their complaint, the Delhi Police arrested another Ugandan woman for extortion and inducement to carry out prostitution.

This small moral victory wasn't to last for too long. On 1 March 2014, the judicial investigation set up to probe the Khirki Extension incident found Somnath Bharti guilty. 'The police were justified in not conducting the raid,' retired additional district and sessions judge B.L. Garg told *The Indian Express*. 'There were no grounds or reliable evidence to conduct the raid. The fact that nothing adverse was found in the tests conducted on the residents also supports their stand.' His findings and recommendations, however, are non-binding on the government.

The mistake that AAP made, according to Yogendra Yadav, was to not put out all the evidence from the Khirki Extension night in the public domain immediately. In not doing so, it lost 'the perception battle'. And by the time it tried making amends, Somnath Bharti had become indefensible even to his own colleagues. In a 23 January 2014 meeting of the political affairs committee of AAP, the party decided not to remove Somnath Bharti from the cabinet, but it did condemn the language used by him against Arun Jaitley and Harish Salve.

Inadvertently, though, within the government of AAP, Somnath Bharti has become the trigger and symbol for a new kind of politics—the politics of agitation, which party members subscribed to as activists, outside the system, and later tried incorporating into a governance model, one that's now gaining traction. While the debate around this issue will linger long, and go much deeper, the 'Kejriwal effect' has begun to mushroom—chief ministers as protesters is becoming a growing trend.

On 5 February 2014, another chief minister, this time from Congress, Andhra Pradesh Chief Minister Kiran Reddy, went on a dharna at Jantar Mantar, a few kilometres from Arvind Kejriwal's agitation spot, protesting against the bifurcation of his state. The currency of his protest was the same as Kejriwal's—a few members of his Cabinet, supporters jumping over barricades and so on.

The next month, on 2 March 2014, Bihar Chief Minister Nitish Kumar went on a dharna to seek special status for his state. His dharna revolved around questions of political largesse:

'What parameters were followed for giving special category status to Seemandhra?' he asked. 'We will not tolerate this and so in spite of being the chief minister, we decided to call a bandh.'

Four days later, on 6 March 2014, Madhya Pradesh Chief Minister Shivraj Singh Chouhan organised a state-wide bandh to seek a five thousand crore relief package for the farmers of his state from the Centre. For a party that condemned bandhs as a tool of protest by serving chief ministers and termed Arvind Kejriwal's Rail Bhawan protest as anarchy, this was a case of the serpent eating its own tail.

'The politics of protest is the politics of problem solving,' Shiv Visvanathan, who calls himself a 'social science nomad', said on NDTV on 5 February 2014, in a programme titled 'India: Now a Republic of Protest', when the streets of Delhi were taken over by two protesting groups—one led by Kiran Reddy and the other by aggrieved north-eastern students, following the death of Nido Taniam. 'But there is one difference. Kejriwal wants to solve a problem while Kiran Reddy wants to make sure that the problem of Telangana remains unsolved. There has to be a dharma of dharna politics.' He raised three questions—one: what is the logic of protest; two: what is the code of protest; and three: how long can the protest last? 'This is not yet clear in Indian politics.' But protest as the grammar of democracy can't be undermined. 'Politics of protest for getting sympathy is understandable,' Shiv Visvanathan said. 'But the Indian politics of protest has not yet matured into a protest of problem solving.'

Atishi Marlena points out that a lot of institutional change does not happen through discussions, letters or dialogues. 'Often, pressure is created by people coming on the streets and protesting,' she says. 'What is one creating? One is creating political pressure.' This conforms to, and is an effective use of the fifth strategy of protest, outlined earlier—nonviolent resistance through the use of physical presence to produce tension.

The Lokpal Bill, she says, came on the discussion table because of the India Against Corruption movement. It was passed in Parliament, after being repeatedly stalled for two years, in the aftermath of AAP's victory, and political parties rushed to take credit. 'In some cases, this (the politics of protest) would have to be adopted, though not for every change…(but) to say that you cannot have politics of agitation just because you are in power is not appropriate,' she says, stealing a quick glance at her watch. Time's up.

Three hours later, unable to make that call, Atishi Marlena drives up to Jangpura, a nine kilometre ride from her Noida residence, to wish her mother on her seventieth birthday, over lunch.

2

BREAKDOWN OF GOVERNANCE

The doorbell rings. It's our neighbours, a young, upwardly-mobile couple working in top jobs, both sound marketing professionals. 'There's a wedding in the family and…you know… the gas cylinder has finished. Could we borrow your spare cylinder?' Of course, we say, here you go. 'We'll return it soon,' they say with much relief and gratitude. Don't worry, just take care of your guests. They painfully drag our second cylinder up the stairs.

At least twice a year, our household becomes a supplier of gas cylinders to our neighbours, family and friends. Perhaps we've come to accept the inefficiency of oil marketing companies, their capacity to throw our carefully calibrated lives totally off kilter. The minute one cylinder runs out of gas, there's a phone call for a new one. Always at the edge of the next crisis that can burst the bubble of urban comfort, we've come to plan ahead. We've managed to maintain our gas cylinder input-output to relative perfection.

But gas is not the only panic-inducing service we use. From water to electricity to drain pipes, the mind-space we accord to things that are considered basic utilities in a modern economy are, when you think about it, frightening. The water inflow doesn't reach our taps, so we need to invest in a pump that pushes it to the terrace, from where it flows down with the required pressure. The need for the smooth flow of electricity has made us purchase an inverter that we need to regulate every now and then. If the storm water drain in front of our house gets choked every year because the municipal corporation is inefficient or corrupt, water flows into our house. Worse, this is a routine part of our lives.

There's a word for these symptoms of stress: misgovernance.

These serial ordeals hit a group of people who are educated, have an income, follow their aspirations and get on with life—the middle class aam aadmi. In the capital of India, in housing societies from Vasant Kunj to Janak Puri, Mayur Vihar to Dwarka, Gulmohar Park to Alaknanda, the glue of misgovernance binds the middle class with far greater intensity than any other factor known to us. Misgovernance meets us at every non-functioning red light, every pavement clogged by cars or vendors, every road potholed by a system that thrives on inefficiency.

'I would say education, health, water are the jobs of the government,' says Arvind Kejriwal, over his morning walk at 7.40 a.m., his voice a little burdened, his breath a little short. 'Basic amenities are the responsibility of the government and governance is about delivering these effectively to its citizens.' The AAP government's promise to give twenty kilo litres of free water every month to Delhi households is probably a step in that direction (but more on that later). Likewise for halving electricity bills, pending the Comptroller and Auditor General audit. The stated objective behind both is fairly broad—giving respite to citizens against rising prices.

But Kejriwal is not rigid about his stances. His ideas on the role of the state in delivering basic amenities is linked to how developed a nation is. 'These are the most basic responsibilities and deliverables for the government,' he says, in between wishing fellow walkers with a polite namaste. 'The other things keep changing with time, environment and civilisation. If it is a very rich and developed country, you could opt to privatise education, but if it is a poor country then education, health or any such basic (provision) is the responsibility of the government. So these issues and responsibilities of the government change and evolve with time.'

Further, he doesn't merely talk of urban creature comforts. 'The government's job is to provide security to its citizens, both internally and externally. But who is talking about maintaining law and order or a safe and secure environment for the citizens? The main opposition party, BJP, is not even talking about it. And how will it talk? It has a terrible track record. The third major responsibility of the government is justice. But neither Congress nor BJP are bothered about that. How will they ensure security or justice?'

And yet, when Arvind Kejriwal tries to bring order into a system plagued by rampant misgovernance, through the Rail Bhawan dharna for instance, he is labelled an 'anarchist'. So deep has the malaise of misgovernance gone into our systems, so much a part of our minds has it become, that we've forgotten what governance is or could be. So habituated have we become to the absence of order, that when someone says the situation needs to change, we drown in the Stockholm Syndrome. So entrenched is this abomination in our consciousness that even when we seek a better India, we are reluctant to step out of the false sense of security misgovernance has given us over the past sixty-seven years.

How do we as citizens deal with misgovernance? By forming our own little republics, our own micro-governments. Each household has its own group of institutions of governance. If piped gas is not available and the supply chain of government-owned oil marketing companies is full of leakages, we buy gas cylinders at prices higher than what the government has set. If power supply is erratic, the inverter comes to the rescue as our own mini power plant that can breathe electricity into homes for six to eight hours at a stretch. The Delhi police is busy protecting and running errands for the VVIP? No problem, we hire security guards to protect our homes.

Our small governments protect us from the change that Arvind Kejriwal is attempting to bring—making the Delhi police more responsive to the citizens of Delhi. Instead, we pounce on the manner in which the change is initiated—the AAP dharna that dislodged our smooth lives for a day or two—and call his act anarchic. So addicted are we to misgovernance, and so far away have we strayed from honest politics, that Lagadapati 'pepper spray' Rajagopal's criminal actions don't affect us—we don't call him an 'anarchist'. Our reversal of labels would have been funny had it not been pathetic. The same mob of 'educated' people who term Arvind Kejriwal's dharna for greater police accountability as 'anarchy', seems not to notice the anarchy of everyday life due to the misgovernance of successive governments. Or should we say 'rulers'?

What is anarchy, if not a weapon that wordsmiths use? 'A situation of confusion and wild behaviour in which the people in a country, group, organisation are not controlled by rules or laws,' is the technical definition that in no way, howsoever hard party-aligned intellectuals stretch the word, applies to what Arvind Kejriwal did at Rail Bhawan, as we explored in the previous chapter. If anarchy is absence of government, it doesn't apply because the AAP government was functioning from the streets. If anarchy is a state of lawlessness or political disorder in the absence of a governmental authority, it does not apply to what Arvind Kejriwal and his cabinet was doing at the roundabout on 20 and 21 January.

On the contrary, if we examine the word 'anarchy' in the context of today's India, it exists in less obvious, seemingly invisible forms around us. It exists in the absence of government, in a 'system' captured by the rich and the powerful, in a framework that allows an MP to get hundreds of gas cylinders a year, while we hustle around for a refill. According to LPG Transparency Portal, industrialist and Congress MP Naveen Jindal's residence in New Delhi was shown to have received 369 refills of LPG cylinders in a single year, news portal *Firstbiz* reported in a 14 September 2012 story. But Naveen Jindal was not an exception. Vice-President Hamid Ansari's official residence consumed over 170 subsidised LPG cylinders in a year; external affairs minister Salman Khurshid and his wife used sixty-two cylinders (under two connections); and Dalit leader Mayawati used ninety-one cylinders under two connections. The list is long.

Perhaps these are symptoms of a systemic failure, examples of governance by the rich and powerful. We have misused the privileges of government posts to a point that loan waivers are allowed to the defaulting cronies of politicians of the governing party (to the tune of thousands of crores). But if one is an average citizen, the aam aadmi, goons come to our doorsteps, abusing, intimidating and threatening us if we miss a couple of home loan instalments. There are a whole host of services that belong to citizens by right, but which are being held hostage by a corrupt and an inefficient system and against whom no government in the past sixty-seven years has taken any action.

As a result, problems such as misgovernance and inefficiency have been compounded by corruption. They have taken root to the extent that they seem like a status quo, something we can take for granted. We send our children to private schools even though there are three government schools within walking distance from our homes. We go to private hospitals even though health centres next door are supposed to offer the same service. In other words, we, as taxpayers, are forced to pay for these services, but as citizens we cannot use them. Fair, every citizen need not use every service all the time.

Move one rung lower on the economic ladder and meet the poor. Here one observes how rusty systems are hurting them every minute—from deficient law and order provisions, to poor water supply, to institutionalised bribery. So far gone is this state of everyday anarchy that if the poor had the option, they would rather suffer intergenerational debt and go to a private hospital than risk the lives of their loved ones in public healthcare; they would rather send children to private schools out of their reach than the government school.

In the thick of the Rail Bhawan agitation, Mithun Gupta, a driver, said that he had filled up the form and become a member of AAP. 'Arvind Kejriwal is doing the right thing,' he said. 'All forty votes in our family will go to him this time.' Mithun Gupta, who lives in Sangam Vihar, a large neighbourhood of poor immigrants in South Delhi, heads one of the millions of households that have been denied governance. There is open sale of unlicensed liquor on the road at night—right under the nose of the police. They've all been bribed, he says. He is now determined to grasp the thin thread of hope that AAP has given him.

Zoom out and what you see is a country that has become a republic of 240 to 300 million households, each forced to form its own government. What we observe is that the entire politico-socio-economic system of the country is geared towards preventing the common man, aam aadmi, from expressing herself. Forming a household government is a survival skill to negotiate a governance system whose foundations have been weakened and are now crumbling. In a country whose spiritual DNA encourages its people to pursue their swadharma, their own-becoming, the hurdles due to the misgovernance of, corruption in, and rent-seeking by an institution called 'the government' are so high that you feel as if the gods have blessed you if you can do an honest day's job and return home.

This is anarchy.

And yet, in the first month of Arvind Kejriwal's Delhi debut, all we had to say was that he can't govern. We, the victims of misgovernance, corruption and rent-seeking, accuse AAP of bringing in anarchy, of indulging in dharnas, of not knowing how to fix citizen problems. We, the educated, who have created for ourselves little bubbles of comfort, have lost sight of what to even expect from the government. So far gone is this capitulation to total listlessness that we don't even know what good governance can be, should be, must be. We've forgotten that in the twenty-first century, good governance is our moral right. Too busy to think about our basic entitlements, too distracted by routine to engage with change, too overwhelmed by the impossibility of transformation, we have been so benumbed that we don't even notice when Arvind Kejriwal talks of governance.

Caught between past benchmarks of what stands for governance and the new charter of disruptive governance that Arvind Kejriwal seems to be scripting, citizens need to make up their minds and take a very tough decision on what 'governance' really means, and whether AAP is on the right track. To do so, citizens need to think about whether the first month of AAP in government has delivered governance or anarchy. On its part, the party takes credit for launching an anti-corruption helpline, ending the VIP culture in Delhi, cutting electricity bills and initiating a CAG audit of power companies' accounts, giving 20 kilo litres of water free to every household and so on—the list is long but we'll come to it later. The question citizens need to ask is whether AAP's achievements in the first month can be viewed as signs of governance, as Arvind Kejriwal contends, or whether everything has been anarchic, as his detractors allege.

Governance Outcomes or Just Big Talk?

Just one month old, AAP is still a toddler that voters are willing to hand-hold, forgive, indulge, accept tantrums from, and help grow. AAP is yet to be faulted for any massive scale of corruption of the kind that has dented the image of Congress; it is yet to isolate any segment of society like BJP has with the Muslim community. As it fumbles through the corridors of power that have been greased with habits of the past, it slips here, it falls there, it dirties itself in muck. But all the while, the electorate patiently picks it up, dusts off the grime and puts it back on track. While AAP has let go of Delhi in forty-nine days, by May, we will know whether its electoral footprint has grown nationally or not.

In his first interview after coming to power, to both CNN-IBN's Rajdeep Sardesai and NDTV's Barkha Dutt, Chief Minister Arvind Kejriwal recited a list of achievements. Barely twenty days in office, he cited fourteen points. Ten days later, he added three more. Whether these actions fit into the framework of good governance or not is a decision that needs the yardstick of time to measure. As of now, we may review these for ourselves:

End of the VIP Culture. By restricting the use of red beacons, symbols of the lal batti culture, that created a master-servant relationship between the political and bureaucratic elite and the people who they were supposed to serve, AAP has accomplished in one stroke what several thinkers and most citizens have been annoyed about for years, even decades now. By refusing personal security, the AAP cabinet is living the idea of egalitarianism and has brought the people closer—though it seems there is invisible security around Arvind Kejriwal provided by the Delhi government. His home and his blue WagonR have become symbols of simplicity, vehicles of public engagement, and a tool for political brand management.

Free Water. Every household that has a water metre will get twenty kilo litres of free water every month. Exceed that by even one litre and the household will have to pay for all the water it gets. For a scarce resource like water, this will not only help poor households, but it will also encourage water savings from the slightly well off consumers, through what behavioural economist Richard H. Thaler calls a 'policy nudge'. This does not apply to households that don't get water in the first place or those that haven't installed water metres.

Control Over the Water Tanker Mafia. The allegations are as follows. Officials of Delhi Jal Board (DJB) create false scarcities of water in various neighbourhoods. Households call up private tankers. These tankers have a nexus with the DJB officials, who then get a cut from their earnings. But what is an exception for middle class homes is routine for citizens on the fringes. For them, with no water pipes or connections, the water tankers are a lifeline. At one point, some of these neighbourhoods did not get any water for a few days, so the issue is more complex than simply ending corruption.

Power Rates Reduced. Prices for the first four hundred units of electricity consumed have been slashed by half. Further, independent agencies have been identified to investigate the cases of allegedly faulty and fast-running electricity metres. Finally, consumers who face issues related to their electricity metres can now approach their sub-district magistrate's office and get their metres investigated. If the CAG audit (next point) shows that the tariffs are backed by reasoned measures, things will change—provided, of course, AAP returns to power in the next Delhi elections. That said, politically, it would be difficult for any future government to raise tariffs after cutting them. We need to see how this moves forward.

Ordered CAG Audit of Power Companies in Five Days. Citing a case in Delhi High Court, Congress government in Delhi did not order an audit of power distribution companies for five years, says Arvind Kejriwal, but AAP did it in five days. The question of whether power companies wrongly raised tariffs has been put on the debating table. Power distribution companies, on their part, claim that the cost of purchasing power from power generation companies like NTPC is now higher and hence the tariffs have risen, as approved by Delhi Electricity Regulatory Commission. AAP, on the other hand, has alleged gold-plating of costs and a fall in transmission losses; as a result, the tariff rise is unjustified and hence the CAG audit is essential. Given a divergence of views, an audit is a fair way to arrive at facts.

Permits to 5,500 Autos to Ply in the National Capital Region Given. A shortage of autos to carry passengers between Delhi and areas like Noida, Gurgaon, Ghaziabad and Faridabad has been a chronic problem. Of the 55,000 autos that ply in Delhi, 10 per cent have been given these permits. Having said that, the bigger problem consumers face is overcharging or a plain refusal to cart passengers by a unionised group that no political party has been able to tame, allegedly because the auto owners are politically connected. Further, even though the Centre had cut the price of gas by 30 per cent ahead of the 2014 elections, AAP did not insist that auto fares fall in the same proportion. Worse, Arvind Kejriwal, in a meeting with auto drivers, promised an inflation-linked annual upward revision in fares—at a time when gas prices had fallen. For a party that has the aam aadmi in its nomenclature, AAP has gone the way of the traditional parties in this case, needlessly turning a blind eye to consumer woes. If this is not addressed, it is going to disappoint a lot of commuter-voters.

One Hundred Rehen Baseras, Night Shelters, for Citizens Living on Roads Opened. Providing a creative twist to entrepreneurial thinking, the AAP government has got abandoned buses to act as night homes for the poor who otherwise have to spend the nights out in the cold. While certainly not all the homeless can be accommodated in these rehen baseras, it is a start and one that brought great respite to some of the homeless in Delhi.

Millennium Bus Depot on the Banks of the Yamuna Shifted, So the Banks Can be Developed into Parks. The depot stands on what is known as zone 'O', where urbanisation is not allowed by the Delhi masterplan (and an issue that the previous government was seeking to change). By moving the depot, AAP has shown a commitment to the environment—in this case a small step in cleaning up the Yamuna. This means a loss of sixty crore rupees and surrendering prime real estate of sixty acres—a difficult call that only a disrupter could have taken.

FDI in Retail Stopped. Depending on which side of the political fence you sit, what your ideologies are or simply whether you are a farmer, a consumer or a trader, you may agree or disagree with AAP's logic of reversing the previous government's action on allowing Foreign Direct Investment (FDI) for multi-brand retail in Delhi. While the mood of the city, and the nation, on this issue is fragmented, AAP had promised a stop to FDI in retail in its manifesto and supported the opposition BJP on this debate. When Commerce Minister Anand Sharma criticised the decision, Yogendra Yadav said stopping FDI in retail in Delhi did not mean it would be stopped in all states. AAP says the decision on whether to allow FDI in multi-brand retail will be taken only after studying the unique dynamics of each state.

Anti-Corruption Helpline Started. For a party that has come to power on an anti-corruption plank, this is a natural first step towards that mission. It's early days, and there will definitely be hitches in the way this helpline will operate. The idea is possibly inspired by the film *Nayak*, where the chief minister installs such a helpline and goes about sacking corrupt officials in the state. It seems Arvind Kejriwal was itching to take that route. According to media reports, the extent of corruption has fallen sharply in the transport department, which is a short-duration governance miracle. But now that AAP government has resigned, will we see a return of corruption? Time will tell.

Private School Helpline for Nursery Admissions Started. Against a rotting government school infrastructure came an explosion of private schools, offering better quality education. However, like all good things, demand for private, quality education exceeded supply and many schools began to move over to the dark side, by demanding huge donations for admissions. This helpline is expected to curb this menace and serve parents.

Complete Mapping of 946 Schools Done and the Schools are Being Given Infrastructure. As a first step towards reforming government schooling, physical infrastructure is crucial. The AAP government has audited the schools for things like toilets, desks and so on, which are crucial in the process of delivering education. Toilets for girl students, for instance, could help reduce their dropout rate, that only rises as they near adolescence. Such a mapping must be done across the country, down to the last school. Ashok Kaushik, a stationery shopkeeper in Vasant Kunj was one of the volunteers who conducted this audit in seventeen government schools and twenty-three private schools.

Apart from giving recommendations for government schools, like conducting regular parent-teacher meetings, he ensures that children of economically weaker sections are provided for in the mandatory 25 per cent admissions quota in private schools.

One Lakh Rupees Offered to Every Government School. An equal transfer of money to all government schools to finance their needs is strange. Do all schools need the same amount of money at the same time? The infusion of money into the schools should have come after the results of the mapping exercise above. The two should have been reconciled. Providing a financial band-aid even as tests were being carried out for a more measured, thought-through treatment seems like a meaningless exercise and could be viewed as being a waste of resources.

Rejiggering the Governing Bodies of All Twenty-Eight Delhi Government Colleges. According to Arvind Kejriwal, all members of the governing bodies in these colleges were Congress incumbents. But instead of replacing them with volunteers or members of AAP, the government put out an advertisement, calling for top academics to take charge of these bodies. Depoliticising universities and giving them a more academic leadership is a good step.

Promise to Introduce Jan Lopkal Bill in the Assembly. The beginning of AAP lies in the Jan Lokpal agitation that was spearheaded by Arvind Kejriwal under the moral eye of Anna Hazare. In AAP's rather naïve opinion, the Jan Lokpal is the panacea to all problems of corruption in India or at least will be an important deterrent. But when he tried to introduce the Jan Lokpal in the Assembly on 13 February 2014, he was shouted down and the bill could not be introduced. Further, Delhi's Lieutenant Governor Najeeb Jung said that the Assembly needed the Union government's permission to table the bill, a claim Arvind Kejriwal contested. He and his government resigned on this issue and now are seeking a larger mandate from Delhi to reintroduce it.

Supporting Contract Workers. Taking cudgels on behalf of contract workers, who live on the edge of the employment hierarchy, the government has set up a committee to look into their grievances. It has also assured them that no jobs will be terminated until the committee delivers its recommendations. A fair move, no doubt. But if Arvind Kejriwal thinks that all employment creation has to be through government jobs, he is gravely wrong. And so far, we have seen no sign of an economic policy that addresses the unemployment problem.

Investigation of Sikh Riots. The government recommended to the lieutenant governor the formation of a special investigation team to review the cases of violence against the Sikh community in the 1984 riots, a long-standing demand.

Clearly a party in a hurry, critics may disagree with some of AAP's decisions above. Economists have lashed out at AAP's free water move, cut in power tariffs and reversal of FDI in retail, for instance. Provisions like rehen baseras have been critiqued by opposition leaders for not being good enough, while ending the VIP culture has been condemned as being populist. Power distribution companies are questioning how the financial gap will be attended to, now that they have to pay power generating companies like NTPC.

The bigger question is whether AAP delivered governance. We believe, it did.

The hurry with which AAP went about doing what in its view is good governance has raised voter expectations beyond reason. The urgency with which Arvind Kejriwal attacked one problem after another only kept pace with the aam aadmi's expectations that were lying dormant. You could say that in less than one month, he opened the proverbial Pandora's box, lying closed for sixty-seven years. With one difference: Unlike the Greek myth, where hope emerged after a rush of evil, in this case, hope has emerged first, and is satiating the hunger of a populace.

'Post 8 December 2013, the kind of surge we have seen is unprecedented and unexpected,' says Pankaj Gupta, who handles AAP's finances. 'Even we had not anticipated it, in the sense that people have suddenly started seeing hope. A hope that the change that they were looking for is now perhaps possible. And it is possible if they participate. That is what is making this phase more and more interesting.'

AAP is unleashing an atmosphere of celebration. 'People have been so frustrated by what has been happening in their lives that when they see even a single ray of hope they want to latch on to it. In Hindi we say, doobte ko tinke ka sahara (last hope for a drowning person),' Pankaj Gupta says. 'Perhaps AAP has given the common man a kind of hope. The failure of AAP will be more harmful to the country than anything else has been, because it will kill hope.'

India is starved for hope, sure. But to say that Arvind Kejriwal is its sole provider is not necessarily true. 'People are looking for a hope,' BJP leader and member of its Parliamentary board Arun Jaitley wrote in his 10 February 2014 blog post. 'They want to redefine standards of probity. Price rise, unemployment and stagnation of economy are disturbing them. It is, therefore, understandable that in traditional BJP strongholds in north, central and western parts of the country (Narendra) Modi should draw an unprecedented response. What does this unprecedented support mean in areas where the BJP traditionally has not been very strong? It is an undercurrent, which is motivated both by anger and also with hope.'

All poll forecasts by various agencies show that the hope Narendra Modi offers is statistically way ahead of what Arvind Kejriwal has to provide.

This hope is twining itself around a tall, thick tree called governance. The question we need to ask is: did Arvind Kejriwal deliver governance in his forty-nine-day stint as chief minister of Delhi? While that question will take time to be answered, what we definitely find in his attempts at governance is good politics. Every point enumerated above is strongly rooted in catering to the aam aadmi. 'Electricity, we promised we will audit, but while that is happening, we have taken an extra effort to reduce tariffs for the first 400 units of consumption. Same with water by giving it free of cost to a certain limit,' says AAP leader Gopal Rai. 'Both these measures will give relief to the common man, who is hit by inflation.'

But it is also important to note that a lot of governance happens behind the scenes, invisible to reporters. 'Governance is happening every day but that doesn't make headlines or (emerge in) prime-time debate,' says Atishi Marlena. 'It may have been when we reduced the water tariff. But now that systematic work is going on in restructuring the Delhi Jal Board or borewells, it doesn't make for news. That is the everyday nature of governance. The appearance that there are things being done recklessly (does not convey) the actual state of what is happening.'

We are witnesssing the evolution of a party as it moves from poetry to prose. 'Till AAP began to govern Delhi, it was all romance, chasing politics as a dream, following the poetry of politics,' political scientist Ashutosh Varshney says, over breakfast at the India International Centre. 'Now, all of that is very necessary, very enlivening, very refreshing, very rejuvenating. All of this will now have to be accompanied and joined with the prose of politics and prose of governance.'

Governance is like a marriage. 'There is a lot of prose, everyday prose, in running a marriage and making a family work,' Ashutosh Varshney says. 'Romance may be the beginning of a new family, certainly in twenty-first century India. But then the prose of running this family will be necessary. The prose of governance, the prose of politics, has to appear very soon... I do think (AAP members are) working on their prose. Some of them have mountains of intelligence around them. And so, let's see what kind of prose appears finally from this poetry.'

3
ALCHEMY OF POWER

The apparent chaos on the streets of Delhi that we saw around Rail Bhawan couldn't have been a spontaneous expression of alleged misgovernance by a political newbie too inexperienced to hold the reins of India's national capital, as the intelligentsia and the media suggested. It was not a politics-by-dharna, designed to ensure Congress withdraws support so that AAP could concentrate on the Lok Sabha polls ahead, as is being alleged by political rivals. Least of all, it was nowhere close to 'anarchy'; both the state and the Central governments functioned—the former on streets, the latter in offices.

This tactic of street protest by a chief minister and his cabinet was part of a well thought-through strategy, a strategy of disruption in the widest sense of the word. Over the past decade in general and the last three years in particular, the word 'disrupter' has evolved. While earlier it carried a negative connotation and was viewed as being so destructive that it would come in the way of a harmonious state, it has today undergone a remarkable metamorphosis in meaning. In the age of Google searches and Twitter streams, of Yahoo before that, and its predecessor Hotmail, the word has accumulated some respect. It is almost aspirational, to use urban lingo, almost 'cool'.

To give it a handle then, it is the beginning of iDisrupt.

Disruption has not been restricted to ways of doing business alone, through the Schumpeterian model of creative destruction.

As a society, political disruption through empowerment by technology has catalysed the Arab Spring and a spate of civil uprisings. From regime change by force (Tunisia, Egypt, Libya and Yemen) and civil uprisings (Bahrain and Syria) to major protests (Algeria, Jordan and Morocco) and minor ones (Mauritania and Djibouti), the past three years have seen unexpected political upheaval in this geographical expanse. Protests that began with a quest for less corruption and better governance soon morphed into movements seeking a political voice.

From August 2011, the Occupy movement took over America; disruption was in the air, with banners such as: 'We are the 99 per cent'. This protest movement was against inequality, against the brazen and drunken abuse of power, against big bankers getting richer at the cost of average citizens. Corruption was the underlying theme in this protest movement. There is a mine of statistics that back this phenomenon—but generally, the top one per cent saw their incomes grow phenomenally, while those of the rest were either flat or, in some cases, even lower.

Disruption has fragmented the politics of Europe since 2009. What began as a financial crisis soon turned into a wider economic crisis that finally ended up being a political crisis for Greece, Ireland, Portugal, Spain and Cyprus. The fall-guy in this crisis was an abstract concept—financial globalisation during the go-go years, from 2002 to 2008, when excessively high-risk lending practices created an asset price imbalance. The real perpetrators of financial crimes, however, continued to draw million-dollar bonuses from taxpayers' money. Unemployment was the biggest contributing factor to people coming on the streets and presenting the idea of 'austerity measures'.

Travel back in history and you will find places and times littered with examples of disruption. India is no different. In fact, it is surprising that despite globalisation and the scenes of prosperity that were beamed into homes after 1991, protest movements took such a long time to mushroom. Perhaps nobody believed he could protest. You could even attribute an inherent state of inertia to this delay. But once the spirit of the aam aadmi was ignited in Jantar Mantar, with the Anna Hazare fast, there was no looking back. Today, disruption has steered the dreams that have resided in this nation's heart for centuries.

'The Arab Spring uprisings are a voice against dictatorships and people thinking that they are being deprived of their rights,' says sociologist Dipankar Gupta. 'But it is (easier) to attack a dictator than to attack a democracy. Across the world, in Brazil or the Philippines or Ukraine, people are saying, "You have to deliver". Citizens are pressuring the state to deliver and the warfare is not between classes, sections of the society, or races.'

It is this warfare, this demand for delivery that Arvind Kejriwal has been able to package into a political voice. But governance outcomes are invisible; it is the street brawls that catch the attention of people. The resultant and intermediate chaos can be seen as a short-cut to change. What Arvind Kejriwal and AAP are trying to do is nothing less than organising a shift in power, using disruption as a lever. And the shift is not merely in institutions of governance or through the creation of disincentives to corruption.

This shift is structural. It is an attempt at realising the dreams that the freedom movement created, dreams that have been forgotten since Independence. Arvind Kejriwal does not simply stand on an anti-corruption platform; he plans to break down, and then rebuild, the platform itself. The theoretical foundations of this rebuilding stand on three legs—anti-corruption, decentralisation of decision making and the devolution of powers, and the right to recall—all three disruptive entities in themselves. Arvind Kejriwal believes that he will not be able to change the system simply by being part of it. The only way forward for him, therefore, is to break the system down.

The Corruption Crusades

At 7.30 p.m., on 10 February 2014, the day Arvind Kejriwal was pushing for two critical laws in the Delhi assembly—Jan Lokpal and Swaraj—a play titled 'Sadachar Ka Tabeez' (Amulet of Good Behaviour) was screened at the Chinmaya Mission in Delhi. This was a play with a difference: every person in the play was an alumni of Salam Balak Trust, an organisation that rehabilitates street children who have run away from their homes. The satire examined issues like inflation, the rise in prices of sugar and onions and basic commodities, poor roads, police accountability, all the way up to corruption in high places.

'I don't know why most of the plays I direct are in some way or the other related to corruption,' Director Kapil Dev thought aloud, sounding like a man who spoke from his heart. 'Perhaps the issue is very close to us who run away from homes. Perhaps if corruption was not there in society, we wouldn't have had to run away.' Then his eyes twinkle with hope. 'Over the past two years, I have seen a dip in corruption.' While this was before AAP came into the political scene, the idea of artistes raising their voices against corruption has been a long tradition. To draw an analogy, it is almost as if millions of such hopes handed the baton of the anti-corruption movement to Arvind Kejriwal, who then translated art into politics.

In the rather simplistic vision of Arvind Kejriwal and AAP, when all laws have broken down or have not been enforced for citizen welfare for decades, and participants have all but dismembered themselves because of a politics that has been captured by vested interests, one new law, the Jan Lokpal—as imagined by AAP and AAP alone, with no space for any wider discussion or debate, whatsoever—will help reduce corruption. They do not claim, as their detractors suggest, that all corruption will end. But even a perfunctory look at this solution, the creation of a small group of people, shows missing maturity. 'Aam Aadmi Party will pass a powerful anti-corruption law, Jan Lokpal, to remove corruption from our system,' is what the party states. 'Under this law, people will be able to complain directly and imprison corrupt politicians and bureaucrats.'

But if that sounds like the song of the naïve, like a group of people playing god in a self-fashioned universe, one has only to observe Indian politics today; one sees the outstretched claws of the powerful, ready to strike down any proposal that threatens their corrupt existence. These claws have to be fought in India's crusade against corruption. More than fifty years have passed since the idea of an ombudsman to oversee corruption came up. The anti-corruption bill through the institution of Lokpal was introduced in Parliament eight times in forty-five years but not passed.

From as far back as 1963—when the idea of setting up an ombudsman first came up in Parliament during a discussion on budget allocation for the law ministry—to as close as 2005 when the second Administrative Reforms Commission recommended that 'the Lokpal Bill should become law with the least possible delay', the reluctance of Parliament to curb corruption tells us far more about its entrenched institutionalisation than anything else. Across traditional parties, corruption has been the handmaiden of democracy.

But for the 5 April 2011 fast by Anna Hazare at Jantar Mantar, demanding the enactment of Jan Lokpal Bill—as drafted by his team that included Arvind Kejriwal, Kiran Bedi and former Karnataka Lokayukta Santosh Hegde—this law would still be trapped in the cobwebs of Parliament, trying to breathe. As the government formed a joint drafting committee comprising ministers and civil society members on 9 April 2011, Anna Hazare ended his fast; 21 June 2011 saw the last meeting deliver two separate drafts.

When the government introduced the bill on 4 August 2011, it was attacked as being flawed. Twelve days later, Anna Hazare began his second fast, this time at Delhi's Ramlila Maidan. It took yet another fast by Anna Hazare, on 10 December 2012, before the bill was finally passed a week later and received the President's assent on 1 January 2014—a new year's gift to India's victims of corruption.

In this tug-of-war, what is glaringly obvious is that instead of creating an institution that checks corruption, the Union government has been reluctant, dragging its feet to bring the corrupt to justice; more than anything else, it is this reluctance that has been virtually institutionalised. Before prosecuting a public servant, for instance, you need the government—Central or state—to give sanction. Although this provision has been designed to protect honest officials from harassment, its abuse is rampant, through a tool called 'delay'.

This can be seen from the following statistics provided by an 8 April 2011 note by PRS Legislative Research that illustrates how the system of bringing the corrupt to justice has been rendered ineffective. As of end-2010, the Central government had not provided responses to 236 requests for prosecution. Of these, 155 requests (66 per cent) were pending for over three months. State governments had not responded to eighty-four requests, of which thirteen (15 per cent) were pending for more than three months. Only 6 per cent of the cases were taken up for prosecution, while 94 per cent were given departmental penalties.

The argument in support of a Jan Lokpal Bill is that corrupt politicians are rarely seen behind bars, partly because of tardy investigation and partly because of the abuse of the processes of law—it can be years before a judgement is delivered. 'In this time, the corrupt politician is re-elected many times over to loot the nation,' an AAP statement on corruption says. 'Many times accused politicians have died before being declared corrupt by the courts.'

AAP proposes to set up 'fast track conditions' under which it will ensure that the investigation of corruption charges and prosecution is done within six months. 'If found guilty, the corrupt official shall serve appropriate jail time from one year to life, depending on the severity of the case, his or her property will be seized, and he or she will be dismissed from the job.' While the intent behind this aspiration can't be doubted, in an institutional set up that takes upto fifteen years to decide on a case, six months seems like a far-fetched fantasy. The answer to whether this is pure fantasy or if there are indeed possibilities of translating these lofty ideas into action lies in a future that looks uncertain today.

Irrespective, other political parties are feeling the heat. The 17 January 2014 resolution of the All India Congress Committee made eleven big points, from economic growth to controlling price rise. It led with its predictable but now tattered theme of 'secularism'. Number two on the list was 'anti-corruption'. For a party that is seen to be an active participant in corruption, this change in stance is a delightful about-turn—the first attempt to fix a bleeding image and an early step towards listening to the aam aadmi.

'The Indian National Congress is deeply aware that the scourge of corruption affects the life of every Indian, and the poor carry its greatest burden,' the 2,520-word resolution states. 'The Congress believes this is unacceptable and has been tirelessly working on an agenda of governance to address this.' It rightly takes credit for turning the Right to Information Act into a law, enacted in 2005, to showcase that agenda. Congress also takes credit for getting the Lokpal Bill passed. Further, the resolution talks about a comprehensive anti-corruption code, consisting of nine new laws, four of which are pending in Lok Sabha and two in Rajya Sabha. It calls upon 'the UPA government and Parliament to debate and enact all six pending anti-corruption bills in the final session of this Lok Sabha, which is due to be convened next month.'

But it defends those actions that other constitutional bodies, the CAG and the judiciary in particular, have questioned. 'In our pursuit to root out corruption we have to be careful so as not to confuse disagreement on merits or even an honest mistake with corruption,' the resolution argues. 'Not everything that we find wrong is necessarily corruption. Several decisions of courts and constitutional authorities rejecting some administrative/ executive decisions, taken with all good intensions, have caused considerable damage to our economy. We are laying down a solid base of legislation to root out corruption and making the corrupt accountable, but equally we have to be vigilant that natural justice is not given a go-by or honest public servants hounded or forced into self-conscious paralysis.'

For BJP, the issue of corruption stands lower in the list of priorities. In the eight-point model of its prime ministerial candidate Narendra Modi, 'anti-corruption measures' come right at the end. And here too, the details are hazy: 'Bring back black money stashed abroad.' In the four core issues, 'good governance' follows development and security, after which BJP offers voters 'a clean government, free of corruption and scandal; a leadership that hasn't reached on top on the basis of connections and cronyism, but on the basis of years of unrelenting work for the masses'. Its manifesto for 2014 is still under construction, seeking suggestions from people (in line with what AAP did in Delhi and is doing for 2014), but in its 2009 manifesto neither corruption nor governance finds a mention.

Clearly, the tornado of disruption unleashed by AAP has moved too fast for either Congress or BJP to negotiate. It is only a matter of time before traditional parties adjust to the new tempests rising in the sea of disruption. But there is no doubt that even before AAP was born or the Jan Lokpal agitation began, it was BJP that had kept the Congress-led coalition under pressure in Parliament and outside on the issue of corruption. Given that the issue has mushroomed, BJP will definitely ensure that 'anti-corruption measures' climb a few rungs towards the top in its manifesto and in its national priorities.

Corruption is no longer an appendix attached to a governance manifesto; in Arvind Kejriwal's politics, an anti-corruption narrative is governance itself.

Decentralisation of Power

Praveen Singh wanted to create a prototype, a model of local governance—decentralisation—that would stand the test of time. 'Our idea was to create a prototype that the world could, over the next fifteen years, emulate and replicate,' says the quiet philosopher, working in the research wing of AAP's policy team. 'We believed that a group of forty to fifty villages together (would be the) right scale. They would capture all the human needs and aspirations that could exist, and so the prototype would deal with all of these. Because over the next fifteen to twenty years, problems are only going to intensify.'

Praveen Singh adds to the galaxy of ideas in the space of governance. 'For the last seven to eight years we had been working on this experimental model of an alternative society with a group of villages. But it was not taking off. There were also several limitations, since this was a grassroots effort. The larger system engulfs one in a frightening manner. We discovered that our utopian local model could operate only in a localised set up, otherwise it was not very feasible. We could create a small ripple through personal charisma, dedication and commitment.' But unless a top-down stream of governance met bottom-up efforts, the process would be incomplete.

They confronted this while dealing with international treaties, for instance. 'Political boundaries are fairly ineffective, economic boundaries these days do not overlap with political boundaries,' Praveen Singh says. 'For example, when we were making the Delhi manifesto we realised that we could not alter much unless there were changes at the national level. But at the national level there are very serious limitations and implications. We realised the limitations of a grassroots initiative when we were experimenting with our prototype model. This movement (the formation of AAP) happened around the time we were beginning to look at how top level changes could be made. It just happened in parallel by itself.'

The two forces—Praveen Singh's bottom-up model, and Kejriwal's top-down governance approach—embraced each other and are in the process of turning harmonious what many see as two ends of the governance spectrum. However, Arvind Kejriwal's choice of words, while endorsing decentralisation, is interesting. The general tenor is, 'No party but AAP will do this glorious work of changing the landscape of India'. As political rhetoric it makes sense. After all, a new party, still wet behind the ears, needs to bawl to catch the attention of voters.

'Concentration of power in a few hands has led to this (corruption),' says Arvind Kejriwal. 'If political power is decentralised, economic power will be too. What we stand for is honest politics and that is what we have set out to do. Now how else do I define AAP or the recent surge? Two words—honest politics—define us and that encompasses everything else. Equitable and inclusive growth, corruption-free environment are some of our basic tenets. Decentralisation of political power is the basic thing that defines our party and corruption is a symptom of that.'

But decentralisation is not a new idea for India. The institution of panchayats has its roots in ancient India. The village as the basic unit of a larger administrative institution, such as a kingdom, may be traced to Kautilya's *Arthashastra*. 'Villages consisting each of not less than a hundred families and of not more than five hundred families of agricultural people of sudra caste, with boundaries extending as far as a krosa (2,250 yards) or two, and capable of protecting each other shall be formed,' the text, written approximately around 350 BC, states. 'Boundaries shall be denoted by a river, a mountain, forests, bulbous plants (grishti), caves, artificial buildings (setubandha), or by trees such as salmali (silk cotton tree), sami (Acacia Suma), andkshira vriksha (milky trees).'

In Independent India, the biggest step towards administrative decentralisation and devolution of powers happened under then Prime Minister Rajiv Gandhi, with the 73rd and 74th Constitutional Amendments that created Panchayati Raj Institutions (PRIs) as tiers of self-governance below the level of the state. These provisions allot responsibilities to different tiers of PRIs. These are also in tune with Mahatma Gandhi's vision of self-governance in villages. These are the blocks that build governance infrastructure. But between this infrastructure and its actual capacity to serve the people of that area lies a wide chasm.

The extent of devolution varies across states. In an April 2013 study undertaken by Indian Institute of Public Administration, titled 'Strengthening of Panchayats in India: Comparing Devolution across States', researchers ranked twenty states based on six parameters—framework, functions, finances, functionaries, capacity building and accountability—to create a 'devolution index'. The results were mixed. On a cumulative basis, the top five states—Maharashtra, Karnataka, Kerala, Rajasthan and Tamil Nadu—were way ahead of the bottom five—Jharkhand, Jammu and Kashmir, Bihar, Punjab and Goa. While the average score of the top five states stood at 57.2, that of the bottom five was 29.8.

But the bigger story lies beyond the numbers. Gram panchayats in Maharashtra, for instance, are entitled to tax mobile towers and windmills, through an amendment in Rule 6 of the Maharashtra Village Panchayat Taxes and Fees (Amendment) Rule, 2011. This change will help the gram panchayats generate more revenues. Further, in order to fight corruption through a change in institutional mechanisms, the state revamped its Integrated Watershed Management Programme Committee and ensured that one gram panchayat sarpanch would be the chairperson of this committee, while the secretary would be elected by the gram sabha. This committee would be responsible for operation and maintenance of watershed works, registering new works, accounts maintenance of expenditure and annual reports of accounts.

In the case of Karnataka, from 2 April 2011, the government enacted a new law, the Karnataka Sakala Services Act 2011, which guarantees delivery of essential civic services to the citizens of Karnataka, within a stipulated time limit, for eleven services pertaining to gram panchayats. These include maintenance of drinking water, street lights and village sanitation, issue of records such as cattle and crop census, and the below poverty line list. The results leave us with optimism: against 1,98,305 applications received since 1 April 2012, 1,83,809 applicants, or an amazing 92.7 per cent of the total, have been delivered.

There are similar stories of devolution of power and its effective outcomes from Congress-governed Rajasthan (strengthening of district planning committees), BJP-governed Madhya Pradesh (receiving consolidated funds based on population to carry out developmental works), BJD-governed Odisha (enhancing institutional capacity of panchayats through administrative and technical support), BJP-governed Chhattisgarh (delivery of public services, action in case of default and an appellate authority). Despite changes in government, this is likely to continue. The contribution of traditional parties to the decentralisation debate is not inconsequential.

While the positive impact of decentralisation is visible, if only as exceptions rather than the rule today, Arvind Kejriwal's disruptive method seems to carry a note of impatience, seeking immediate action and overnight results. In the incrementalist approach, one policy change at a time, the list above has the potential to increase the devolution of power to the villages. But the process will be slow. To seek instant change is a lofty ideal; but if the foundations holding that ideal are not in place, it has the risk of crumbling.

'Decisions affecting millions of common Indians are taken by a few select leaders of the ruling party in Parliament,' AAP states. 'We believe that good governance happens when people have the power to influence decisions that shape their life. This is a major change that India needs badly. No present day party will usher in this systemic change. Today all big and small decisions that affect the nation are taken by a few select members of this body of governance.' The goal of AAP, it says, is to give power back in the hands of the people of India, give them Swaraj or self-rule.

According to Arvind Kejriwal, to fix the problem of absentee teachers in rural schools or absentee doctors in rural hospitals, we need to devolve power and give salaries to the panchayats. Panchayats, he argues, will know what is best for the children of their village, or the ailing. So, if a teacher is missing from school, he doesn't get his salary. Do this for three months and the problem will be solved. But in a system that has misused privileges over decades, can one stroke of a pen, backed by the might of the state, change the future?

Not necessarily, says BJD leader Baijayant Jay Panda from the Biju Janata Dal. 'You go to any village, any slum, you have a private school run by volunteers with very shabby infrastructure. But this offers far better education than the government-run school. It may have shabby infrastructure because it doesn't get government funding. Parents pay a pittance to the teachers and they work. If you had given vouchers to parents, that is, instead of the government giving money to government schools, we give money to the end user, and they decide whether the child should go to a government school or some local private school, this would change the paradigm. This would empower the aam aadmi in enormous ways.' This is a different way to look at the same problem with a similarly-empowering outcome.

'One of the most attractive things but one of the most difficult hurdles in the way of decentralisation is the gram sabha,' says social activist Nikhil Dey, while boarding a train to Rajasthan for a gram sabha meeting. 'Attractive, because every citizen is a voter, every voter is a decision-maker, and so it is like the general assembly of all the citizens of the country broken up into each gram sabha. So, it is extremely attractive. But when you start discussing participation in decision-making, there are questions regarding who gets involved, how much, where the safeguards are, what the modes are. It becomes far more complex.

Participative democracy is easier said than done. That is because any form of decision-making needs an institutional structure.'

Arvind Kejriwal's proposal is to bring about a change in administrative responsibility through the devolution of power. That's a simple way of doing things, and it will bring some benefits. Baijayant Jay Panda's way is more radical and attempts to change the incentive structure. In either case, opposition will come from incumbents, teachers' unions, for instance. The rise of the aam aadmi through devolution of powers to the panchayat is only a case of partial empowerment. The circle of empowerment gets completed when the incentive structure is changed.

Clearly, nobody is denying that decentralisation is a worthy ideal to pursue. But to say that decentralising decision-making by granting power to the smallest administrative unit is a panacea for all problems is overstating the expected outcomes. There is danger of losing economies of scale that large projects demand. Or, when a national project is being implemented, the Delhi-Mumbai Industrial Corridor for instance, if one is compelled to negotiate with innumerable gram sabhas, regarding each bend in the road and each industry around it, the delay that gets written into the project will be debilitating.

The bigger problem with devolution of power lies in the way it is being perceived—as giving excessive force to the democratic urge, at the cost of the country's republican needs. How will one deal with a village, for instance, with traditional systems of caste in place, that segregates the lower caste children in schools? How will religious minorities stand up to the brute force of a majority? Who will grant them the protection needed—and for which India calls itself a 'republic'? What if there are oversights by the gram sabha leaders? Who is to say that the corruption we see everywhere else will miraculously vanish the moment the institution of a gram sabha or a mohalla sabha is created? What are the safeguards to prevent a repetition of what AAP wants to change in the first place?

The answers lie somewhere around the change Praveen Singh is seeking, where a top-down operation meets a bottom-up institution to derive the best from decentralised power. They lie in institutions that work within the confines of and in harmony with the Constitutional provisions that protect the last marginalised Indian. If these requirements aren't met, it won't take time for a democracy to turn into a mobocracy, and for the new system of devolution of power to get hijacked by old entrenched operations.

Right to Reject, Recall

The third leg of accountability that Arvind Kejriwal's politics of disruption stands on is the right of the electorate to reject all candidates and recall an elected representative. That is, if an electorate finds none of the candidates up to the job, it can reject all candidates and seek a new election. Further, if the elected representative the electorate voted for is found to be wanting, the people can divest him of that authority, through its right to recall, and go for re-elections. For a people tired of corruption and cynical about the system, both these tools would be worthy experiments in offering political respite.

'When we go to cast our vote, we know that almost all the candidates are either corrupt or criminals,' AAP says, clearly passing a rather rash and hurried moral verdict on most elected representatives, displaying the immaturity of an impulsive upstart. 'But our current voting system forces us to choose any one candidate and waste our vote on someone we know is unfit for the job,' it goes on, once again continuing with the generalisations of its previous statement as it attempts to display the resultant helplessness of those being forced to elect the corrupt to power.

AAP's solution: giving people an alternative—a reject-all option in the voting booth. If most of the electorate takes this option, the election in that constituency will stand cancelled and new elections will be held within a month. To see the proposal through, those candidates as well as the parties they belong to will 'forfeit their right to contest again in re-elections'. This option was given to all the five states that went to polls in late-2013, but with a notable difference from what Arvind Kejriwal seeks: votes of those exercising the reject-all option would not be counted in the final tally. As a result, the option is ineffective.

The proposal that will have an impact, the right to recall an elected representative, is not yet in force but, if implemented according to AAP's wishes, will bring in greater accountability. 'Today, we give our vote to a candidate, he or she wins the election, and then they disappear from our life,' AAP says. 'And in the current electoral system, the people have no choice but to suffer this candidate for five years. We want to create an alternative. We will enact a Right to Recall law wherein the common man does not have to wait for five years to remove a corrupt MLA or MP from office. People can complain to the Election Commission anytime to recall their representative and call for fresh elections.' As a democratic tool in the hands of the people, the right to recall, theoretically, ensures greater accountability of inefficient or corrupt representatives.

A good idea, no doubt, but how practical is it? For this, we need to look beyond India to see if there are any benchmarks. In the US, there are eighteen states that permit recall elections to remove state officials, notes the Constitution unit of University College London. 'Only two governors have ever successfully been removed: Lynn Frazier in North Dakota in 1921, and Gray Davis in California in 2003. Some states require specific grounds for recall, and the most common threshold in terms of signatures required is 25 per cent of the total number of votes in the last general election.'

Dissatisfied voters of provincial districts in British Columbia (Canada) can petition to have their MLA removed from office. Corruption is not a necessary condition for recall. All a proposer, known as the proponent, has to do is give a reason in less than 200 words as to why the MLA must be recalled. Once the petition is accepted, the proponent has sixty days to collect signatures of 40 per cent of the electorate—the most challenging aspect of converting the idea of recall into practice. As a result, since its first use in December 1997, there have been twenty-two recall efforts, 'of which only two were submitted with enough signatures to proceed to the verification stage. One lacked sufficient eligible signatures; the other achieved its purpose when the MLA in question, Paul Reitsma, resigned when it looked as if the recall attempt would be successful.'

The first experiments in India are delivering results. In June 2008, three municipal bodies in Chhattisgarh initiated the successful recall of presidents of three urban bodies. Chhattisgarh and Madhya Pradesh are the only two states—both governed by BJP—that have the option to recall elected presidents for non-performance. The process, however, is cumbersome. It starts when three-quarters of the total number of elected representatives within the urban bodies write to the district collector and demand recall, writes Vinod Bhanu of the Centre for Legislative Research and Advocacy, in a 29 December 2007 article in *Economic and Political Weekly*. 'After verifying the circumstances, the district collector can report to the state government. Once the report has been considered, the state government can recommend that the state election commission conduct an election to recall the presidents.'

There have been two learnings from this recall, Vinod Bhanu

writes in the same journal on 4 October 2008. One, it has sent 'overt messages to the elected representatives about the risks of ignoring the development concerns of their electorates'. And two, it has shown that the process of such recall can be mishandled. 'The ousted independent presidents were reported to have stated that both BJP and Congress councillors formed an alliance to initiate the process of recall, and there have been allegations from the ousted presidents of the local bodies about misuse of legitimate provisions of the recall. The ground responses also seemed to feature reports of allegations of political bias, supposedly influencing the decisions of the state administration which recommended that the Election Commission perform recall polls.'

It is not without reason that then Chief Election Commissioner S.Y. Quraishi said that recall is not possible in India. 'It will destabilise the country, everywhere where there is discontent, people will start recalling,' he told CNN-IBN, days before he met Arvind Kejriwal along with Shanti Bhushan, Prashant Bhushan, Manish Sisodia and Kiran Bedi on 31 October 2011. S.Y. Quraishi explained the various implications of implementing the recall suggestion to them. His concerns included: the minimum percentage of voters who may file the petition for recall; verification of authenticity of thousands of signatures; whether those signatures have been given voluntarily or under coercion; minimum time after which such petition for recall could be presented. 'He also mentioned that such a move would bring instability as the losers could start such a campaign from day one,' the subsequent press release from the Election Commission stated, showcasing practical hurdles that lay between initiating recall and enforcing it.

However, instead of getting completely overwhelmed by the seemingly crushing hurdles in the path of a recall process, it is important to acknowledge the advantages of a system of a recall. First, an elected representative will be forced to engage with his constituency throughout his five-year term—and not just towards the end, with elections around the corner. Second, the practice of injecting cash and drinks into the electoral system will scale down, since the investment could have a shorter gestation period, given the risk of recall. Third, it could help check corruption— the knowledge that a long-term risk could confront him if he pursues short-term gains would help keep a corrupt politician in control, his own self-interest driving checks and balances. As a result, it could infuse greater accountability into the constituency and the system.

But on the flip side, the right to recall can lead to a draconian democracy that may not be needed and keep the elected representative under the constant threat of being recalled. To prevent that from happening, the incentive of representatives would be to keep their constituents contented. This, in turn, could lead to taking decisions that would pander to the majority— again, leaving marginalised sections vulnerable to the brute force of democracy. Constant re-elections could destabilise the government, as S.Y. Quraishi said. Finally, there is the challenge of transplanting a system that has successfully worked in small countries like Switzerland or Uganda onto a large and complex democracy like India.

'This whole notion of direct democracy has to be thought through,' says Ashutosh Varshney. 'India cannot be Switzerland. Even the city of Delhi is larger. So, for what issues should you have direct democracy and for what issues should you take decisions on your own and submit yourself for a citizens' review every five years, as other parties do, needs to be seen carefully. Representative democracy is inadequate but not irrelevant and not entirely to be wished away. It has its purpose, it has its logic.

It basically says that people go for citizens' consultation every five years and in those five years they take decisions which will then be reviewed in elections. The basic idea is insufficient but not wrong.'

The debate is still to open out.

'Going forward there are a lot of things that we want to do,' says Pankaj Gupta. 'A corruption-free society is what we look forward to. Fighting a larger election becomes a means to this end. If we win the elections, is our work done? No. The objective is to create those sort of checks and balances in government, those kinds of processes that support the distribution and decentralisation of power, which is the central motive of the party. To ensure that power goes back to the public, to the people. Whatever Arvind and this team are doing in the current government is oriented towards that. Ultimately, if we achieve the objective that people can decide what they want, decide how best the budget is to be spent, if we can make them masters of their destiny, then we have achieved our target.'

Arvind Kejriwal, takes the idea of power and turns it around. 'Power is the ability to influence the lives of many people through your decisions. You are an instrument to influence the lives of other people. People in public offices have this power and that is why power should not reside or remain concentrated in a few hands,' he says. 'People who are directly impacted by these decisions should have a say in the decision-making.'

But in the land of Mahatma Gandhi, how did we lose sight of this simple objective, how did we lose the alchemy of power? How and when did the political class begin to 'rule' rather than 'govern'? How did we lose our freedom?

4

CORRUPTION OF FREEDOM

When Arvind Kejriwal raises the clarion call for swaraj, independence, it borders on the weird. His slogans, 'Bharat Mata Ki Jai!' or 'Inquilab Zindabad', that have been and continue to be invoked in every rally, every meeting—he began his first speech as chief minister of Delhi with these two slogans—sound out of place. It is almost as if he is summoning ideas of past struggles for Independence to brand his political enterprise. The slogan worked when India fought the British for freedom. But on 15 August 2014, when India will celebrate the 67th anniversary of that Independence, the question to be asked is, what is the relevance of the idea of swaraj today and why is the Indian electorate dancing to this rebel rallying cry?

'Our representative seeks the power of our vote with obsequious postures and folded hands,' Arvind Kejriwal writes in his book *Swaraj*. 'Once voted as the representative, he immediately sheds this posture and becomes a despotic ruler.' Further, the executives, who report to representatives and not the people, are virtually untouchable as far as the law goes. Finally, the third leg of democracy, the judiciary, is unable to deliver justice in time. 'This,' he says, 'is not Swaraj. After the British quit we are now the slaves of this deception known as democracy.'

What is swaraj? Arvind Kejriwal gets into the epistemology of the word. 'It is a Hindi word,' he writes. '"Swa" means "my" and "rajya" means "kingdom". Swaraj means "my kingdom".

If it is my kingdom, then it is I who will govern the way I want. "Swaraj", therefore, stands for "self-governance". We are a democracy, which is governed by the people, of the people and for the people. In other words, we are part of this process of taking decisions for our welfare by ourselves.'

Translating this into institutional frameworks, Arvind Kejriwal suggests that swaraj implies giving people the power to recall elected representatives; making government officials accountable for acts of omission and commission; decentralising power and distributing it to people at the level of gram sabhas in rural areas and mohalla sabhas driven by Resident Welfare Associations (RWA) in urban centres; controlling the flow of government funds and their use; and declaring people as owners of national wealth like land, forest, waterways and minerals—most of which we have already discussed at length in the previous chapter. As a philosophical statement, Arvind Kejriwal's understanding of the word means handing power back to the people.

But if citizens have elected their representatives, how is democracy being smothered? In Kejriwal's worldview, there is a two-headed monster lording it over India today. One head eats the hearts and minds of India's people through corruption, drawing power from the police. The other head, more dangerous but invisible, eats the bodies and vitals of India through misgovernance. Enslaved between the two are a people, institutionally free but still slaves of the processes set up by the British and perfected over the years by successive governments.

'The entire police force was built during the colonial times, where the police was created to cater to the colonial masters and rule over the people. It wasn't designed to be responsive to the citizens,' says Atishi Marlena, in context of the police inaction in the Somnath Bharti case. 'In that sense, the entire police system needs to be overhauled.'

She echoes the words of brilliant actor-intellectual Balraj Sahni. 'I am sure there must be some police officers in this country who in their hearts want to be regarded as friends rather than enemies of the public,' he said in a 1972 convocation speech to students of Jawaharlal Nehru University. "They must be aware that in England the behaviour of the police towards the public is polite and helpful. But the tradition in which they have been trained is not the one which the British set for their own country but the one which they set for their colonies. So, the policeman is helpless. According to this colonial tradition, it is his duty to strike terror into anyone who enters his office, to be as obstructive and unhelpful as possible. This is the tradition which pervades every government office, from the chaparasi to the minister.'

The need to change the system politically is a narrative that's not restricted to Arvind Kejriwal. The other challenger to Congress, riding a similar anti-corruption, good-governance plank is Narendra Modi, the prime ministerial candidate of Bhartiya Janata Party (BJP). He too plays with the word swaraj. His slogan, 'from swaraj (self-rule) to surajya (good governance)', encapsulates both the ideas that Kejriwal proffers, corruption and misgovernance. But he takes it a step further, making it more specific through 'sushasan (good administration)'.

'Even after decades of Independence, the country has not been able to make the important transition from swarajya (freedom) to surajya (good governance),' he said in a 9 January 2014 speech to non-resident Indians. 'The last decade in particular has witnessed unprecedented depths of petty politics, self-interest and exploitation, undermining the exalted principles of inclusive and sustainable nation building. A deteriorating economy, unrelenting stream of scandals and corruption exposes, poor delivery of basic services, policy paralysis, stagnating society and an overall atmosphere of divisive politics has severely hit the people's perception of, and trust in, the government and its leaders.'

Narendra Modi brings in a new word into the corruption-misgovernance vocabulary—trust, or rather the loss of trust. Further, he has a clearer idea about the role of the state—that must evolve 'from merely carrying out regular day-to-day business of the government to strategically guiding the nation towards a brighter future through governance.' These electoral weapons are missing in Arvind Kejriwal's armoury.

And yet, today, it is Arvind Kejriwal and AAP that are more strongly identified with the two heads India is fighting. Of the two, corruption is the noisier one. And even though it is the mass of people that has brought their leaders to power, in the fight against corruption, battles are lonely, it is each victim for himself fighting against the entire might of an elected state and an entrenched bureaucracy. Worse, the victim fights not one but a network of institutional frameworks. Complain about corruption in a municipal body and the culprit's cousin from the water department will hound you; try and get your wealth-destroying water bill looked into and you are up against official arrogance and institutional frameworks that back it. The official is smug in the knowledge that he will be protected, come what may.

In the hot summer of 1996, I had gone to the electricity office of Noida to complain about the huge bill that I had wrongly been presented with. On day one, I was told that the concerned authority was not in office and there was no information about when, and if, he would come. Come day two, I had armed myself with patience and waited from 11.00 a.m. to 5.00 p.m. generally loitering in the area, depleting my energies, my enthusiasm, my strength. On the fourth day, one of the officials finally pointed at a long, black Cielo and said, 'There he is.'

As he walked up the stairs, I waited for him.

'Sir...' I began but he swooshed past as though I did not exist. I followed him to his room. The guard stopped me. I was at that point of anticipation where I was convinced that I would finally be able to speak to this man and receive redressal. My mind had weakened in the past three days, but my will was still strong.

After an hour or so, the man walked out. I followed him. 'Sir, I need to speak to you.'

'Come tomorrow,' he dismissed me with a wave of his hand.

'Sir, this is the fourth day that I'm here, can you please give me just one minute?' I asked, the bills in my hand fluttering.

'Oh, you've come for four days?'

'Yes, sir...'

'Come for two more days,' he concluded and walked down the stairs.

I didn't know what had hit me, but I followed him blindly to his car, in a daze. He sat there with a property broker and drove off, the only memory of his presence being the dust that settled on me as I looked on with acute frustration and a profound unsettling rage. I vomited at the gate. But if mine is the banal example of an aam aadmi being throttled, the apparent khaas aadmi fared no better.

'Any government office you go to and put your finger in is festering,' says Vinod Rai, the former Comptroller and Auditor General. 'Any office—death certificate, ration, electricity, water—anywhere you go, you have to grease palms.' He narrates a personal incident when his wife went to the DDA to get a freehold for their apartment. 'I was a secretary in the finance ministry. The official said that about twenty-four thousand rupees were due. My wife showed the receipt and said that it was already paid. The official said "register mein nahin chada hai" (it is not showing in the register). On asking what she could do since it was a lapse on the part of the DDA, the official said "agar maine ye register khol diya to ye chaubees hazar aratalees hazar ho jayega" (if I open the register, the twenty-four thousand will become forty-eight thousand). He was threatening her. My staff member had gone along and when he disclosed his identity, the official said, "Delhi mein sab VIP hote hai, humara kya hoga?" (In Delhi, everyone is a VIP. What will happen to us?) It's as brazen as that.'

What makes government officials behave in this manner? What makes them believe that they are masters of citizens? With Arvind Kejriwal and AAP, these questions I asked seventeen years ago have come full circle today. From teachers in government schools who don't come to teach and doctors of government hospitals who don't heal, to owners of ration shops who steal rations meant for the poor and a police that doesn't register cases, Arvind Kejriwal's list of cases of corruption and misgovernance is long—enumerating cases of passport officers, revenue department personnel, birth and death certificate officials and so on. 'You can do nothing against him,' he writes of the corrupt official, 'except seethe with an impotent rage.'

Each of you reading this book will have his or her unique story to tell of being scalded by the system. The question is: How did we get here? Is it something to do with India being nicknamed a nation of the corrupt? Is this phenomenon new to this subcontinent? While the topic is as wide as it is deep, of two things we are clear. One, the phenomenon of corruption is certainly not unique to our times—history provides us with evidence. And two, India is not living in isolation—across the world, corruption has unfortunately been an indispensable part of economic development.

Landscape of Corruption

Before we contemplate the time and extent of corruption, it is essential to define it. Pause for a moment and ponder over the idea. Can you define the word? Not the symptoms, but the idea? In seven small words, the World Bank attempts a definition of corruption as: 'Abuse of public office for private gain.' Another definition comes from Transparency International, the body that tracks perceptions of corruption across the world: 'Corruption is the abuse of entrusted power for private gain. It hurts everyone who depends on the integrity of people in a position of authority.' This, according to the body, has a range that almost mirrors the government itself. From defence and oil to public procurement and judiciary, it extends to and infects all possible institutions.

Then, again, there is the tendency to make the definition simplistic or gloss over the complexities that define the phenomenon. Map the scholarships that children of senior Indian civil servants procure against the overall sample and you will in all probability see numbers that make no sense, unless you admit that there are illegal allotments.

At times, it is more brazen. According to AAP leader Yogendra Yadav, if corruption is an issue in Delhi, it is 10 times more so in Haryana. 'Corruption characterises virtually everything you see in Haryana, beginning with land—land acquisition or non-acquisition, compensation for land acquisition,' he says. 'If you look at jobs, government jobs, everything is up for sale. Look at the recent announcement of Haryana Civil Services—incidentally, a constitutional body, but functioning like any other government department. Of the thirty candidates who have made it to the state civil services, the equivalent of the IAS at the national level, twenty are related to leading political parties of Haryana or the OSD (Officer on Special Duty) of the chief minister. The whole thing is so brazen that all this happened when Congress was trying to bring in the Lokpal Bill, when Rahul Gandhi was asking for the Adarsh scam to be looked into.'

Corruption can be broken down into five large fragments—bribery, theft, political and bureaucratic fraudeulency, isolated and systematic mismanagement, and corruption in the private sector. For a long time I did not subscribe to the view that private sector misdemeanours should be classified as corruption. After all, corruption is the misuse of public office, I surmised, not private. In any case, while investigating a corrupt official, investigators would catch the private entities. But now, with Indian companies growing, particularly in the financial services, corruption in the private sector could influence money laundering even for terrorist activities. The public-private nature of infrastructure partnerships is another instance where careful observation is needed.

The driving force behind the audit of private power distribution companies in Delhi that AAP has initiated is just that. Here, not only has the government given a virtual monopoly to two companies that supply electricity to citizens of Delhi, it has done so in a sector it regulates and is a shareholder of. When the company overcharges consumers by using meters that have allegedly been tampered with, for instance, it amounts to corruption. When the city's electricity supply was under the government, citizens faced one kind of corruption, at the individual level; today, the fear is that it has been commercially institutionalised.

One can spot similar instances of open, brazen, rampant corruption in the way that autorickshaws overcharge or refuse to go where citizens want them to. The tariff an autorickshaw can charge is regulated by the government. When that is breached—and there are no institutional mechanisms to control this rampant abuse—it amounts to corruption. This is a constituency that helped AAP come to power in Delhi; autorickshaws were used as vehicles of communication during elections. The rickshaws have now aligned themselves with other parties.

Further, corruption need not be limited to a financial transaction. For example, directing public funds to the constituency of leaders of parties in power could be seen as political corruption. Here, there is no personal gratification. But using the exchequer's money to fund an energy research organisation in a spoilt constituency, twisting a straight industrial corridor so that it passes through the decision-making minister's constituency or building a swimming pool in a village when the rest of the state is reeling in poverty could be cases where the definition might be extended.

Vito Tanzi, in an International Monetary Fund working paper, 'Corruption Around the World: Causes, Consequences, Scope, and Cures', defines seven categories under which acts of corruption can be classified. Corruption, he says, can be bureaucratic (or petty corruption); cost-reducing or benefit-enhancing; briber-initiated or bribee-initiated; coercive or collusive; centralised or decentralised; predictable or arbitrary; and involving cash payments or not. The definition could be critiqued for being technical and being of value only to scholars, but every Indian can identify the nuances of this note, having experienced every shade and hue of corruption.

All forms of corruption ultimately get their signals from the political leadership, says Vinod Rai. As far as bureaucratic corruption goes, there are three kinds of perpetrators—white, black and grey, he says. The white are totally above-board. The black are beyond redemption. The bulk is grey, which is 50 per cent. They are fence-sitters, who are waiting for signals from the top. 'If the signal from the top is white, they have no difficulty in turning white, and 75 per cent would be white. The black guys are responsible for policy paralysis; they have sided with the politicians and have made a buck. And they make the biggest noise.' As a result, having a political leadership that's corruption-free is an important tool towards building a corruption-free society.

Arvind Kejriwal says pretty much the same thing; the only difference is in the statistics. 'There is no dearth of money within the government,' he says. 'What is lacking is honesty and good intentions. Rank and file are a part of this rot and corruption. But if you send a right message from the top, many of these people are willing to change—10 per cent are those who are born corrupt and they need to be jailed; another 10 per cent are born honest who will not change and succumb even when there are pressures; and 80 per cent of the people go with the wind. They wait for signals from the top. And it is very easy to bring in a change if the signal from the top is clear.'

Finally, we come to the issue of international corruption, a practice that goes beyond the aam aadmi and enters the realm of foreign policy and global actions. Even as the dust is to settle on the recent diplomatic incident involving India's Deputy Counsel General to the US Devyani Khobragade, the fact is that the misuse of diplomatic immunity has become a malaise that is crying for reform.

In 'Cultures of Corruption: Evidence From Diplomatic Parking Tickets', Raymond Fisman and Edward Miguel observed that because of diplomatic immunity, the thousands of diplomats posted in New York faced zero enforcement as far as parking violations were concerned. 'Diplomats from high corruption countries (based on existing survey-based indices) have significantly more parking violations,' they conclude. On that front, India fares about average, with a ranking of 79 out of 146 countries surveyed.

With 6.1 parking violations per diplomat, India ranks comfortably better than Kuwait's 242.5, Egypt's 139.6 and Chad's 124.3. Among equals, Brazil's diplomats, at 29.9, had higher violations. So did China at 9.5, South Africa at 34.0 and Indonesia at 36.1. Only Russia, at 2.0, had a lower score—even though corruption within Russia is rampant.

The issue here is not specific to India but points to the institutionalisation of corruption by sovereigns. This is now beginning to be addressed by the Group of 20 (G20) nations. In its September 2013 declaration at St. Petersburg, the G20 intensified its fight against corruption. 'Corruption is a severe impediment to sustainable economic growth and poverty reduction and can threaten financial stability and the economy as a whole,' the statement said. 'Corruption is corrosive, destroying public trust, distorting the allocation of resources and undermining the rule of law.'

The G20 encouraged its members and other countries to ratify and implement the United Nations Convention against Corruption (UNCAC), a sixty-five-page document that carries the theoretical aspirations of nations against corruption—prevention, criminalisation, international cooperation, asset recovery and so on. While the convention was adopted by the General Assembly of the United Nations on 31 October 2003, India signed it two years later, on 9 December 2005. But it took more than five years before it finally ratified it on 9 May 2011, a period during which protest politics had brought the issue on the streets, forcing the government to wake up and respond.

This was the period during which the anti-corruption agitations by Yoga guru Baba Ramdev and activist Anna Hazare were at their peak. Baba Ramdev raised a furore when he said that India's corrupt politicians and bureaucrats had stashed away upto $1.5 trillion of the country's wealth in Swiss banks.

Calculations on how India's poverty could be ended once and for all if this money were to be brought back began to fill the national discourse; the issue struck an emotive chord and gathered political momentum.

'This is a ridiculous figure,' then Swiss ambassador to India Phillippe Welti told me over tea at his Chanakyapuri residence. 'Take any economic indicator and it will be impossible to go with this figure. This number could be representing Indian money worldwide, not in Switzerland alone. As per our estimates, the money owned by Indians in Switzerland is $2 billion.' Besides, just because the money is in a Swiss bank doesn't mean it is illegal. There are legitimate businesses operating there.

Also, getting money from there back to India or revealing the identity of Indians and their bank accounts goes against Swiss laws, he said. 'There may be cases where ownership is very complex. But don't blame Switzerland for it. As far as we are concerned, the assets must be located in Switzerland and they must be identifiable.' The Indian government has tedious work cut out for itself.

Between Baba Ramdev's cries for bringing money back and Switzerland's reluctance in the matter lies a more dangerous phenomenon—the legitimisation of sovereign corruption. When countries like Switzerland, Cyprus and Mauritius make laws that attract investments or become pass-through zones for money to flow under the veil of secrecy, it amounts to another kind of corruption that no other country can fix. Again, the G20 has focussed its attention on this crime. The 2010 Toronto Summit, for instance, clearly stated: 'We stand ready to use countermeasures against tax havens.' Much needs to be done on this front, however.

For the moment, agitations against corruption, like Baba Ramdev's or Arvind Kejriwal's, need to focus on the rot within.

Litany of Laws

Arvind Kejriwal's is a politics of articulated angst. By highlighting corruption in his narrative, he has touched a raw nerve of the aam aadmi, for whom a corruption-free or at least a corruption-reduced world is beginning to become a matter of significance. Arvind Kejriwal's belief is that setting up an anti-corruption agency called Lokpal, effective from 1 January 2014, will be the most effective means to ending corruption. The promise seems exaggerated to some. Will it work?

Like every other law in general, and anti-corruption laws in particular, there is no dearth of legal remedies available to Indian citizens. With six large acts of Parliament—Indian Penal Code, 1860; Prevention of Corruption Act, 1988; Prevention of Money Laundering Act, 2002; Right to Information Act, 2005; Central Vigilance Commission Act, 2003; and Lok Ayukta Acts of states—the issue of corruption has been largely addressed through laws. And yet, corruption continues unabated.

The biggest paradox while tackling corruption in India, in fact, is that despite a litany of laws, corruption has only increased. The corruption that bothers the Indian voter today is not so much the abuse of power by the super-rich to get governments to allocate land, mines, spectrum, oil blocks or other natural resources. These make good fodder for headlines and talk shows. While the Congress-led UPA government managed to deliver these to perfection in the past ten years, it is the office of Comptroller and Auditor General (CAG) which got a new lease of life under Vinod Rai, even as he exposed governmental excesses and helped coalesce the anti-corruption sentiment that is now gaining political strength.

In his first interview after taking charge, he told me he was not interested in pursuing petty vouchers. 'It is not worth CAG's while to look at hundred rupee telephone bills or two hundred rupee staff car bills,' he said. 'Our job is to improve governance or administration. We have to recommend how we can improve efficiency of administration. For instance, if hundred rupees leaves the government's coffers, how do we ensure it reaches beneficiaries?'

All leakages need not be corruption and hence governance becomes an important tool to fix the problem. 'In the 1980s, Rajiv Gandhi said that out of every rupee the government spent, only fifteen paise reached the citizen, eighty-five paise went towards expenses and corruption,' says BJD leader Baijayant Jay Panda. 'People don't know what the recent figures are, I can cite one Planning Commission figure of the PDS (Public Distribution System). Out of every rupee spent on the PDS, only twenty-seven paise reaches the beneficiary. So, in thirty years, you've gone from fifteen paise to twenty-seven paise. Still seventy-three paise is being lost on every rupee.'

Arvind Kejriwal is hoping to fix the problem through the empowerment of the aam aadmi, as a bottom-up solution. Devolution of power to enable local village or urban resident welfare associations to take local decisions, for instance, would help fix the problem, as they would know the best use of the money and would be able to track it better through results that reach them directly. But a top-down solution, brought into the system by reformers through the use of technology, would not be out of order.

The Rich...

And then, there is the supply end of mega corruption—business. Just as the dominant chronicle in Arvind Kejriwal's fight against corruption rests on the public official who now rules rather than serves, the flip side of this coin is the business fraternity. Nobody is shedding any tears for it, however. Caught between a closed economy of controls on one side and playing the politics of patronage on the other, businessmen haven't exactly covered themselves in glory as far as corrupt practices go.

In his continuing battle against corruption, on 11 February 2014, Arvind Kejriwal brought the issue at the doorstep of India's largest business conglomerate, Reliance Industries Ltd. He ordered the Delhi government's anti-corruption branch to register first information reports (FIRs) against petroleum minister Veerappa Moily, Reliance Industries Ltd chairman and India's wealthiest man Mukesh Ambani, former petroleum minister Murli Deora and former director-general of hydrocarbons V.K. Sibal for alleged irregularities in the pricing of natural gas from the Krishna-Godavari basin in the Bay of Bengal.

Arvind Kejriwal said the move was prompted by a complaint his office received from former cabinet secretary T.S.R. Subramanian, former expenditure secretary E.A.S. Sarma, retired admiral R.H. Tahiliani and advocate Kamini Jaiswal. He quoted the complaint and said Reliance Industries Ltd and the Central government had colluded to almost double the gas prices to $8 from $4.20 per unit.

Denials followed. 'The complaint and each of the allegations on the basis of which the Delhi government has taken such action are completely baseless and devoid of any merit or substance whatsoever,' a Reliance Industries Ltd statement said. 'I sympathise with his (Arvind Kejriwal's) ignorance. He thinks that it's just like taking water through a bucket from a well. He cannot take oil like that,' said Veerappa Moily.

While it is easy to point fingers and raise issues like corruption, particularly against the rich and powerful in an overall atmosphere of mistrust, proving them in court may take more rigour; mere allegations are not enough. This means Arvind Kejriwal and his team will have to engage with the intricate economics of oil exploration in this case. Further, since the nexus of big business with politicians is likely to be a running theme in his discourse he will have to understand how business functions better.

He will also need to keep in mind the impact such decisions have on investments. If a nexus between big business and politicians is proved, well and good. But if not, it could, and effectively would, lead to uncertainty and scepticism in the public mind. In the India of tomorrow, an India that expects economic growth through large manufacturing and delivering jobs for its young populace, ignoring or shunning this constituency would be a matter of great concern. As the texture of politics begins to change and it gradually becomes 'uncool', even risky, to be corrupt, industry will inevitably adapt—or seek out other corrupt destinations abroad. For now, the indications are leaning towards change.

A 2013 survey of two hundred senior executives titled, 'Bribery and Corruption: Ground Reality in India', by industry lobby group FICCI and consulting firm Ernst and Young, came up with the following findings. Eight out of ten respondents said that cases of bribery and corruption can negatively impact foreign direct investment (FDI), the most vulnerable sectors being infrastructure and real estate, metals and mining, aerospace and defence, and power and utilities. More than half the respondents agreed that it is the reluctance to obtain licenses and approvals through authorised channels (which may take longer), that leads to bribery and corruption. Nearly half the executives said their companies lost business to their competitors because of the latter's unethical business practices. Most importantly, almost nine out of ten executives felt there should be greater enforcement of laws to curb the proliferation of bribery and corruption.

You might want to take the survey above with a pinch of salt. In any transaction, there is the taker of a bribe and the giver—the bribee and the briber, the demand side and the supply side. Given that the focus group of such a survey is corporate executives—many of whom may provide the supply pipelines to corruption—one could question the motives guiding their answers. But the last point about most of them seeking better enforcement of anti-corruption laws should serve as a smoke signal of changing times.

'You are right, it's mostly the privileged who benefit from corruption, but corruption affects everybody,' says Baijayant Jay Panda. 'Among the business people, if you ask those who are technocrats, if you ask those who have ambitions of taking on the world, doing business is tough. There are businesses that thrive on rent-seeking. Just like there are bureaucrats and politicians who thrive on rent-seeking. And there are businesses like the IT industry that thrive on creating something. They thrive on building value. If you thrive on building value and creating something, you will be very handicapped by a corrupt system. Corruption hampers everybody.'

Perhaps the pendulum of day-to-day functioning has swung so far towards corruption that even beneficiaries are uncomfortable. Now, the pitch against corruption has been raised so high that we look at even legitimate businesses with suspicion. An equilibrium is needed—and business is playing fair ball. 'I have spoken to some big industrialists in the past few weeks and some of the biggest ones have told me that they appreciate the changes that are going on in India today,' Baijayant Jay Panda says. 'They are fine with a fair system, where everybody has an equal chance. Many of these businesses have a problem with a corrupt environment, since there will always be somebody with a better bargaining chip, some connection to somebody to get spectrum or something else. It is only in an open and transparent system that the best businesses can thrive.'

It is not as if AAP does not understand this or has a view that all businesses and businessmen are corrupt and beneficiaries of graft. 'It is wrong to assume that the rich are not agitated by corruption,' says Pankaj Gupta. 'They might have to follow the system. Perhaps they are into corruption because the system is asking them to. But a majority of Indians I would say, if given the chance to do business without corruption, would like to do that. They would like to follow the norms. Unfortunately, our existing system does not allow them to perform that way.'

...And the Poor

But corruption of the higher echelons of society finally hits the poor and middle class aam aadmi. Corruption in road contracts, for instance, means rising tolls. Some of these excesses, combined with the fact that India does not take well to user charges, are showing up through protest politics, as in Maharashtra and Gurgaon. Corruption in real estate through a change in land use means higher prices of houses for the aam aadmi. Combined with unaccounted-for money chasing real estate deals, affordable housing has all but disappeared. Graft in power means the aam aadmi has to pay higher tariffs for electricity; broaden it to cover water and spectrum, and tariffs there rise too.

As far as the corruption the aam aadmi has to deal with is concerned, former Chief Economic Advisor and current Vice President at World Bank Kaushik Basu has an interesting solution—let the bribe-giver go scot free, punish the bribe-taker. The simplicity of this solution is in stark contrast to laws that were created to encourage petty corruption and protect incumbent bureaucrats, officials and politicians. Focussing on 'harassment bribes'—withholding of a tax refund, signing off on land allotted by government and so on—that play a large role in breeding inefficiency and have a corrosive effect on civil society, he says 'we should declare the act of giving a bribe in all such cases as legitimate activity. In other words, the giver of a harassment bribe should have full immunity from any punitive action by the state.'

The reasoning is that once the law is altered, the interests of the bribe-giver and the bribe-taker will diverge. 'The bribe-giver will be willing to cooperate in getting the bribe-taker caught. Knowing that this will happen, the bribe-taker will be deterred from taking a bribe.' What is the institutional solution? Revoke Section 12 of Prevention of Corruption Act, 1988. 'Whoever abets any offence (pertaining to bribery),' it says, 'shall be punishable with imprisonment for a term which shall be not less than 6 months but which may extend up to five years and shall also be liable to fine.' The paper is gathering dust but maybe Arvind Kejriwal could revive it and explore its potential.

However, corruption alone is not to blame. There are other, related issues that accompany the politics of moral corruption and the aam aadmi is raising his voice against this.

Plethora of Privileges

Another issue provoking disquiet among citizens is this—the stream of legitimised benefits, paid for by taxpayers, enjoyed by politicians and bureaucrats time and time again. From palatial bungalows in the centre of Delhi that are spread over acres of prime land, and the security cover of dozens of police, to the abuse of lal battis (red sirens) atop luxury cars, so traffic is at a standstill till the cavalcades pass by, the VIPs of India have done all they can possibly get away with. In the process they have rubbed the nose of the angry citizen to the ground again and again.

These privileges may not be classified as corruption. When they have been accorded to VIPs by law, the question of illegality doesn't arise; backed by law, they are technically legitimate. But to an electorate that's now waking up, this legitimacy is oppressive. These are being viewed as practices of a bygone era, where the British 'rulers' had to keep a safe distance from the Indian 'ruled', the 'natives' had to stand at a distance. And as far as legitimacy goes, the 'laws' that dictators in other countries have written technically legitimise their privileges too.

After freedom, the idea of 'rulers' should have been squashed and been replaced with governance. Instead, what we see is a perversion of that thought, that aspiration. Not only has the usage of the word 'governance' been missing from political discourse (the past three years being an exception), but the abuse of the term has also been rampant.

Arvind Kejriwal has been able to capture this ruptured status and convert it into a political tool. Every privilege is now under the scanner. While the traditional parties, Congress and BJP, offer lip service, Arvind Kejriwal and his AAP team of ministers in the Delhi cabinet walked the talk in their forty-nine days of power by refusing to live in large bungalows.

When the BJP asked why Kejriwal, as chief minister, was moving into a five-bedroom apartment, the latter quietly asked the central government to give him a smaller house. His colleague and cabinet minister (for education, PWD, urban development, local bodies and land and building) Manish Sisodia moved to a two-bedroom apartment in his constituency. Curiously, while Leader of the Opposition in the Delhi Assembly Harsh Vardhan was aggressive about Arvind Kejriwal's house being too large, he was equally indulgent about his own colleague V.K. Malhotra when the latter did not vacate his government accommodation as per rules. The excuse made was that he was getting his plush Greater Kailash house ready. Truly magnanimous.

The question is, is Arvind Kerjriwal and his cabinet's shunning of privileges mere symbolism? Maybe. But AAP leaders are not alone in this drive. Manohar Parrikar (BJP), the chief minister of Goa, routinely hitches rides on scooters, lives a simple life. Manik Sarkar (Communist Party of India), chief minister of Tripura, takes home a monthly salary of Rs 9,200. Mamata Banerjee (All India Trinamool Congress), the chief minister of West Bengal, is the epitome of frugality; her predecessor Buddhadeb Bhattacharjee neither owns a house nor a car and has a net worth of Rs 5,000.

These are not easy principles to adhere to on the long road to politics; the weight of these symbols could cripple the best of intentions. For every outlier in every party, there is a mob of vested interests. So far, AAP has shown resilience and strength in avoiding unfair privileges. For the moment it also seems that this will continue. But for a nation exhausted with the burden of brash ostentation, a little cynicism wouldn't be out of place.

Lessons from History, Gleanings from Geography

Corruption is not new to India. If literature is any indication, it has been pervasive across time. About 450 years ago, a corrupt guard allowed a citizen to enter and meet the Mughal king Akbar only if the citizen promised him half the reward that he would get. The citizen asked for fifty lashes from the shocked king. But after twenty-five lashes, he asked the guard to be brought in to get his 'share' of the reward. Of course, the guard was given the balance twenty-five lashes and five years' imprisonment. And the citizen? Legend says the citizen was Birbal.

Travel further back in history—2,300 years ago—and reach the time of King Chandragupta Maurya and his minister Kautilya. In his masterpiece on public administration, Arthashastra, he was convinced about the fickle-mindedness of people and held forth on many kinds of corruption. From forty kinds of embezzlement to judicial corruption, Kautilya had seen through it all and planned accordingly. Any analysis of his work on corruption will be huge and beyond the scope of this book but if we are searching for evidence of the ubiquity of corruption, it is to be found in abundance. Around the same time came Manusmriti, where the punishment for stealing from the royal treasury, storehouse or armoury was death. Clearly, ideas about ancient India being a land of the virtuous are imaginary. The cold fact is that corruption was an innate part of India as far back as two millennia ago. And it still lingers on.

Equally, to say that India is alone in being a corrupt nation, that its citizens are lonely victims, that its officials are solitary animals of prey, is incorrect. No civilisation has been spared this malaise. From ancient Greece, Rome and China to modern nations like the US, Australia and countries in sub-Saharan Africa, nothing binds people as strongly as corruption. From Dante to Shakespeare, poets and philosophers have tracked it, condemned it. Even in Sweden, the third-least corrupt country in 2013, according to Transparency International, corruption flourished in the second half of the eighteenth and early nineteenth century, notes Assar Lindbeck in his paper, 'Swedish Lessons for Post-Socialist Countries'.

A comparative study of corruption in four countries suggests that Indians are just too used to and hence have a high tolerance for corruption. 'The results from India suggest that exposure to high levels of corruption may lead to a tolerance of and perpetuation of corrupt behaviour,' Lisa Cameron, et al, conclude in 'Do Attitudes Towards Corruption Differ Across Cultures? Experimental Evidence from Australia, India, Indonesia and Singapore'. 'Moreover, comparing Australia and India suggests that lower levels of exposure to corruption may not result in a decrease in the propensity to engage in corrupt behaviour, but may result in an increase in the propensity to punish corrupt behaviour.'

According to them, the differentiator between India and Indonesia—a country as corrupt—is that in the latter case, the tendency to engage in and the willingness to punish corrupt behaviour is not much different from Australia. You could, therefore, conclude that better enforcement of anti-corruption laws is the key to having a corruption-free country, a line of action Arvind Kejriwal seems to have taken in his enthusiasm to clean up the country. 'Corrupt officials should either reform or they will perish,' he warned the bureaucracy of Delhi, a day after he launched his anti-corruption helpline on 8 January 2014.

'Two important things have happened,' says AAP leader Gopal Rai, a fortnight later. 'Corruption from top to bottom has broken because the person on top will not protect the corrupt. The sting operation call also has brought fear. The system has been broken.' Vinod Rai attests to the efficacy of a sense of fear. 'I don't know whether it is impacting the central bureaucracy, but it is definitely having a deterrent effect. The person who was indulging in corruption earlier now feels that the risk involved is much higher. So either the risk-reward phenomenon starts operating. Or, if he is brazen, he will lie low—50 per cent of the bureaucrats are lying low today.'

According to Ashutosh Varshney, today, corruption is a low-risk and high-return activity. In the near future, and probably because of AAP, corruption will morph into a high-risk and high-return activity. And once you cross that phase, you may finally be able to say that it will become a high-risk and low-return activity. 'He (Arvind Kejriwal) will certainly have an impact,' he says. 'I think the proposals and the new thrust will reduce corruption significantly.' But this is still a dreamer's world. 'A discourse or an environment which encourages corruption has the story of in India for some time. Now, if the discourse or environment changes, you raise the odds of being caught. Therefore, a number of people will behave in a different manner. As of now, the system has corruption at its heart. It assumes that the corrupt will not be caught. If you begin to believe that you might be caught and might have to pay a high price for it, you will change your behaviour. Right now there is impunity. That impunity might begin to go.'

But a word of caution comes from another paper, 'The Economy, Corruption, and the Vote: Evidence from experiments in Sweden and Moldova.' Here, Marko Klasnja and Joshua Tucker conclude that in a 'high corruption country (Moldova), voters react negatively to corruption only when the state of the economy is also poor; when economic conditions are good, corruption is less important.'

The economy is an aspect that Arvind Kejriwal has given scant attention to but could profit greatly from—something Narendra Modi is doing very well. Extrapolating the conclusions of this paper, it is not just corruption that has got the aam aadmi on the street, voting for change. It is the simultaneous slowing of the economy over the past five years that has catalysed it. Would Arvind Kejriwal have got the support of the aam aadmi had economic growth continued on the upswing? That's an open question with no answer, but one worth pondering over.

'In the traditional discourse, corruption was seen as an obstacle to economic growth,' says Ashutosh Varshney. 'In the new discourse and the new understanding that people are developing now, it is clear that corruption also accompanies very high growth. It's not that high growth clears the polity of corruption. So, especially when rural society modernises and rapidly develops and rapidly urbanises, a lot of corruption accompanies that process and has historically done so.'

If corruption is neither new to modern India nor is an aberration across the world, why did the electorate of New Delhi embrace this idea so strongly in December 2013 and give Kejriwal's AAP 30 per cent of its votes and twenty-eight out of seventy seats in the assembly? How is it that if corruption has been gnawing at the insides of India's psyche for more than six decades, it took just one man to put it all together and package it into a political narrative that has given hope to the aam aadmi? What makes this man dare not only the Congress-led governing coalition but challenger BJP together?

What does one man amount to? Why has the aam aadmi linked its audacious hopes and aspirations to him? Who, to put a face to the idea, is this Arvind Kejriwal?

5

POLITICS OF ENTREPRENEURSHIP

It takes the non-regular viewer of prime time Indian news a lot of effort to connect each of the talking heads in tiny four inch squares to their political affiliations. One has to wait for either the super script at the bottom of the screen or for fawning references to their leaders—Rahul Gandhi for Congress, Narendra Modi for BJP. One party is an exception to this rule. Identified by the white Gandhi cap with the name of the party in black on one side, and the party symbol, the broom, on the other, this party has made a statement. For a newly-born party to have a symbol that crashes into prime time so audaciously, there must be a hungry entrepreneur staking claim to the market he has identified.

For Arvind Kejriwal, the topi is more than a mere cap. 'Yeh topi mera conscience keeper hai (this cap is my conscience keeper),' he says. 'It will keep reminding me that I am a common man and work for the common man.' Sitting with Prashant Bhushan in his Noida home, two or three neatly folded aam aadmi topis wait on the side table. 'I wear them when on a television show or at a press conference,' he says. 'It helps me identify with the rest.' For spokespersons such as Prashant Bhushan, the cap is not the identifier, but for unknown faces in the crowd, the topi is an invaluable beacon.

The relationship of Yogendra Yadav with the topi is similar to Arvind Kejriwal's, though he wears it only occasionally, when political situations so demand. During a volunteer meet in Karnal in Haryana, Yogendra Yadav paused, took out his cap, placed it carefully on his head and only then moved on to the stage to address the volunteers, a sea of bobbing topis.

'I must have lost more than a hundred caps,' says Pankaj Gupta, as he interrupts his conversation with an NRI on how to help with party funding; his topi is missing. 'Why? Because if I wear it and go, someone will ask for it and I will just give it to him. And it's not just me, it's everyone. A person, who is sitting on the street selling chai or samosa, he is also asking for the cap. That is the disruption you are talking about and I'm referring to. They feel that they are now part of the party. They are becoming part of a family.'

The idea was born during the freedom movement—the source of AAP's inspiration. 'In Congress, the Gandhi topi was significant but it has become a part of customary practice, worn on special occasions,' says psephologist Ashish Talwar, who currently oversees the AAP campaign. 'For instance, an organisational man like Sardar Patel never wore the cap, although Nehru wore it as part of his style. You will see people wearing it at a Congress adhiveshan and that too mostly workers. For AAP it has come to play a unifying tool. For one, it gives the message powerfully that we are the aam aadmi. More importantly, it is part of the uniform. The moment you wear the topi, it helps unite and bring a sense of ownership. No matter who you are, there is no segregation in the uniform.'

What was merely something AAP inherited from the Jan Lokpal agitation under Anna Hazare—the caps then sported the slogan 'mein hoon Anna Hazare' (I am Anna Hazare)—has today become the party's calling card, its identity, bordering almost on the religious. With one difference: the topi has grown in stature. Every AAP volunteer sports this cap, and every cap is a moving emblem of change, a powerful visual statement of hope. The cap accords a feeling of camaraderie, it gives a sense of purpose, imparts a bond of strength.

The cap and its use speaks the language of political entrepreneurship. But can politics be entrepreneurial? We examine this by defining who an entrepreneur is and by looking back in time to identify other political entrepreneurs.

Entrepreneur

Looked at through the traditional, economics-focussed lenses of analyses, entrepreneurship is often called the fourth factor of production, after capital, labour and land. But who is an entrepreneur, what does she do? Let's begin with what an entrepreneur is not.

A capitalist has the following traits—she controls ownership; is passive in her stance, prefers the well-beaten path and is averse to risk; she also explores alternatives to deploy her capital. In the Indian context, the Tata group, under Cyrus Mistry and Ratan Tata before him, are capitalists. They seek out opportunities across the world, evaluate the risk, and take decisions to set up businesses that can scale up and serve a global consumer. You could say they are entrepreneurial in the sense that they are working in a new paradigm of global competition. But in essence, they are capitalists—their job is to preserve and grow capital on behalf of shareholders.

The capitalist uses another entity to meet her goals of wealth creation—the manager. On her part, the manager administers resources given to her; is risk averse; is rational about how to go about managing a business; and creates and maintains what is known as a competitive advantage of a business. A flood of professionals, graduating from business schools, help grow the business that the capitalist has invested in with as little risk as possible. Accountability to the capitalist ensures and sharpens the manager's risk-averse nature. Star managers like K.V. Kamath of ICICI Bank or Indra Nooyi of PepsiCo fall into this category.

The entrepreneur, on the other hand, generally has a vision that goes beyond creating wealth or managing risk. She looks beyond the boundaries, identifies gaps in the market, sets a vision, pursues innovation not merely by defining and creating products and services but through processes. Of course, she seeks wealth. But the prime motivation doesn't come from money. An entrepreneur turns every obstacle into an opportunity. A lack of resources typically means that she will be supremely efficient; she will unleash better products at significantly lower costs, or will put a spin on an existing product, so it is viewed as having greater value, and can therefore be priced high—something like what Starbucks has done to coffee.

In the field of Indian business, no name can come close to Dhirubhai Ambani in the space of entrepreneurship. Ambition coursing through his blood, Dhirubhai Ambani was able to break into the cosy clubs of big business and government to create his own disruptive relationships. Would he have been successful had he been seeking opportunities today? Definitely—his skill was not merely in creating alliances with government, financing and creating the equity boom, but in a vision that looked beyond today. To make the distinction clear, his sons, Mukesh Ambani and Anil Ambani are capitalists.

Entrepreneurship has largely and wrongly been limited to business. But the entire sector of social entrepreneurship follows the same norms, the same principles, the same concepts. We see entrepreneurs during war, in schools, in hospitals, in religious institutions. In AAP, we are seeing this entrepreneurial spirit charge the atmosphere of Indian politics. But within the arena of politics, where participating gladiators fight for eyeballs, mindspace and votes, wielding ideas as swords, flying on the chariot of ideology—history illustrates that the AAP experiment is neither novel nor permanent.

A successful entrepreneur is essentially a disrupter. She is someone who pushes the boundaries either by expanding market size, by snatching away markets from existing businesses or by introducing new categories of products and services. Can we extend this view of entrepreneurship to politics?

A political entrepreneur is a player who seeks to gain political and social currency or pursue an ideology by providing common and public goods that can be shared by an unorganised citizenry. In a democracy, the political entrepreneur proposes to change public goods or the manner in which those goods are provided, including law and order, and economic policies, though votes. Even Gandhi, who said he was no politician, played in the political field. All of them dismantled theoretical stereotypes of entrepreneurship—they were neither in business, nor were they new and small. But they also strengthened the stereotype—all of them took great risks.

Dynast, the Capitalist

Applying these principles to the field of politics, the two large parties of India, Congress and BJP, but equally smaller ones like DMK, SP or CPI-M, have their capital in place, and we use the word 'capital' broadly. If not money, there is an ideology. If not an ideology, there is an ideologue. Some have a mix of the three. When an individual wants to make a political debut from one of these parties, she has behind her institutional support. If the candidate making a debut is the son or daughter of the controllers of these parties, the support gets cushioned with goodwill or a quick advance to public office.

Much of this support, however, is abused. The entire debate around dynastic politics—from Congress and BJP at the centre to SP, DMK, NCP, Shiv Sena and the large alphabet soup that is the universe of Indian political parties—converges around this abuse. The merit of an individual is often overlooked, and the son or daughter of an existing leader is propped up instead.

This trampling goes across parties, across demographics (the young are more dynastic), and gender (women have more members in political families) and any other metric. In fact, the metric of blood, gene, chromosome or family goes beyond and binds political parties like nothing else does—not enterprise, not creativity, not brilliance, not even loyalty. As many as three out of ten members of Parliament (MPs) in Lok Sabha had family connections in politics, notes *The India Site*, a website run by author Patrick French, who explored the phenomenon of dynastic politics in his 2011 book, *India: A Portrait*.

When this data was further sliced, it revealed that almost seven out of ten of women MPs came into politics through family connections. If the 33 per cent reservation for women in Parliament comes into force, this number is expected to rise, the site forecasts. When the analysis touches upon age, the conclusions get depressing—all, repeat all, MPs below the age of thirty were found to belong to political lineages; more than two-thirds of MPs below the age of forty had political pedigree.

The uglier truth of India politics is the concept of hyper-hereditary—that is, MPs who have several family members in politics. Twenty-seven MPs were found to be hyper-hereditary, with nineteen of them, or seven out of ten, in the Congress. It is almost as if, in this backdrop, the playing field of politics was waiting for an entrepreneur to make non-dynastic politics his calling card. Narendra Modi, a leader who has reached the top through his own merit and grit, loses no opportunity to slash at the dynasty-worshippers in Congress, even as dynasts litter his party, BJP. But it has taken an Arvind Kejriwal to take such rhetoric all the way and make an attack on dynastic politics a part of his politics. AAP tickets are given to only one person from one family.

That the political landscape is loaded against those who enter politics for the first time can be seen from an analysis of the average age of politicians. While the average age of a hereditary MP is forty-eight years, that of an MP with no significant family background is fifty-eight years. 'Since a hereditary MP is likely to join parliament at an early age,' the site states, 'this translates into a decade of political advantage for him/her.' A dismal state of politics by any yardstick. But to suggest that India is alone in this game, where the odds are loaded against political entrepreneurs, would be myopic and incorrect.

'In politics, power begets power,' conclude Ernesto Dal Bo, of Haas School of Business at University of California, Berkeley et al in a May 2007 paper, 'Political Dynasties'. After studying political dynasties in the US Congress since its inception in 1789, they documented historic and geographic patterns in the evolution and profile of political dynasties, the extent of dynastic bias in legislative politics versus other occupations, and analysed the connection between political dynasties and political competition. 'We find that legislators who enjoy longer tenures are significantly more likely to have relatives entering Congress later,' they wrote. And here's a finding that is even more dangerous for a democracy: 'We establish that this relationship is causal: a longer period in power increases the chance that a person may start (or continue) a political dynasty.'

It's the same story in Japan. 'Our model predicts that, as compared with non-dynastic legislators, dynastic legislators bring more distributions to the district, enjoy higher electoral success, and harm the economic performance of the districts despite the larger amount of distributive benefits they bring,' says Yasushi Asako of the School of Political Science and Economics, Waseda University, et al in their May 2013 paper, 'Dynastic Politicians: Theory and Evidence from Japan'.

The case of Philippines is no different. 'Representatives from political dynasties account for 70 per cent of the jurisdiction-based legislators in Congress,' notes Ronald U. Mendoza, faculty, Asian Institute of Management et al in their January 2012 paper, 'An Empirical Analysis of Political Dynasties in the 15th Philippine Congress'. Their results are depressing: 'On average, they (representatives from political dynasties) possess higher net worth and win in elections by larger margins of victory compared to non-dynastic representatives. Dynastic jurisdictions are also associated with lower standards of living (as measured by average income) and lower human development (as measured by the Human Development Index), and higher levels of deprivation (as measured by poverty incidence, poverty gap, and poverty severity).'

Clearly, when a political entrepreneur enters the chessboard of Indian politics, as in the rest of the world, she is up against rivals, first within her own party to get a legitimate square to stand on, before the real battle even begins; most fall by the wayside as mere pawns in the larger game being played by dynasts. Had Arvind Kejriwal aspired for political office as a member of the Congress or even BJP, which is relatively more democratic and less dynastic, chances are high that he would have been rejected. There was only one way he could test the conviction of his ideas in the political arena: by disrupting it.

Entrepreneur, the Disrupter

But in order to cause disruption, Arvind Kejriwal had to think out-of-the-box. He had to think and act like an entrepreneur. In which case, we need to get deeper under the skin of the entrepreneur to understand how she or he functions. Economist and sociologist Werner Sombart said, the entrepreneur, with his vital energy and creativity, brings to life other economic factors such as labour and capital, which otherwise might be considered dead-weight. Sociologist and philosopher Max Weber said that the entrepreneur is the beholder of an 'instrumental rationality', which makes him capable of linking systematically some goals (the pursuit of economic gain) with the most proper means.

Philosopher and philologist Friedrich Wilhelm Nietzsche underlined the difference between those who are far ahead of the conventional wisdom of their times and those who don't do anything else but adapt to it, thus highlighting the role of individuals who follow a path that does not appear rational; they are moved by willpower. But 'economic theory and the entrepreneur have never made easy travelling companions,' wrote J.S. Metcalfe in his paper, 'The Entrepreneur and the Style of Modern Economics'. If scholarly evidence is to be relied upon, it is difficult to capture the spirit of the entrepreneur in a cohesive theory.

But, arguably twentieth century's most profound thinker, Peter F. Drucker (1909-2005), did just that. In his 1985 book, *Innovation and Entrepreneurship*, he dissected the idea of the entrepreneur. According to him, the entrepreneur looks at seven sources of innovative opportunity—unexpected; incongruity; innovation based on process need; changes in industry structure or market structure; demographics; changes in perception, mood and meaning; and new knowledge. When we examine Arvind

Kejriwal and his party through these windows, it becomes easier to place the man and his work.

The opportunity that Arvind Kejriwal pulled out of thin air was unexpected. Fed up with the corruption of UPA2, the seventy-four-year-old Anna Hazare began his fast unto death on 4 April 2011. That fast, and the resultant negotiations with the government, brought what was known as Team Anna, then comprising Arvind Kejriwal, Manish Sisodia, Prashant Bhushan and Kiran Bedi. It also brought the man and his ideas to TV screens.

Team Anna's relentless, obstinate and unflinching focus on the Jan Lokpal bill as a law that would permanently and absolutely end the rampant corruption in the country was once again the unexpected. In politics, a little give-and-take is the currency of discourse. But when Team Anna refused to change even a word, the resultant response from the UPA2 government was predictable—talks failed and it reverted to its defensive stance. People outside and in homes, watching the discourse on TV, began to align themselves with Arvind Kejriwal. They were not interested in the complex technicalities of the bill; all they saw was how a small group of people were fighting to clean up a system mired in corruption.

The party's incongruity came from the fact that it stood out in a political environment that had been hijacked by political families, and by those who benefited from, and therefore, supported that hijack. They were oddities in a space governed by government contracts, the abuse of privileges using the exchequer's money and crony capitalism. Worse, the extant political class was completely unaware of the disgust the common man, aam aadmi, nurtured against them. Kejriwal and his team shattered the belief that politics is the profession of scoundrels, a profession that well brought up citizens should steer clear of.

Consequently, a large number of young citizens began applauding the disruption Arvind Kejriwal brought. In a country, where more than half the population is below the age of twenty-five and about two-thirds below the age of thirty-five, the young form a significant constituency, one that needs nurturing. They are idealistic and there are no chains binding them to the past. Both Congress and BJP speak about the young, BJP being a few steps ahead of Congress in this. But it took a seventy-four-year-old man, Anna Hazare, to capture the imagination of this segment.

When Arvind Kejriwal finally got working and joined the political process by forming the Aam Aadmi Party (AAP), he introduced lessons in innovation, particularly in the way he went about canvassing for votes—using autorickshaws as his medium, getting volunteers to stand at crossings and flyovers with banners and so on. Above all, it is in the area of electoral funding—from the people, in an open, transparent manner, disclosing every rupee generated online—that Kejriwal's innovative steps have scored a strong and replicable victory.

Hussein Muaaz Hussein from New Delhi, Sukhwinder Singh from Fatehpur Sahib, Mukesh Kumar from Nalanda, Pooja Jethwani from Mumbai, Mufti Khawar from Srinagar, Amna Nashit from Vellore…these are not high-profile financiers or names that you may see glorified in newspapers. These are instead the common people, the aam aadmi, whose donations of Rs 2,014 stand tall on the AAP website, shoulder-to-shoulder with larger donors. For the Delhi elections, the party did not accept any corporate donations, a tactic they're changing for the national elections.

Such transparency in funding goes beyond what we have been seeking from traditional parties—to disclose their books of account. While Congress and BJP fight the pressure to disclose, AAP has gone ahead and bared all, in real time—the collections of the day, cumulative collections, countries with the highest donations and so on. By mid-January 2014, it was collecting funds at the rate of twenty to twenty-five lakh rupees per day. But to reach the two hundred crore mark for the Lok Sabha elections, the party is now targeting corporate executives in their individual capacity.

'AAP is attempting to fundamentally change how political parties and elections work in India,' is the message that greets you when you open the donations page. 'AAP will not put up any candidates with criminal backgrounds. It will also not put up more than one person from the same family. With your support, AAP will be able to launch a formidable challenge to the established political parties and provide the much necessary political alternative to the people. We seek clean money from people like you, so that we can make a difference for you.'

This innovation of processes goes beyond funding. It binds every aspect of the party, from the organisational structure to creating its manifesto. In the attempt to take a ground zero look at the needs of the city, the party went to individual constituencies to understand what the people there wanted. Two months after the party was formed in November 2012, formal background studies for the city-level manifesto were initiated with a small team of eight to ten members, led by Yogendra Yadav.

The group made detailed studies on the city's policy needs, from public service provisions and the state of housing to transport systems and employment. These were then collated and sector-specific proposals were made. The city-level manifesto that was finally released in November 2013 took all these proposals and compressed them into a political statement. This broke the manifesto into two parts. The Delhi Manifesto looked at the issues pertaining to the city; the Constituency Manifesto examined the local issues.

AAP volunteers met with various neighbourhoods and conducted Jan Sabhas (people's meetings) throughout the city. When issues such as inadequate water supply, rising electricity bills, lack of sanitation and the need for high quality schools and healthcare emerged in all areas, the party put those under the city manifesto.

The volunteers conducted about twenty meetings in every constituency and across neighbourhood types—planned colonies, unauthorised areas, resettlement colonies, slum clusters, and rural and urban areas. These inputs were compiled and mapped to understand local issues, which in turn formed the basis of the constituency-level manifesto.

AAP claims that this is the first time in the political history of India that such an exercise has been undertaken, one that seeks inputs from people regarding what they want, what they need at the city- and neighbourhood-level. 'A small step towards the realisation of Swaraj that the Aam Aadmi Party is committed towards,' the AAP website states.

The enterprise of AAP mirrors what Peter Drucker defined as the seven primary characteristics of an entrepreneur. AAP has used each of these characteristics to build its political pillars:

Characteristic 1: Doing something new.
AAP: Anti-corruption stance, decentralisation of power, right to recall.

Characteristic 2: Replicable at an economical cost.
AAP: Being a bootstrap operation, every idea can be, and is being, replicated by traditional parties.

Characteristic 3: Satisfy a specific need.
AAP: Fixing the governance deficit, bringing isolated citizen back into politics, giving the aam aadmi dignity.

Characteristic 4: Application of information, imagination and initiative.
AAP: The bottom-up look at governance, asking what people want, using new ways to reach out to voters.

Characteristic 5: Satisfy the needs and expectations of customers.
AAP: The speed with which it went about delivering what it called governance (and what its detractors called anarchy).

Characteristic 6: Create new markets.
AAP: An entirely new constituency of voters has brought AAP to power; more offshoots are springing up across the country.

Characteristic 7: Space for imitators.
AAP: Weakness in governance is not restricted to Delhi or to the states; it is observed at the village level, leaving the doors wide open for vested interests and imitators. Further, imitators are not just new entrants—an entire stream of governance changes can be observed in traditional parties due to the AAP effect.

The innovation AAP is bringing to governance and politics is not evolutionary in nature. We do not see a slew of continuous changes through incremental advances in technology or processes. No one methodical step follows another. The innovation the party is bringing is more in tune with the personality of its founder, Arvind Kejriwal, and is hence, unusual in its texture, discontinuous in its approach—and disruptive in its philosophy. The new power purge that AAP is bringing rests on four entrepreneurial strategies.

Hit First, Hit Hard. Arvind Kejriwal was the first to initiate a bottom-up form of governance. When it came to anti-corruption, he lagged behind BJP, which had already raised the pitch in Parliament but had not done much beyond seeking the resignation of the prime minister and making life uncomfortable for Congress. BJP was doing what was expected in the space of traditional politics—making the governing coalition look bad in order to extract political mileage. It took an Arvind Kejriwal to convert the corruption of Congress and the pitch of BJP into a political statement on Jantar Mantar with the Jan Lokpal bill. Since the ground was set, it took a little nudge to bring the people together. Kejriwal may not have been able to 'hit first', but he hit hard and captured the issue.

Hit the Gap in the Market. Again, while corruption was a burning issue, both the large parties were too busy fighting one another, in a circular case of *et tu*. Congress was defending the interpretations of CAG on spectrum, Commonwealth Games, Adarsh Housing Society and mining, with BJP aggressively cornering Congress in Parliament and on all debates. As the two parties danced around the opportunities that allegations of corruption provided, a positioning gap emerged that Arvind Kejriwal easily occupied. For him, the idea of an anti-corruption plank was waiting for political expression.

Finding and Occupying a Niche. The stage was set for the anti-corruption brigade: the atmosphere was charged, there was a face for the cause, and there was space for a party. Earlier, Baba Ramdev had taken up the corruption issue rather successfully, until he was driven off, first by the police and then out of the minds of the people. Frustration with corruption filled the air, elections were getting closer, and an anti-Congress wave—combined with an anti-incumbency wave against the party's ten-year stint at the Centre—was beginning to rise. This is the niche that AAP occupied. Being a new party with no history, it was easily done.

Changing the Economic Characteristics of a Product, a Market

or an Industry. Following the occupation of the anti-corruption niche, Arvind Kejriwal and AAP began to change the political discourse. The traditional parties began to realise that graft was no longer a weapon that swung the baton of power from Congress to BJP; it was a far more serious issue. Overnight, the market of politics changed in favour of the newbie, AAP. And this was not restricted to the existing electorate; the new and young voters, who began to register themselves in droves, had already decided to change things. Now, the anti-corruption positions of both Congress and BJP are supposedly morphing to serve these new voters. Unfortunately, traditional parties continue to join hands with individuals who carry criminal backgrounds.

When we analyse the theories by focusing on three ideas—politics, entrepreneurship and innovation—we get a peek into what's going on in society. We understand who the change agents are, the mavericks, and the mad men. To answer a question like who is a political entrepreneur, for instance, we need to ask another question: What is political change?

Standing at the cusp of a new era in Indian politics, it seems the aam aadmi is aching for a change that no longer follows a step-by-step handbook. Before her is a dream opportunity—the distinct possibility of breaking down the walls of old politics to create a new world. At such a time, a political entrepreneur will present herself as an alternative to old, deep-rooted ways of thinking.

'Political scientists have been increasingly interested in entrepreneurs—individuals who change the direction and flow of politics,' wrote Mark Schneider and Paul Teske in their paper 'Toward a Theory of the Political Entrepreneur: Evidence from Local Government'. They identify several conditions that affect the probability that an entrepreneur will emerge in a local government, 'especially slack budgetary resources that the political entrepreneur can reallocate. We also find that the probability with which an entrepreneur is found in local government is a function of the difficulty of overcoming collective action problems in a community.'

Delhi law minister Somnath Bharti's attempt to fix the problems at Khirki Extension, an unauthorised neighbourhood in South Delhi, for example, is a prime example of how an entrepreneurial political party, whose weapon of change is disruption, has to negotiate each and every step with particular prudence. When residents of the colony alleged that some migrants from Africa living as tenants in this neighbourhood were running a drug-and-sex-racket and the police was not doing anything, Somnath Bharti, in the middle of a cold Delhi winter brought the police there and asked them to take action.

Before any executive action could be taken, however, the project turned into a fight between an SHO and a minister. Lost in translation was the fact that the residents had been complaining for years about these goings-on. They had written letters to the police commissioner as well as to the home minister of the central government, under which the Delhi police functions. They had written to the lieutenant governor. Arvind Kejriwal at this point went for the jugular and, citing the statement of former Home Secretary R.K. Singh, accused Home Minister Sushil Kumar Shinde of being part of an organised network of bribery. Arvind Kejriwal overlooked the fact that R.K. Singh had joined the BJP.

What Arvind Kejriwal and Somnath Bharti did in this one example disrupts the step-by-step ladder of change that most of us are used to—that ideas shape institutions, institutions shape incentives, incentives determine actions of participants, actions determine outcomes. In this case, Somnath Bharti's error was arriving at outcomes directly after the conceptualisation of an idea. Even if the outcome had been positive, his disregard for institutions created pockets of disappointment among political analysts, and of course, political rivals.

'Political change happens when entrepreneurs notice areas of weakness in the structure of ideas, institutions, and incentives, and then find ways to change the institutional rules in those areas,' wrote Wayne A. Leighton and Edward J. Lopez, in 'Madmen, Intellectuals, & Academic Scribblers'. 'In a democracy, this requires making it in the political interests of the existing powers (the madmen in authority) to change the rules accordingly. Political entrepreneurs strive for that right political moment, for the time when the right idea can take hold.' Was a cold winter night, with temperatures of close to ten degrees Celsius the right moment to play the change game? Time will tell.

But even as we look at the future to assess the present, not having a political past helps political entrepreneurs like Arvind Kejriwal. The electorate sees in their stance a future of promise and opportunity, and the entrepreneurs themselves are unencumbered by history. With little to lose but short-term reputation, political entrepreneurs have the power chess-board at their feet. If they win, it is a step towards their goal of wresting politics out of the hands of the firmly entrenched dynasties. If they lose, they will be given another chance for this will be kindly viewed as their first debacle. Its forty-nine days of governing Delhi proved to be a half-way house for AAP. Will national politics head the same way?

For the moment that seems unlikely. All surveys are pointing to BJP coming up as the largest party, followed by Congress, with the balance being made up of all other parties, including AAP. A repeat of Delhi, with Arvind Kejriwal coming to power with the support of Congress seems a distant possibility. More tangible is the way in which AAP has positioned itself as a party of political entrepreneurs, who have established themselves in the highly-competitive, hugely-segregated Indian political landscape.

While AAP may have to wait for Elections 2019 to get enough seats as an anchor party, supported by other parties, the resonance of AAP's politics will echo all around. Through the power of enterprise, imagination and innovation, it has already changed the political discourse—anti-corruption, clean candidacy, decentralisation of decision making and devolution of power are ideas that Congress and BJP have begun to engage with but will take time to implement. The prime example of Arvind Kejriwal's success is how Rahul Gandhi and Narendra Modi have started building their manifestos ground-up instead of imposing them from a high command or a central authority at the top of the organisational hierarchy.

As someone entering an arena occupied by two fighting Goliaths, incumbent Rahul Gandhi and challenger Narendra Modi, political entrepreneur Arvind Kejriwal has to find empty spaces to stand in without being crushed. But instead of joining the fight and being pulped, Arvind Kejriwal as a disrupter has shifted the arena itself. By focussing on aam aadmi issues like inflation, power and water, the marketing and packaging of his enterprise has been sharp. While BJP too has been keeping the government under pressure on the issue of prices, the credit of highlighting the political mire in Delhi has slipped out from its hands and to AAP.

Reliance Industries Ltd. founder Dhirubhai Ambani sold cloth, going door-to-door on his bicycle in hot summers, before the high and mighty began to line up at his door. Nirma Group founder Karsanbhai Khodidas Patel sold handmade detergent, also on his bicycle, before managing to challenge giant Unilever Ltd. Arvind Kejriwal is no different—his door-to-door campaign through tea party drives by local prabaris or larger Jan Sabhas are steps in the same direction. But doing this in high-density areas like Delhi, the metros or even large cities is one thing; repeating it in villages scattered across India would be quite another.

AAP had displayed its resilience in the door-to-door operation earlier. With a fluctuating media support, for instance, they innovated by going to the very source that would grant them power: the people. 'We said, forget the media, it's not in our hands,' says AAP's Gopal Rai. 'We will go to the streets, direct communication to people.' How they deal with a dissipated electorate in villages though needs to be seen.

As far as leadership goes, Arvind Kejriwal and his team act as symbols of hope. By taking a tiny house, as a chief minister, Arvind Kejriwal is relaying a clear message to incumbent Sheila Dikshit, and all the CEOs who talk of cost cutting but fly business class and keep their bonuses. Congress and BJP call this cheap symbolism and point out scattered cases of their leaders living similarly. The truth is, it is easy for one man or two men to live simply, not for the entire officialdom. Before traditional parties point fingers, they need to vacate their large palaces and walk the talk—difficult for practitioners of the old school of politics to do. Since his daughter has to take exams, Arvind Kejriwal will pay market rent for the house allocated to him. It would be interesting to know how many MPs or MLAs have overstayed their welcome in government accommodations over the past ten years (or more) and of them how many paid market rent. An RTI should help get that information.

The symbolism is simple, stark and substantive. While the topi creates a strong visual presence, the broom is recognised by every household. Translating these symbols into a political rhetoric—clean up the corruption in India, for instance—is easy. Most likely, there may not even be any strategy or plan guiding these symbols. Starved for resources, AAP has had to take what comes its way and run with it, like an entrepreneur would. What we see as a conscious act may simply be quick-fix solutions.

Traditionally, entrepreneurs begin small and then scale up. But in the age of technology and instant communication, AAP is attempting to disrupt that idea as well. There is no time to make a larger plan and then walk towards it, one step at a time. That luxury is at least one election cycle away. It could work in the Haryana elections in October 2014. But with less than two months to prepare for the general elections, the only way forward is through the currency of audacity.

Finally, one of the biggest challenges before AAP is that of a qualified leadership. It is very well to pull out new leaders, fresh faces from among the aam aadmi. But despite giving them every concession possible, we can clearly see that a Somanth Bharti or a Kumar Vishwas is not an Arvind Kejriwal, a Yogendra Yadav, a Prashant Bhushan, a Pankaj Gupta. Going national means having faces that can bridge the future to the present. And even though the party is becoming what many call the only option for those people from the non-political class who wish to join and participate in the national politics, pulling talented individuals out, training them and most importantly, giving them time to hone their experience is going to be an uphill task.

'As the party expands at an exponential rate, (there will be questions about) the people representing the party—how will they be selected, how will their credentials and records be assessed, and how will they get rid of the bad apples, who should speak and who shouldn't—these are issues the party needs to grapple with,' says Ashutosh Varshney. 'For example, support for plebiscite in Kashmir or support for Maoism will sink the party. It will gift the election away to Mr Modi. Even if you are intellectually convinced that that's the right thing, you will have to carefully assess the political value of the conviction. Being intellectually convinced about something is one thing; presenting it on a political platform is an analytically separable issue.'

At some point, the institutionalisation of entrepreneurship will have to take place and an organisation built. For this, one will need two arms that aid growth—political managers, who will help transition the party into a larger establishment; and political capitalists who will ensure risks around it are taken care of. But the moment AAP moves in that direction, its sharp entrepreneurial edge will be dulled, its capacity for disruption will fall, its shrill vocabulary of change will slip an octave or two. It may still retain its anti-corruption soul, but its body could get weakened by its own bureaucracy and internal fiefdoms.

While that would be good news for its rivals, what boggles the mind is another question: Why aren't the traditional parties being enterprising enough? What's stopping Congress and BJP, with all the resources, intellectual and political, at their disposal, from looking at politics afresh? Why are they allowing the impression to persist that they are steeped in the past and may never get out of the quicksand of corruption and dynastic rule? Politicians are among the smartest people in the system and both the traditional parties have ideal candidates in this regard—a P. Chidambaram, a Salman Khurshid or a Jairam Ramesh in Congress; a Shivraj Singh Chouhan, an Arun Jaitley, a Manohar Parrikar in BJP. Both Rahul Gandhi and Narendra Modi are positioning themselves as change agents. And yet, outside their traditional bastions they are unable to capture the imagination, beyond tinkering with peripheral issues they are unable to innovate. It couldn't just be complacency or hubris.

Most importantly, AAP has set the ball rolling for other political entrepreneurs—not necessarily aligned with either AAP or with its values—to benefit from the opportunities it is throwing up. It has shown that in order to pursue what many call the most fulfilling profession in a democracy, politics, you don't need to either have an incumbent daddy or be a criminal. If your idea is strong enough, if it engages voters, if it seeks to solve real problems, your enterprise will get the support it needs. You can pursue the politics of values, the politics of change, the politics of disruption, riding solely on the courage of conviction and a strong sense of self.

But that can happen only after deciding to take a plunge into full-time politics, with the formation of a party. How did a bunch of entrepreneurs, led by Arvind Kejriwal, take that step? This is the question we hope to investigate.

6

CHALLENGE OF PARTY

It was almost 1.30 a.m. on 20 September 2012. The last few hours had been agonising and painful for seven people deliberating into the wee hours, as they sat at the Constitution Club in Central Delhi, barely a kilometre from Parliament. The group of seven—Arvind Kejriwal, Gopal Rai, Yogendra Yadav, Sanjay Singh, Kumar Vishwas, Prashant Bhushan and Manish Sisodia—had spent the last few hours mulling over their decision to join mainstream politics.

A day before, following a marathon nine-hour meeting with more than forty activists, Anna Hazare had announced his opposition to Arvind Kejriwal's plan to launch a political party. Along with Justice Santosh Hegde, the anti-corruption ombudsman in Karnataka who between 2008 and 2010 uncovered the rot of illegal iron ore mining in the state, and supercop Kiran Bedi, the mascot of Maharashtra walked away, asking Arvind Kejriwal not to use either his name or his photograph in his party or campaign. 'It is our misfortune that the team has split,' newspapers reported him as saying. 'I didn't want a political party to be formed but if people want (that) then they should go ahead. We will go our separate ways.'

Anna Hazare's rather abrupt and typically blunt exit shook the team and its decision. While most of them were certain that there was no alternative, having exhausted all options of dialogue, pressure and public discourse, the moot question for many of them was whether just entering the fray would give them solutions. While members like Yogendra Yadav, who had spent a large part of his life working with several social movements, were more certain that the way forward was to mainstream their activities, for Arvind Kejriwal, it was all about overhauling the present system.

'We respect Anna Hazare, he is our guru and father,' Arvind Kejriwal told reporters the next day. 'Yesterday's developments came as a complete surprise. It was shocking, unbelievable, unfortunate and sad.' It was an emotional moment for those wanting to take forward the work that India Against Corruption (IAC) had done under Anna Hazare's leadership. 'Anna's photograph and name are printed in our hearts. We will continue to take his blessings and touch his feet. Anna's five principles will become the foundation of our party.' The five principles are shuddh achar (clean conduct); shuddh vichar (clean thoughts); nishkalank jeevan (life without blemishes); jeevan mein tyag (a life of sacrifice); and strength to face insults without flinching.

Their unquestioned face and leader till a few days ago, now Anna Hazare had raised three crucial questions. One, entering politics would force them to participate in mudslinging; how would they resist that? Two, political activities need money; who would fund the party and how would it be possible to finance elections through white money? And three, how would they ensure that the candidates representing the party would not be corrupt? 'After all, did Jayaprakashji (Jayaprakash Narayan, activist and political leader who opposed Indira Gandhi in the 1970s) know that Lalu Prasad would be a part of the party that followed his movement?' he had asked.

But relationships, particularly those forged while facing strong adversaries, are not easy to let go of. They tug not only at the heart, but also make one question the mind and its decisions.

'We had developed a special bond with him, having spent long hours together over the past few months,' Gopal Rai recounts, saying how Anna Hazare's exit was a painful decision that haunts him even today. 'We had begun to work as a family and it was difficult for us to opt for a path which he did not agree with.' The mood was sombre, reflective and even unsure. As the hours ticked by, most of them sank into deeper silence, each one looking for the right answer in the recesses of his mind.

'By around 1.30 a.m. it was clear, though none of us spoke,' Gopal Rai says. 'We had decided to take the plunge and form a political party even if it meant getting stained (as Anna Hazare had described it). We had taken two decisions that night. One was to join the political electoral battle, the other was about Anna Hazare himself. We resolved that we would not speak against him even if provoked (us).' He pauses to recollect the night's decision. 'I am glad we have held on to both (resolves).'

It was a decisive moment that was to open a new chapter in India's democratic history. While there was little doubt about the path they had chosen to change the political landscape, which was by participating in the electoral process, the separation from Anna Hazare, their leader in the IAC movement, was not an easy decision. Gopal Rai, who has spent the last eighteen months toiling each day to give shape to AAP, chokes, doing little to hide his emotions, while referring to how Anna Hazare opted out of their decision. 'It was very difficult for us to think of moving on without Annaji. He was our face, our strength and our leader,' he says while describing the fateful September night.

For Arvind Kejriwal, the move to a political platform was the next logical step, the shift to politics from protests was inevitable. In any democracy, both are legitimate instruments for expression—protests usually raise the issue within the confines of a geographical space, a community or a social grouping; politics pushes the edges of those confines and widens the idea. Those who support democracy usually focus on, and have a greater enthusiasm for, the strengthening of civil society and protest movements. While these are important and can help enforce rights within a democracy, it is the joining of the political process by the formation of parties that delivers sustainable change.

For supporters of the anti-corruption battle that Arvind Kejriwal was leading, the long night of 20 September 2012 was decisive. It was here that team Arvind Kejriwal and the Aam Aadmi Party decided to unleash a new wave in the country, now being labelled as the alternative political force. 'If we decided against the political party then the movement may have stopped, ended there, and the new hope you see today may not have been there,' Gopal Rai recounts. This decision that has forced India's political discourse to change needed conviction, courage and the willingness to take a risk. After all, these men were talking of rewriting the rules of the game, challenging the existing system, even turning it on its head and taking on the mighty establishment where friends and foes came together as one force when it came to resisting change.

Politics has come to be just like any other enterprise, quite unlike the initial post-freedom-movement days when political discourse rode high on dedication and passion. It has now become a profession in its own right. Whether that's a good thing or not is an open-ended question. But incumbents sense the change. President Pranab Mukherjee during his stint as the finance minister had once told a young student how politics today is about taking calculated risks. He had explained that a citizen could do proud his country in many ways, as a sportsman, an artist, a businessman and so on, as opposed to the days of yore when politics was the only way to serve one's country. He had detailed how politics today is a risky game where your work may go unnoticed.

It is this structure that Arvind Kejriwal and his team were set to disrupt.

Birth Pangs

The issuance of the birth certificate for this political outfit was still a few weeks away as Arvind Kejriwal and his core team got down, for the first time, to 'dirty their hands' in politics. Decision taken, these men knew little of what they had set out to do. Arvind Kejriwal, who would go on to trounce three-time chief minister Sheila Dikshit in his maiden ballot race, was still grappling with the idea of being a politician. 'I am still trying to understand the transition from a campaigner, to a civil activist to a politician,' he said, sitting cross-legged on a broken cane chair at the Kaushambi party office in Ghaziabad, days after declaring his intent to form a party on 2 October 2012. 'I am not a politician yet. I do not think we will ever be able to become politicians.'

Sitting at the end of a long table in a poorly lit room amid a string of visitors, ranging from an aspiring IAS candidate who had travelled from Pune ready to give up his career to volunteer for the new party to a businessman who was willing to give his fleet of cars to take him around, Arvind Kejriwal explained how there was a marked difference in the way people looked at them after 2 October 2012, the day the party formation was announced. The flood of volunteers giving up their day jobs or putting their aspirations on hold was a sign that AAP had captured the aam aadmi's imagination. Wearing his trademark half-sleeved cotton shirt, sipping tea from a glass tumbler and drinking water straight out of a plastic jug, Arvind Kejriwal came across as the man next door who one could bump into at a street market or at a parent-teacher meet.

'We have seven thousand volunteers working for us,' he would tell the charter members of The Indus Entrepreneurs (TiE), a not- for-profit organisation dedicated to fostering entrepreneurship, in a 29 June 2013 speech. 'Who are these seven thousand workers? They are young men and women. Software engineers who have left their jobs. Some have closed their companies and joined us. The secretary of our party, Pankaj Gupta, used to run a company, he has shut it down and is now working with us. Many boys and girls who came to Delhi to take the civil services examination have postponed their exams for two years.'

It was amply clear that although they had taken the plunge into politics and had declared their intent to form a political party, the evolution from a movement to a political party was still a work-in-progress. Sixteen months from then, in January 2014, Yogendra Yadav, one of the tallest leaders of AAP who is billed as the next chief minister of Haryana by his supporters, said AAP expects to be declared the seventh national party, post Lok Sabha elections 2014, joining the ranks of Congress, BJP, BSP, NCP, CPI and CPM, a quick march on a steep cliff. According to the rules prescribed by the Election Commission of India, a political party is considered a national party if it is recognised in four or more states where it has contested elections, which is linked to winning a certain number of seats or bagging a certain vote share in each state. At the time of writing this, AAP plans to field about 300 candidates for the 545-member Lok Sabha in the forthcoming general elections in 2014.

The short history leading up to the birth of AAP was coloured with all the elements of drama, dissent, deceit and dogma. This played out in minute detail across 24x7 TV screens and social media. Failing to get the Lokpal Bill passed in Parliament, the IAC movement had decided to take a different route in August 2012, when Arvind Kejriwal, Manish Sisodia and Gopal Rai undertook a fast at Jantar Mantar, demanding a special investigation team to probe allegations of corruption against fifteen Congress leaders. This was an intentional strategy to expose the double speak of the political establishment against corruption.

The Lokpal Bill was going through the regular motions of passing through a Parliamentary committee without much of a timeline in sight. The demand for the special investigation team and the agitation at Jantar Mantar, where Anna Hazare joined in a few days later, finally ended with the protesters deciding to deliberate on a new path. 'It was clear by this time that the government or other political parties were in no mood for a dialogue,' Gopal Rai says of that tumultuous time. They ended their hunger strike after ten days on 3 August 2012, at Jantar Mantar, a protest ground of sorts a few kilometres away from Parliament that has incubated several movements, including Anna Hazare's first hunger strike for Lokpal in April 2011.

The decision then was to deliberate on an alternative way to force political pressure; this included forming 'a political party to take their campaign to Parliament,' Arvind Kejriwal said. Anna Hazare then had said that while he would not contest elections, he would support such a process. 'We will keep fighting. Change is needed. I won't fight elections, but I am ready to support. I have decided this now,' Anna Hazare said on 3 August 2012, explaining how their decision to call off the hunger strike was driven by the need to find an alternative. Five weeks later, it was this exact alternative approach that forced the two, Anna Hazare and Arvind Kejriwal, to part ways.

And Aam Aadmi Party (AAP) was born.

Movement to Party

The origins of the party lay in the India Against Corruption movement. But AAP's success, according to social activist Nikhil Dey, also owes something to the many civil society movements that worked doggedly, without any ambition or desire to come to power, to give a greater voice to people. 'What is happening today does not surprise us so much because I think things were opening up,' he says. 'So, it's like when something gets rolled over a hill and it suddenly gathers momentum, sort of that tipping point.'

AAP's roots, in the Jan Lokpal movement, were of a non-party people's movement. 'But suddenly, they turned the tables to say that we have to get into the system to get things done,' says Nikhil Dey, who is a member of the Mazdoor Kisan Shakti Sangathan (MKSS), a non-party people's movement. 'And now, what AAP does for itself will stand for itself, full and fair.' He points out that all parties, including Congress, BJP and BSP, grew out of a movement, or a series of movements, but have kept growing more and more distant from those origins.

Nikhil Dey himself came into this space, thirty years ago, hoping to join some political party because he believed that's where change comes from. 'But I found that party structures do not allow that kind of real political change. And this is my personal view.' He terms the work he does as 'political', but makes the distinction of it being 'non-party political work', implying that it is not guided or shaped by a pursuit of power. Indeed, MKSS, whose two best-known faces are Aruna Roy and Nikhil Dey, has done some stellar work while being outside the system, including on landmark legislations like the Right to Information Act (RTI) and the National Rural Employment Guarantee Act (NREGA).

A prime example of far-reaching change brought about by the

non-political actors is RTI. The law, now billed as UPA's biggest weapon to weed away corruption as it forces transparency into the governance system, was a result of several movements. The National Advisory Council, set up by UPA Chairperson Sonia Gandhi, which brought in domain experts from different fields to work on the social agenda of the party and the government, has played a significant role in impacting crucial laws that have empowered citizens. The UPA government owed a large part of the credit for its flagship policies like the right to food, education and work to the painstaking work carried out by the NAC, despite the brickbats it faced within the government for derailing fiscal discipline.

Nikhil Dey maintains that MKSS could never have achieved what it has if it were a part of a political party. He feels party structures do not allow real political change as parties are victims of their own constitution. For example, he argues the necessity of contesting elections can in itself pose a problem. 'There is a certain party discipline they have to follow and they do eventually have to fight for political power. You cannot have a political party saying, "We don't want to come to power". Which means, parties must function in a particular way. There are certain things that go with the territory. Today we may not see these signs in AAP but it's a very new party. We will see many of those things down the line. It's written into the DNA of that structure.'

While Nikhil Dey insists that there is nothing wrong per se in joining politics, he says it is not the only way to bring about change. 'There is a space for citizen movements, which are now playing a definite role in bringing change, and that will continue.' What is helping such movements is the growing realisation and mobilisation around this new space termed as non-electoral political power. 'Those spaces were largely left alone by political parties,' he says. 'Political parties spend all their energy capturing power. People like us have spent decades working within the spaces outside. We have been in dharnas for six months, years, not to capture the seat of power, or gaddi. And this is not to say that is bad. But I am only highlighting what people and pressure from outside can do.'

To Party or Not to Party: The Larger Debate

So while pressure has to be built to usher in change and shift the status quo, what remains a dilemma is whether mainstreaming through the formation of a political party is the best way to do so. This question is pertinent not just to civil society movements, as is clear in the recent case of technocrat entrepreneur Nandan Nilekani, founding member of Infosys who joined Congress and mainstream politics to pursue his goal of being a change agent.

It was this very decision to join the mainstream that attracted people like Yogendra Yadav to AAP. 'Politics is the highest form of human activity and to be a part of it is highly satisfying,' he says. Not one to only preach and craft policy directions for AAP, the social scientist believes in testing the ballot route himself. 'I know that I cannot recommend elections to everyone in the world and say "but I don't want to contest". Yes, I would like to run from Haryana,' he says, defying popular belief that he will restrict himself to being a brain behind the party.

Yogendra Yadav had been a supporter and sympathiser of India Against Corruption ever since its inception, though his occasional appearances on the stage with Anna and team for a few words of encouragement would leave one unsure of whether he was ready to take the plunge. The savvy psephologist, who was a regular commentator on every poll by the Centre for the Study of Developing Societies, where he was engaged, is a soft-spoken man who can fool many with his appearance. Ready with a rebuttal, taking on even the most aggressive of television anchors or political pundits, he is a raring political leader and orator, who takes to street meetings and volunteer gatherings like a bee to honey.

'I don't see such a radical break as most people think and make it out to be. Politics and ideas are two things that have been with me and fascinated me all my life. For the last thirty years, I have actually been involved in a lot of activism. One-third of my life was given to activism, except that it never made it to the media, and so mercifully I could travel all over the country as a part of social and people movements. What this change has done is to turn that one-third of my life into the whole and more. This is something I really wanted. In some ways, my life, so far, retrospectively can be seen as preparation for what I'm doing now. In that sense, I have no regrets irrespective of consequences,' he says, now a man who has found his true calling as a member of AAP. 'I am a political animal who had drifted into political science. I am happy that I am released.'

He is not alone. Praveen Singh, a little-known backroom brain, who details policy documents and researches reports to help form the party position on economic, foreign and other policies, came into the AAP fold while looking for systemic changes from the top. Having tried to decentralise power and empower people through an alternate model—one that entailed organising a group of forty to fifty villages in Madhya Pradesh to create a community that existed in harmony with nature—Praveen Singh realised the bottom-up approach had its own limitations. He, along with his partner, Atishi Marlena came to Delhi in 2012 to take stock of their lives and reapproach the issue of top-down change. He found his answer in AAP, which has adopted as its central theme the devolution of power. It can be conjectured that life has turned a full circle.

After an IIT education, Praveen Singh worked in the space of software. He then went to IIM (Ahmedabad), and after graduating, worked in a management consultancy for five to six years. But he was restless as he could not find meaning in his life. 'The basic story is that ever since I left college, I was perturbed about my role in the larger scheme of things,' he says. 'The truth was, I managed to study and get here with a job because I knew a bit of English. But if you look at the larger system, you are very much part of the problem as well. So, I had these questions that bothered me, particularly when I saw injustice and inequality. I was looking for ways to find sense in my own life.'

So, Praveen Singh quit his job in 1998, and entered the world of non-profits, which also did not match his expectation. 'They are all working on some isolated problem, one symptom of a larger issue. And that had its own limitations, they could only get so far,' he says. 'I felt the fault lay in what we judged as "a good human life". Inherently, the criteria we had established would not get fulfilled. Unless we created a different set of aspirations for ourselves, this external manifestation will not change. So, our first effort was to create a prototype of a harmonious community.'

Singh and his group decided that a construct of forty to fifty villages would be the right scale for their social experiment, and set about creating such a community. But as they went along, Praveen Singh discovered the limitations of a grassroots effort—the larger system engulfs the smaller ones in an almost frightening manner. 'We soon realised that our utopian local model was not very feasible. We could create a small thing through personal charisma and commitment,' he says. But what then?

'It was clear to us from our little experiment that our model would have to be accompanied by a top-down effort as well. Some things you cannot alter at the grassroots level; and even so, there are serious implications, particularly with regard to say, international treaties. When we were making the Delhi manifesto, we did realise that we could not alter much unless there were changes at the national level. But at the national level, there were very serious limitations and implications.'

Call it a quirk of fate or sheer coincidence, but Praveen Singh and Atishi Marlena landed in Delhi, bag and baggage, looking for top-down change just when the Jan Lokpal movement was peaking. 'It just happened in parallel by itself,' says Praveen Singh, as he describes himself as a person who is still trying to deal with the changes in his life at a philosophical level.

The couple met senior AAP leader Prashant Bhushan at an institute he is involved with, the Institute of Public Policy and Politics at Palampur, in Himachal Pradesh. 'We were exploring what they were doing and what role we could play,' says Praveen Singh. 'At one of the seminars, Arvind Kejriwal and team came and made a presentation, and we met them. A dialogue began and we got involved.'

Even as he transits from a non-party political space to a party political space, Praveen Singh sees a lot of relevance for activists like Nikhil Dey and MKSS. 'If fifty or five hundred people enter the mainstream, it does not mean that all non-profits or civil society shuts down. There is a need for those to continue,' he says. 'I think it's also about people taking personal calls. I would have refused (to work in a party political space) if asked fifteen years ago. At different times in life, there is a different call.'

For many, it was the sheer charisma and simplicity of Arvind Kejriwal that drew them in. Such was the case for Nimmi Rastogi, a gynaecologist, who has also been working with civil society organisations, like People's Action. 'Arvind Kejriwal is a magnet. It is very difficult not to notice him, his enthusiasm, his persistence, his grit,' she says, sipping warm milk during a late night conversation. 'Normal human beings have a gut length of six metres. Arvind Kerjiwal's gut is sixty metres.'

What intrigued her was that while they would face a difficult time trying to get people to join their movement or come for meetings, Arvind Kejriwal would get people 'in hordes'. She began to study him. In the severe monsoon of 2013, when Delhi was facing its worst deluge, she got a call for a meeting. 'I rushed and saw a simple, dark man who couldn't even reach the podium. But he had the most amazing smile, he smiles without any guile. Someone introduced me to him and he said, "We need doctors, I need a doctor all the time."'

Small actions showed the depth of his person. 'When I came to the meeting, there were no chairs to sit on. Arvind Kejriwal got up to offer me his seat. I was so deeply touched.' On the way back, as traffic progressed at a snail's pace, she texted him, saying she would like to join his party. 'Doctor saab,' he wrote back in less than thirty seconds, 'we have to change the world. Together we can do it. Alone I can't.'

At a meeting with residents of Hauz Rani, a Muslim-dominated area in South Delhi, 'he laughed and spoke to them as if he was one of them. When they got together to give him "dua", blessings, everyone was quiet. Arvind Kerjiwal too became silent, in meditation. I thought this man is not only sensitive to gender but also religion. Ye lambi race ka ghora hai (he is in this for the long haul).'

Asif Rameez Daudi, an English lecturer teaching in Saudi Arabia's Jubail University, who has made the jump from his village in Begusarai in Bihar, sees in Arvind Kejriwal a hope of alternative politics. 'Right now voters don't want Congress,' he says in a coffee house just five minutes away from AAP's Hanuman Road office. 'Even minority voters don't want Congress. But they can't vote for BJP. And the image of regional parties is very bad.'

So, why AAP? 'Anyone who fights corruption will also be secular. If you mix religion in politics, that too is corruption, it is moral corruption.' The community has its problems with AAP. 'Right now, complete Muslim support is missing because there is no Muslim in Arvind Kejriwal's cabinet. But gradually, Muslims are coming towards the view that we can't have a better candidate than him. They need to get organised.' Two weeks later, there was no AAP government, so the story of political inclusion still needs to play out.

Asif Rameez Daudi talks about the corruption in his village. The school he opened for the underprivileged, for instance, was being harassed by the police following an accident of the school bus with a motorcycle. He had to speak to the local MLA to get the bus released from the police. 'Arvind Kejriwal may not be able to fix corruption immediately, but there is something called "fear of the law". In Saudi Arabia it is not easy to trouble a girl or steal. Rules are implemented. Arvind Kejriwal is a source of fear for those breaking the law. If AAP members continue to work honestly, India will change.' But he warns that the hopes of the people have risen so high that 'if fulfilment doesn't happen, disappointment will set in.'

Foundation Stones

The question of forming a political party was also driven by other considerations that had begun to worry some of the leaders of the IAC, now leading AAP. Experiences while dealing with the government and politicians had forced the decision, Arvind Kejriwal had said soon after the formation of the party. There was apathy and cheating at every stage, he claimed. 'We tried everything, from pleading before them, meeting, writing, fasting, and it can go on. We did everything possible but they did not listen to us, or even adhere to their commitment on the floor of the house. So we were left with no option but to completely overthrow the system.' This presaged what they would do while assuming office in the Delhi government. A pointer to his disruptive proclivities.

While the movement was all about passing the Lokpal Bill that would help restrict corruption by bringing in more accountability and transparency in the highest offices, the agenda was larger than just passing this law. The idea of forming a political party had also been driven by the realisation that laws alone could not bring change; their efficient and honest enforcement was key. Examples of earlier movements like that of Jayaprakash Narayan, and V.P. Singh during the Bofors scam, showed how the Indian electorate was ready to engage with alternatives. That they continue to experiment shows that despite failures, the aam aadmi harbours hope for change.

Lokpal was just one focus point and AAP soon realised that they needed to change the whole system to usher in alternative politics; it couldn't be done in fragments. That's because the existing political system itself begets corruption. How can a salaried person join the political process if he is required to spend ten crore rupees to contest elections? He is forced to take unaccounted-for money and this in turn forces him to accommodate his financiers with favours. 'Corruption is deeply rooted in the political electoral system,' Gopal Rai says, sitting in the party's office, an old, two-storeyed building given to them by an AAP member at a rental rate of one rupee per year. 'We needed to amend the electoral system if we had to change things. And for this, we decided that we needed to alter political systems, the ways in which people get elected.'

The other guiding force for the political party was what Arvind

Kejriwal describes as swaraj. Mani Shankar Aiyar, the Congress leader who, by his own admission, often ends up with his foot in his mouth, claims to have read the swaraj document when Arvind Kejriwal met him some months ago. 'His idea of swaraj is like a school boy writing an essay in a school magazine,' Mani Shankar Aiyar says, despite being one of the biggest voices supporting decentralisation and Panchayati Raj. Arvind Kejriwal, in one of his media interviews, admitted that former Prime Minister and Congress leader Rajiv Gandhi had made the first attempt towards decentralisation through the 73rd and 74th amendments of the Constitution. While the move for decentralisation was laudable, particularly in view of the party's aims to empower people, its modus operandi has led to a new debate today.

Sociologist Dipankar Gupta says that while decentralisation is useful to keep track of how the government is functioning, and helps bring these issues to the notice of those in power, big policies have to be taken at the top. 'You can come down to the local level to feel the pulse and gauge if policies will be accepted or voted out,' he says. 'But you can't have policy decisions being taken at the local level.' Many of the swaraj principles that guide AAP are still to be tested.

But just like the move to join the political mainstream attracted leaders like Yogendra Yadav into the party fold, some other leaders who play crucial roles as backroom men and women were drawn into AAP on the decentralisation plank. Take Atishi Marlena, the party spokesperson who is also deeply involved in the policy committee. Empowering people and giving voice to the marginalised to ensure greater equity is what appealed to her in AAP.

The idea of creating seventy different manifestos in Delhi to reflect the aspirations of multiple people was one method of decentralisation that she likes to speak about. 'In the Delhi manifesto, we went out and spoke to people in each constituency,' says Atishi Marlena. Similarly with candidate selection, where people from constituencies chose their candidate for the polls through a secret ballot system. 'We will take inputs from people of that state and consult the people of that district. So, it will be more consultative.'

AAP's attempts to make the manifesto crafting process more participative during the Delhi state elections is now being emulated by traditional large parties like Congress and BJP. Congress Vice President Rahul Gandhi is holding meetings with representatives from local governments, groups like railway porters and women, to get their suggestions on the party's manifesto. BJP's Narendra Modi is holding a 'chai pe charcha' campaign to get a feel of what voters want in their manifesto. As part of this, Narendra Modi visits a tea stall and interacts with common people over a cup of tea, while the interaction is relayed through satellite and social media to around a thousand tea stall locations across the country.

The coming together of ideas as well as people happened all at once for AAP. Suddenly, a door to an alternative politics was pushed ajar. For a lot of people, this alternative became a viable option to engage with politics without the baggage of dynasty, polarisation or corruption.

New Akhada

While Congress and BJP have established party organisations and structures, AAP is working towards creating them, empowering political novices like Atishi Marlena and Praveen Singh with large responsibilities. 'Arvind (Kejriwal) is the most important public face. But it doesn't mean that he is the ultimate decision-maker; besides that won't work,' Praveen Singh says. 'How can you retain good people if you do not give them responsibilities? It cannot be a one-man-show and, most importantly, you have to have democratic processes. There is much to learn. So far, people who come and perform also get into positions of responsibility.'

At the leadership level, according to Praveen Singh, AAP has a two-pronged structure. The national executive—currently comprising twenty-four members—is its supreme body. Then, there is a political affairs committee, of nine people, all of whom also belong to the national executive. 'This is the operational decision-making body, but the national executive is the overarching body,' says Praveen Singh.

Another AAP leader who did not want to be identified points out that the party is also novel for the many kinds of people it has brought together. 'It has a range of characters. Arvind is about brinkmanship, he pushes you to the edge. He is that angry young man on the brink. Prashant Bhushan, on the other hand, is a liberal, whose views on human rights go too far. Yogendra Yadav belongs to a different background. Even Kumar Vishwas. There is a class bias against him. But he has a huge following among people, who see in him a representative of their class. If Pankaj Gupta brings in a corporate worldview, Gopal Rai and Sanjay Singh bring in a different complexion to the discourse. The core group crosses class barriers and adds that diversity.'

The complexities within the party are an open secret. But contradicting the popular perception, party insiders believe this diversity is a strength. Entry-level membership is open to all, though it comes with little power. The actual scrutiny comes in at the second level where active membership is given after a screening process that requires nominations and introductions. One thing that has been sacrosanct is the party's stand that it will not compromise and induct criminals or those with corrupt histories. Any member will have to first declare any pending case or charge that has been filed against him or her.

AAP has set the ball rolling and is today being pushed by the high expectations and aspirations of the disenchanted, who have found in the party an alternative platform away from traditional national parties like Congress and BJP or regional parties. The trend that began with caste empowerment and the empowerment of regional voices in Parliament is set to consolidate further.

'Neither party (Congress or BJP),' write Pradeep Chhibber and Ken Kollman in their 2004 book, *The Formation of National Party Systems*, 'has been successful in articulating a national policy program that unites disparate regional factions within its party or absorbs enough regional or state parties to form a winning national party. And neither party can overcome the most difficult obstacle to national power—namely, the perception that the delivery of public goods and services such as electricity and clean water are the purview of state governments.'

For all practical purposes, the age of unfocussed mass parties is over. They cannot exist at a time when individuality and specialisation are being privileged. Political parties in restricted geographical areas or those focussed on sharp issues like anti-corruption (in the case of AAP) are here to stay. Larger parties will find themselves unable to be representatives of such smaller groupings—their canvass is too large for smaller issues to stand on their own. They may persist due to past momentum for a few elections, but with a new, young and impatient populace, whose reactions to inter-generational voting patterns carry a note of rebellion, it will be smaller parties that will recognise their aspirations. The upshot: a constantly-fragmenting democracy may deepen the actual democratic process, with the aam aadmi disrupting both caste and regional politics. It is in the aam aadmi's parlour, aam aadmi's akhada, training ground, that the foundations of politics will now be set.

Following the lead taken by AAP, both Congress and BJP are looking at redesigning manifestos that speak directly to the aam aadmi. Perhaps, over the next few elections, they might even succeed in repackaging themselves as parties that have a national face backed by local action. As far as the aam aadmi is concerned, Congress seems to have lost the plot and BJP is readying itself to carry the baton in Elections 2014. But it is AAP that has ignited the fire, and whose performance will be studied closely. Either way, none of the three parties will gain in legitimacy if they, over the long term, are unable to guarantee accountability, ensure devolution of power, and deliver governance.

For a representative democracy, it is the word 'democracy' that will matter more than the word 'representative'. As a result, it will be the setting up and enforcing of processes that serve the interests of aam aadmi which will carry the weight of legitimacy, rather than vision statements of a fuzzy future, howsoever grand they may be. The biggest hurdle in the way of a party trying to be representative is size; size carries the risk of distance. The glamour of grand policymaking at the top, away from the 'unwashed masses' is embedded in this size—leaving citizens frustrated that the only decision in their hands is the right to vote every fifth year. The gap this distance has left has been filled by civil society organisations, like IAC, that hear the voices closely. The transformation of such organisations into political parties is the next step that Arvind Kejriwal has taken. Whether he too will drown in the compulsive alienation that large parties suffer from, remains to be seen.

While arguing in favour of civil or people's movements, Nikhil Dey articulates his views effectively, saying the going could be easier for AAP because they are in an empty playing field where they set their own rules of their game—small is easier. 'It could be a big disadvantage if AAP were on the other side where rules have already been set,' he says. Arvind Kejriwal further stated in October 2012, 'We have to pull them into our "akhada" to fight. We have to fight with our rules. If we are able to pull them into our "akhada", they will not be able to stand.' The akhada he talks about is not representative democracy but direct democracy—a platform on which neither Congress nor BJP can stand today.

With AAP, Arvind Kejriwal created that disruptive akhada. But if setting up the akhada was an arduous, exhausting task, the peak of success is still higher. How will Arvind Kejriwal and AAP carry the aam aadmi there?

7
ANATOMY OF SUCCESS

With the decision to form Aam Aadmi Party (AAP) firmly in place, it was time to fight elections and shift from protest to politics. The party—in the early stages of its formation and making its debut in Delhi—was preoccupied. A coronation was hardly on the minds of the party's leaders.

Survival was.

Belief was.

Structure was.

Their shift—from being outsiders knocking at the gates of power to bring change to entities in the same room as insiders seeking votes with folded hands—was not easy. There was no organisation, no cadre, no talent. With no experience in the rough-and-tumble of politics, here was an audacious new party flexing its puny muscles, even as it was trembling inside. How did they get here? What prompted them to participate in what they had condemned? What was the turning point that transformed this group of people from activists to politicians? Not one, not two—there were ten turning points in this journey. And if the walk from activism to politics was a fall into the frying pan, participation in the electoral process was a jump from the frying pan into a raging fire.

Turning Point 1: September 2012, Anna Walks Away

On 2 August 2012, after failing to achieve their goal of having a strong anti-corruption legislation passed in Parliament despite the intense Indian Against Corruption (IAC) movement, Arvind Kejriwal and a few other leaders decided to enter politics and launch a new political party. After some debate and many confabulations, in early-September 2012, Anna Hazare—their natural leader, their capital, the one around whom they bandied— decided he would not join them and walked away. 'He felt, by entering politics, we would be stained,' recalls Gopal Rai, one of the figureheads of AAP who was involved in setting it up. 'Our view was that even if we were stained, in the process if we changed things in society and in our country, it was fine. Change in society and in the country is bigger than the concerns of our individual lives. And we could not see change through protest movements.'

About a month later, on 2 October 2012, the 143rd birth anniversary of Mahatma Gandhi, the idea and intention of forming a new party was announced. Also announced that day was its first electoral goal—Delhi was to be the epicentre of the IAC anti-corruption movement and one of the nine states that was to see state-level polls in 2013, before the big, national one slated for mid-2014. 'Electorally and politically, Delhi made imminent sense,' says Yogendra Yadav.

The choice of Delhi is one of AAP's many moves that make Santosh Desai, brand consultant and social commentator, feel the party's rise was not just happenstance—being at the right place at the right time with the right message—but that a lot of design went into it. 'As a strategy, the choice of Delhi to make its political debut was extremely sharp,' he says, from his perch in Mumbai. 'That's where the energy was. It is a contained space that allows for greater impact and yet it gets disproportionate media coverage. To a degree, it's because the media resides there and political action resides there.'

The leadership of AAP saw Delhi as their debutante akhada, their first battlefield, as we have explored in the previous chapter. They also saw it as a testing ground for the new politics they were advocating. 'We wanted to establish a role model,' says Gopal Rai. 'So, we decided to implement our complete philosophy in Delhi. We said we would choose candidates from the people, including those who had never contested. We would ask people to give contributions in white and we would put up their names on our website. Whoever is courageous enough to give—give to change. And we have to win—we have to fight with honesty and we have to win. We will focus all our energy on Delhi.'

For those following national politics, the difference AAP brought was stark. 'We have shortlisted our candidates and have announced the first list,' Arvind Kejriwal told charter members of The Indus Entrepreneurs. 'In other parties, you can get a ticket for two crore rupees. Another five crores goes in the campaign. Once he gets elected he will earn thirty crores over the next five years. It is from here that the politics of corruption begins. It is here that we want to put barriers.'

The process was not easy. Any candidate seeking an AAP ticket needed to get one hundred signatures from his constituency. 'This,' Arvind Kejriwal told entrepreneurs, 'is not so easy, as an Australian NRI discovered. Despite this, five hundred people have applied for seventy seats. And the candidates are varied. Some are very poor, rickshaw pullers, daily labourers. But at least they have begun to dream. Could you have imagined a rickshaw driver seeking a ticket in any other party?'

Apart from the positive anti-corruption message that he conveys, he also contrasts it against the tenor of traditional parties. 'In our Lok Sabha today there are 163 MPs who have cases of serious crimes against them. In the Delhi Vidhan Sabha there are sixteen Congress MLAs and nine BJP MLAs with serious allegations of crime against them, including rape and murder. We will have no criminals contesting elections from our party.'

Turning Point 2: October-November 2012, 'Scam' Season

But instead of talking about Delhi, and the issues the capital city faced, the party-in-waiting stuck to its anti-corruption agenda, still under the banner of IAC, and raised the pitch. Instead of speaking about corruption in broad generalities, it started making specific allegations about crony capitalism and influence-peddling against the rich and the powerful. And it did so in a way that made it the object of attention—through press conferences that, initially, a hungry 24x7 media relished and covered generously.

A certain amount of planning was evident in these press conferences, which happened between 5 October and 9 November. They came in quick succession to maintain recall, continuity and shock value, but were spaced out adequately to let an issue simmer. They were announced a day before and members of the media were sent invites; sometimes a subtle hint was dropped, a discreet mention made, on the 'target' of the day.

Leading on the dais would be Arvind Kejriwal, wearing the white cap, spewing fire, holding up papers, pointing fingers, venting and invoking the name of country. Seated next to him would be Prashant Bhushan, a Supreme Court lawyer known for filing Public Interest Litigations (PILs) and another founding member of the party, making additional points, fielding follow-up questions and explaining nuances in his typical slow, measured, deliberate style. The party did not always put out new allegations in the public domain. What it did, and rather effectively, was load a lot more information on what was already known, raise the pitch and compel the rest of the media to go hunting for more.

Essentially, the idea was to make the issue political and make it resonate with the aam aadmi.

They started with the biggest scam, alleging sweetheart real estate deals between India's largest real estate company DLF and Congress President Sonia Gandhi's son-in-law Robert Vadra. It prompted Robert Vadra to post a Facebook comment, 'Mango people (a literal play on "aam aadmi") in a banana republic', that he later deleted, but not before it became a punch line, used to attack India's first family of politics.

About a month-and-a-half later, after the flames of this issue had died down, Arvind Kejriwal announced the name of their new party—Aam Aadmi Party (AAP). It was a brilliant move, reckons Santosh Desai. 'AAP has the confidence to do something which is otherwise extremely counter-intuitive,' he says. 'Why would you go and call yourself Aam Aadmi Party when that is the Congress plank? It's a gamble that played out. It's a huge feat that worked to their advantage.'

Eleven days after they put out Robert Vadra's business dealings, AAP trained its guns on the excess allotment of land in Maharashtra to an entity belonging to the Purti Group, owned by then-BJP President Nitin Gadkari. The media latched on and started an intense scrutiny of Gadkari's business interests, which revealed a box of shell companies and sharp accounting practices. About two months later, against the backdrop of an income tax investigation into the Purti Group, Nitin Gadkari decided against a second term as party president and resigned.

AAP followed it up with allegations of misappropriation of funds meant for the disabled from a trust run by External Affairs Minister Salman Khurshid's wife Lousie. Then, in two press conferences spaced out over ten days, it alleged irregularities in the Krishna-Godavari gas project of Reliance Industries Ltd, causing a loss to the exchequer, and accused Mukesh Ambani, the promoter of the company and India's wealthiest man, of holding black money in Swiss banks. The press conferences were creating a buzz for this yet-to-be-formalised political party. They were capturing media time, something they had in abundance when the Anna Hazare movement was at its peak but that had slipped away after he left.

They would see media time slip away again. In mid-December, Reliance Industries Ltd. and Mukesh Ambani sent a legal notice, but not to Arvind Kejriwal or Prashant Bhushan, who had addressed the two press conferences in question. The legal notice went to several TV channels for broadcasting these press conferences. It said: 'In the course of above press conferences, several and false and extremely defamatory statements were made by Mr Arvind Kejriwal and Mr Prashant Bhushan relating to our clients, amounting to very serious libel on our clients. (The TV channel) provided a platform and instrumentality for wide dissemination of the false and defamatory statements and allegations made at the said press conference.'

The company raised the threat of defamation. 'Telecast of these press conferences amounts to permanent publication of defamatory material relating to our clients by you... Each of the two press conferences were telecast live without making any attempt to verify the truth or veracity of the statements and allegations being made during the press conference. Apart from having telecast the press conferences live, (the TV channel) in the course of several television programmes and televised debates that followed after the said press conferences, continued to telecast, transmit and retransmit the defamatory footage of the press conferences.'

A combative Arvind Kejriwal raised questions about the target of the legal notice, through a letter to Mukesh Ambani. 'I find it quite perplexing,' the letter, which was made public on 24 January 2013, began. 'If you felt that you have been defamed by what Prashant Bhushan and I said, then we are the real culprits and, if you had to send a defamation notice, it should have been to us. The TV channels merely broadcast what we said. It is evident that your sole purpose of sending this notice was to steamroll the TV channels into subservience.'

While the party put up a brave public front, in the AAP backrooms the pressure was palpable. 'In its immediate aftermath, we felt the government put a lot of pressure on the media. The media blacked us out. It was sudden,' says Gopal Rai. 'They had been broadcasting our press conferences live, but such was the pressure, some internal pressure, that even a line in the papers became difficult.'

That overnight disappearance from public attention raised doubts among leaders, more so since the new party, unlike mainstream parties, lacked organisational structure and a cadre base. It needed the vehicle of the media to spread the word for it. 'That was a moment of doubt when we wondered whether we could go forward. We were uncertain about the future,' says Gopal Rai. 'Then, we sat down and discussed. The support among reporters had not changed, but pressure had been imposed on media owners, and that changed the way the press started covering us—that was our understanding.'

Ironically, as had happened a few times before and would happen more in the coming months, necessity would become the mother of invention for AAP, in powerful, defining and sustaining ways. In this case, it set them on a path that liberated them from depending on others, and gave them the chance to create, nurture and control outcomes. It took them to the very source that would be the ultimate force multiplier for them: the people. 'We said, forget the media, it's not in our hands,' says Gopal Rai. 'We will go to the streets, opt for direct communication to people.'

Turning Point 3: March 2013, Bijli-Paani Signature Campaign

When it came to chiselling the 'idea' of AAP—what it wanted to do and how it wanted to do it—this phase would be the most important step in the journey. This is when the organisational strength of the party in Delhi, and to a small extent beyond, was built. This is when volunteers, supporters and candidates were discovered and identified, strengths and weaknesses of constituencies were marked.

This is when the message of AAP started reaching the people, across the seventy assembly constituencies, which could be further broken into 272 wards. 'We started going to all wards directly, holding meetings, small groups, discussions, door-to-door campaigns,' explains Gopal Rai. 'We took the fundamental problems from the lives of people—electricity and water—and planned protests around them.' The base for these protests was a signature campaign against allegedly inflated power and water bills. AAP volunteers went from door to door, locality to locality, asking people whether their bills were inflated, and urging them to sign up submissions that confirmed that they would not pay their power and water bills.

Even as AAP volunteers were fanning out on the ground, Arvind Kejriwal started another fast at a modest house in Sunder Nagri, a resettlement colony on the outskirts of East Delhi. 'It was on 6 April 1930 that Mahatma Gandhi had broken the salt law. Taking inspiration from him, I have also started the civil disobedience movement,' he addressed the 3 April 2013 gathering on the eleventh day of his fast. But there was a difference between this fast and the ones that preceded it, under the IAC banner. The earlier ones, at Jantar Mantar or Ramlila Maidan, were exercises in crowd mobilisation. 'This time, we planned local protests,' says Gopal Rai. 'We did not encourage supporters to come and join Arvind. We said, "Go to your wards." We made centres in all wards, started meeting and taking signatures.' The target was ten lakh signatures.

AAP was gradually building touch-points with the people of Delhi, especially the poor and marginalised. 'People liked AAP as we were fighting against corruption, talking about the aam aadmi,' says Gopal Rai. 'But they did not have faith in us. They would say to us, "I am with you, but who else will support you? You are a new party. The others distribute alcohol, money. How will you cope? You don't know politics, you don't know what happens here." They were speaking from experience.'

According to Gopal Rai, something changed as Arvind Kejriwal continued his fast at Sunder Nagri, eventually fifteen days long, and AAP volunteers fanned out deep and wide, especially in localities where people lived a hand-to-mouth existence. The volunteers, he says, collected signatures from ten lakh households, during this period. At three people a household, that is thirty lakh voters.

But it wasn't the poor alone that were affected by those hugely emotive moments. 'When I was on an anshan, a fast, a big industrialist came and got very emotional,' Arvind Kejriwal says. 'He said he wanted to give us ten crore rupees. But, he insisted, his name could not come on the website because the government would harass him. I said, no sir, we don't need money from you. Give us your blessings. I can't take your money, because if you give me money today, your name will come up tomorrow. Many people don't give us money because if their name comes up on our website the government may harass them. Someone who had given us twenty-five lakh rupees was harassed by the government.'

When he broke his fast on the fifteenth day, a visibly weak Arvind Kejriwal—who is diabetic and had lost 8.5 kg during his fast—addressed the people assembled. Behind him sat Manish Sisodia, Kumar Vishwas, Prashant Bhushan and Gopal Rai. He started by thanking the many doctors who had attended to him during this fast. Next, he thanked Santosh and his family, whose house he was fasting in; he acknowledged the generosity of this family of seven in giving him the bigger room in their house and adjusting in the smaller one.

'The coming elections will be fought on the issues of electricity and water,' he said. 'The government that cannot give these will not be in power.'

The fast and the signature campaign were just the first phase of what AAP had planned. Arvind Kejriwal outlined the second phase in his speech. AAP would hold a rally in Jantar Mantar and then walk to the residence of Sheila Dikshit to hand over these ten lakh signatures. The signatures also held some political implication. Party leaders were looking at a statistical correlation, and they liked what they saw. 'In the last (2008) elections, the Congress came to power with 24.6 lakh votes. And here thirty lakh people had signed against Sheila Dikshit. That gave us confidence,' says Gopal Rai. 'Also, we had highlighted this electricity-water campaign in jhuggi-jhopris and resettlement colonies, areas where news does not filter in through the media, where people don't read papers or see news channels. That gave us confidence that there is a discontentment among people regarding corrupt politics.'

According to Arvind Kejriwal, news that most of us take for granted as it reaches us instantly does not reach the slums. 'In the slums nobody knows us. But they know the hand (symbol of Congress) and lotus (symbol of BJP). You will be surprised to know that some people in slums say they will vote for Indira Gandhi because she had given them these plots. Fighting this in two or three months is going to be very difficult for us. The hand is ingrained in their minds, while nobody knows about us. I asked one of our prabharis—a person who is in charge of twenty-five households—who she would vote for. She said, "You". I asked her, what is our party? She said, Congress!'

The ten lakh signatures went a long way towards making the party politically relevant. A monitoring committee was asked to verify each signature, which served two purposes. One, it gave inputs about households in a particular ward—who were the people there and their contacts. Two, it helped the party identify interested and engaged volunteers, who too were on a voyage of discovery, learning intimately about colonies that so far had just been names in their minds. Separating the interested from the uninterested, the engaged from the detached was very important, says Yogendra Yadav. He cites the example of Uttar Pradesh about a decade ago, when the number of registered Congress members in the state exceeded the votes polled by the party in an election. 'This happens when there is a membership drive as opposed to our model of volunteers,' he says.

Turning Point 4: April to June 2013, Army of Volunteers

In a matter of months, AAP went from being a media-led and media-amplified movement into being a ground-up political force. 'It was entirely deliberate and a remarkable feat,' says Santosh Desai. 'Currently, political branding is divided between the old-school megaphone way or rallies, and using social media as the centrepiece. The AAP strategy is a third view: a more engaged exercise, ground-level activity carried out by volunteers who are believers. The bottom-up approach.'

AAP expanded by means of how it came across. It grew by word of mouth. During the signature campaign and in its immediate aftermath, while the media was not looking, AAP intensified its search for volunteers and sharpened the way it approached canvassing. 'We started putting together a volunteer base for booth management,' says Gopal Rai. 'The door-to-door campaigners were already there. We additionally identified volunteers who would give us two hours a day, or Saturday and Sunday, or full time.'

Volunteers were imparted training on the issues at hand, the party's stance regarding them and how to engage with the people. A set of party workers was trained at the first level—the seventy assembly constituencies. This set, in turn, was assigned the responsibility to train people at the ward level (272 wards). The engagement of the second set with the people revolved around a pamphlet whose pitch was: If you want to change the country, give us some time. It talked about three things—swaraj, the Jan Lokpal bill and corruption. The volunteers at the ward level were asked to do, what Gopal Rai terms, 'tea parties'. 'If you are a supporter or a volunteer, you had to call four to five people in your neighbourhood, and serve them tea and read from the pamphlet,' says Rai. 'Slowly, a team started stringing together to cover each booth.'

'We created a group of three teams,' says Nimmi Rastogi. 'First, a team of two at the booth, a manager and a substitute. Second, the teams outside the booth. And three, the welcome teams, who would go house-to-house to get people out to vote.'

A distinctive feature of AAP as a political party is its volunteer base as opposed to membership count. Unlike most parties, which draw workers by going on a membership drive, AAP was created as people joined the party—in many cases, giving up jobs, and making families and life as they knew it second priority. 'A lot of what AAP managed to pull off is because you had passionate believers who were willing to do things that people who were paid would not do,' says Santosh Desai. 'This included funding, the effort and the actual volunteering work, which increasingly political workers and parties have stopped doing, because for them it is a job.'

AAP members didn't join the party grudgingly. They joined in spirit. Yogendra Yadav recounts an anecdote, when a volunteer gave a pamphlet to an individual who read it and threw it away. Immediately, the pamphlet was picked up another volunteer. 'Asked by a passer-by why he had picked up the crumpled leaflet, the volunteer said: "My party does not have money and we cannot afford to waste." It is their sheer idealism and conviction to be the change (that inspires us),' Yogendra Yadav says.

Arvind Kejriwal likes to say that the party did not design a low-cost campaign. AAP saved money because the common man decided to campaign for a fellow common man who was representing him. This was in stark contrast to other parties, who hired people to do this. 'I am told a person is hired for five thousand rupees per week,' Arvind Kejriwal said after the Delhi results. 'So, other parties would spend about two crore rupees just for hiring people for campaigning. But ours was a people's campaign.'

As part of its outreach programme and in an effort to capture mind-space, AAP also started putting out visual publicity material. 'Many did not even know the name of the party,' says Gopal Rai. 'Some people knew Anna Hazare, a fewer number Arvind Kejriwal and even fewer AAP. And we did not have an election symbol yet.' Yet something was going on here, something invisible, almost as if people were drawn to a political pied piper, following him wherever he led them.

Despite the overall sense of mission-madness, visual publicity wasn't an easy task. AAP's first attempt at visual publicity was a disaster, according to Gopal Rai. During the electricity-water protests, the party put up boards at traffic intersections. 'At the Centre, there was a Congress government. At the municipal level, it was a BJP government,' says Rai. 'Overnight, they took off the boards and ripped them apart. Not one board was spared. We were worried. No media to support us. And now money, raised via donations, down the drain.' For a party that was saving money by reusing crushed pamphlets, this was a blow.

By then, the numbers of volunteers and supporters had reached a critical mass and new volunteers were increasing steadily. For visual publicity, the party decided to tap into this goodwill that was building. It started a new campaign after the tea party campaign—local prabari (in-charge).These were people with jobs, and they were given the task of canvassing with ten to twenty households in their neighbourhood. In addition, they were also to be carriers of a visual message. A standard AAP poster, with space to write a person's name and telephone number, was pasted outside their house. 'People started to see, interest grew. These came up in every galli and mohalla,' says Gopal Rai. 'Now, this was on the person's house, and so the Congress and BJP could not touch the posters. Starting in April, within a month, we had about a lakh-and-a-half local prabari.'

According to Gopal Rai, the posters vaulted the party from an abstract space into a real one. 'The BJP would say of us, "It's a chaar aadmi (four-people) party",' says Rai. 'But people started thinking, "I know four people in my locality who are associated with the party".' In time, many of these posters were also torn. AAP replaced them with a board that listed what it would do on six key issues—Lokpal, corruption, utility bills, education, women, and employment. These boards would later fall afoul of the Election Commission, which disallowed political parties from putting up boards outside homes as it amounted to defacement of property.

The ground-up, door-to-door work done by the party, when it was not in the media glare, set the stage for something bigger. By June 2013, AAP's message had gone far enough for it to hold public rallies. 'About three thousand to eight thousand people would come for these rallies, where we would discuss electricity-water and manifesto issues,' says Rai.

Turning Point 5: Strengthening the Backroom

Even before the party launched in earnest, through the signature campaign, a small group of key people in charge of various functions were in place and were quietly marshalling things in the background. Some of them carried the protest passion of the India Against Corruption movement. Others came from beyond, drawn by the novelty of AAP. But some things were common to all—they were young, they were restless, they were idealistic, they were keen to dirty their hands in the business of nation-building. All of them were expressions of an abstract entity referred to as the aam aadmi.

Like Atishi Marlena, thirty-two, the key policymaker and manifesto writer of AAP. She studied history in Delhi's St Stephen's College, and went to Oxford as a Rhodes scholar, before returning to India to teach in Rishi Valley School, and work with a string of non-profits and associations. Through one of these associations she met Prashant Bhushan, an AAP founder. She watched the IAC movement from the sidelines, but gradually was sold on the AAP idea after meeting many of its functionaries. She was the point-person for the thirty-one policy committees that gave inputs to AAP's overall manifesto and the seventy constituency-specific manifestos in Delhi. 'This is a historic juncture in our democracy and I am happy to be a part of this,' Marlena says.

Like Durgesh Pathak, twenty-five, who was in charge of door-to-door campaigning. A resident of Allahabad and with a Master's degree in English, he was preparing for his civil services examinations in Delhi when he joined the IAC movement in June 2011 and then, with some hesitation, AAP when it was formed. It wasn't long before he found his calling—being on the ground and meeting hundreds of new people everyday.

Like Ankit Lal, twenty-nine, who left his job as a software engineer in a company in January 2012 to help the IAC movement with its social media outreach programme. At AAP, he was given charge of the party's social networking strategy, where he engineered, among other things, the constituency-specific Facebook pages and a coordinated Twitter campaign that depended on a team of about hundred AAP volunteers and supporters across the world. 'When we joined Twitter, we were up against a highly-organised BJP presence on it. But we soon realised that after a certain point in time, nobody can control Twitter.'

Like Ashish Talwar, forty-four, who Yogendra Yadav rates as a better psephologist than himself. For nine years, between 1996 and 2004, as part of Congress, he visited households and walked the streets of Delhi. Talwar has an intimate knowledge of every ward in Delhi—its social and economic construct, streets, infrastructure, milieu, problems—and he eventually became the go-to man for AAP candidates on strategy. In his Congress days, Ashish Talwar volunteered at poll booths, handed out electoral slips, worked on electoral rolls, assisted legislators. This was the period when he learnt the fundamentals of mapping polling booths. Typically, an assembly constituency has about two hundred polling booths spread over thirty to forty polling centres. 'It is about working on each of these centres, ensuring voters have their voter cards in place and are in the voter list,' he says.

Ashish Talwar tutored candidates, supplied them with key inputs about their constituencies and the composition of voters in each ward, helped them understand what voters wanted and how to channel that. 'The youth played a big role in the AAP campaign, and it shows,' says Talwar, who has a family business. 'AAP boasts of ten of the eleven MLAs elected in the twenty-five to thirty-five age group. These are the leaders of tomorrow, the next generation.'

These are but just some of the people who plugged into the budding AAP network, motivated by little else than a powerful desire to change things. The vehicle of the new political party gave them the opportunity to propel transformation. There were students, working professionals, business folks, homemakers, social workers, retired bureaucrats. 'People came from all spheres of life, from the US, from Singapore, from London, from Karnataka, from Tamil Nadu…they came leaving their jobs, their businesses,' says Pankaj Gupta, who is now using his skills as an entrepreneur to raise funds for the party. 'They were not worried. I have at least fifty people in the team here and in different offices in Delhi, who must have left their jobs and businesses. If you ask them what is going to happen to their business, they say, "We'll see".'

Turning Point 6: Campaign of Innovation

From people like these, and the team assembled around them, came some innovative campaigning ideas, which were mostly embedded in the economy of cost or in the philosophy of people participation. 'We also had a lot of talented people who quit their well-paying jobs to be with us,' Arvind Kejriwal said after the Delhi elections. 'Their creativity helped make up for what we lacked in terms of resources.'

There was the 'human banner', a milder version of guerrilla warfare. Short of funds to rent billboards, they hung massive seven foot by eight foot AAP banners on the sides of flyovers from 8.00 a.m. to 11.00 a.m.—a time of day that was high on traffic and low on cops. The banners that sported a carefully-chosen picture of the angst-filled face of Arvind Kejriwal or a giant broom could not be missed. A volunteer always hovered near the banner. If a cop came and asked him to remove it, he would quietly unstring it, and go put it on another flyover, or come back the next day. A cat-and-mouse game had begun between the cops and the AAP volunteers, who would mix and match timings and flyovers to retain an element of surprise. People stopped to see.

There was the autorickshaw campaign, where AAP posters started appearing on the back of these vehicles. The idea originated from the need for more places where AAP posters could be put up for free. Over time, Arvind Kejriwal had built a certain amount of equity with the community of auto drivers, and AAP consequently reached out to them. A special team of volunteers would stand at CNG gas stations, coaxing auto drivers to let them place the AAP poster on their vehicles. Soon enough, the posters became an integral part of the green and yellow three-wheelers.

There was the decision to have, in addition to a city manifesto, a manifesto for every constituency. 'Preparing seventy manifestos itself was a unique but back-breaking exercise, which sometimes took sixteen hours a day as elections neared,' says Atishi Marlena, who was coordinating that endeavor. While the constituency manifestos followed a broad template, they gave space to the candidate to address local issues as well as bring in his or her vision. For example, the manifesto of AAP MLA Saurabh Bhardwaj from the Greater Kailash constituency—a patchwork of mostly relatively upscale colonies that also houses the contentious proposed Reliance mega mall at Alaknanda—ran into sixteen pages.

It also contained small sub-sections for certain localities in the assembly constituency. For Greater Kailash-II, an extremely affluent neighbourhood, it outlined a review of the experimental Bus Rapid Transport (BRT) corridor, which lay less than a kilometre away and had become a major traffic bottleneck, and the removal of telecom towers, among other things. For Savitri Nagar, which stood at the opposite end of affluence from Greater Kailash-II and struggled with more basic amenities, the manifesto promised last-mile connectivity of water pipes into the homes of residents, and an inquiry into, and subsequent repair of, the area's sewage and drainage systems. The promise was governance at the local level, tailored to local problems and issues.

Before the framing of manifestos, AAP had replicated that same thought on social media. Other political parties had a national page and state pages on Facebook. AAP's social media team launched seventy pages, one for each Delhi constituency. In the process, they went against the advice of Facebook representatives, who felt that it would be tough to manage seventy pages and who cited US President Barack Obama's campaign in 2012 that did not have local chapters. In the end, the idea of having constituency-specific pages meshed with the idea of constituency-specific manifestoes as people had a forum to raise questions about and make conversation on local issues.

In the way the AAP team went about establishing its social media footprint, and the engagement its volunteers encouraged around it, there were parallels with US President Barack Obama's 2012 campaign on social media, where he scored big over his rival Mitt Romney. For example, research conducted by Pew Research Center's Project for Excellence in Journalism showed that the Obama campaign posted about four times as much content as the Mitt Romney campaign, and was active on nearly twice as many platforms. Obama's digital posts also drew twice the number of shares, views and comments from the public than Romney's.

In the Delhi elections, AAP, too, scored big over other parties on the fundamental metrics of social media. It posted much more content than its rivals, with the constituency-specific Facebook pages being one example of platforms that were sharply positioned and encouraged a certain kind of information dissemination and sharing of views. AAP's sharp social media strategy turned viewers from passive consumers of content to active participants and co-creators. AAP's strategy was to engage with fence-sitters, says Ankit Lal, sipping his first glass of filter coffee. 'After fifteen days, they became converts.'

It also channeled super-users for good effect, exemplified by its Twitter strategy, which was marshalled by a core team of about fifteen people and executed by one hundred volunteers across the world. The central idea of this strategy was to keep AAP active in online conversations. To make an issue trend on Twitter, the AAP team of volunteers would first decide a topic, its hashtag and the time when they would tweet about it together. That first coordinated burst would give them visibility on Twitter counts and other Twitter users would pick it up. The team's high point came on 29 November 2013, when all the top five trends from India on Twitter were either related to Arvind Kejriwal or AAP. Since then, the two—along with the negative tweets around Somnath Bharti—have been regulars on top ten Twitter trends.

Turning Point 7: June 3013: Arvind Kejriwal Dares Sheila Dikshit

By June 2013, Arvind Kejriwal and AAP, despite being the underdogs, were making a lot of ground in the perception battle. AAP was in full poll mode, with volunteers silently trawling across the city, dominating the conversations on social media, a steady stream of crowd-funding flowing in. 'We had said that we would decide our candidates early,' says Gopal Rai. 'So, we started the process of candidate selection on 15 April.' This was for an election about which the only thing that was known was that it was likely to be held in November or December.

On 2 June 2013, addressing a convention of AAP workers, Arvind Kejriwal announced that he wanted to have a straight electoral fight against Sheila Dikshit. 'If she decides to avoid such a contest in New Delhi constituency (her assembly seat then) out of fear and moves to another, I will also move to the seat from where she is contesting,' he said. It was a delicious political moment: the anti-establishment crusader wanted to take on the establishment—in the fortress of the establishment. The New Delhi assembly constituency is the biggest concentration of power in the country: ministers and Parliamentarians living in bungalows the size of football fields; bureaucrats and government employees at various levels living in lavish row houses. But above all, and glossed over by many, there's also a smattering of slums.

To some, Arvind Kejriwal's decision seemed foolhardy, even hasty. One of the naysayers was Arvind Kejriwal's close aide Yogendra Yadav. 'I was then in the US and I would have surely advised him against this,' he says. 'And it would have been my biggest mistake.' Arvind Kejriwal's straight and public challenge to go head-on against Sheila Dikshit—the chief minister for fifteen years, who was seen as a provider of good governance in a party that wasn't—helped AAP in the psychological and perception game. It established AAP as the principal opposition party, ahead of the BJP. And it told the people that AAP was not scared to lose. 'It was like giving the perception that you were ready to put your seat at risk,' says Santosh Desai. 'At that time, they were looking at a single-digit performance. So, it also needed political wisdom.'

Arvind Kejriwal's political wisdom behind this choice, when he did express it, invoked the words of a philosopher, the wordplay of a martyr and, seemingly, the idealism of a reluctant politician. 'My victory lies in my loss,' he said in September 2012. But how would he change the system from within if he was not there in the first place? This battle was more than just about a seat, he explained; this battle was about proving that professionals could enter the political system and contest without money or muscle power, and that people power was enough.

A glimpse of the formidable power of the people came on 22 September 2013, as Arvind Kejriwal, rooted in passion and driven by data, explained the maths. By AAP's estimate, there were about thirty thousand households in the New Delhi constituency, accounting for a total of 1,12,000 votes. By that time, roughly the half-way point of the campaign, Arvind Kejriwal and AAP had made contact through a door-to-door campaign with 23,600 families. About six thousand houses, including those of the country's biggest politicians and bureaucrats, were beyond their reach. About twelve thousand families in this region had donated money to AAP and it had contact details of fifty-five thousand voters in its database.

Arvind Kejriwal's challenge to Sheila Dikshit intensified the war of words between the two. It spilled on to other platforms and moved into new territories. On 20 June 2013, her political secretary Pawan Khera wrote to Kejriwal, admonishing him for disrespecting Sheila Dikshit, for running an 'uncouth campaign on auto rickshaws', for using 'language unbecoming' of him against political rivals, for being an outsider and showing a 'lack of understanding of either the issues or the culture of the city', and more. It ends by saying: '...since you have made a career out of rumour mongering, here is a piece of advice: those who live by the rumour, die by the rumour too.'

Shallow in its content, patronising in its tone, naïve in its political understanding, it was a piece of communication crying to be ripped apart. Kejriwal obliged. Five days later, he delivered a 1,632-word riposte addressed not to Pawan Khera, but to his employer, Sheila Dikshit, written in Hindi. It was part repartee, part jibe, part critique, part insinuation.

'Smt Sheila Dikshitji, I have received a letter written by your political secretary, Mr Pawan Khera, in which you have raised certain issues,' the 25 June 2013 response stated. 'This letter answers those questions. However, I am perplexed (about) why you did not write to me directly instead of using your staff member's name. A few months back, you did the same thing. I had stated in a public meeting that you are a broker of electricity companies. You probably took offense to it. Even at that time, instead of filing a defamatory case against me in your name, you did it using Mr Khera's name. There is a saying in English, "a leader should lead from the front". Hiding behind someone, or firing from someone else's shoulder, demonstrates the weakness of a leader...'

Responding to a provocation, Arvind Kejriwal seized the moment. The rest of the letter alternates between answering the charges levelled by Pawan Khera and tearing into the Delhi chief minister's leadership, decisions and politics. He referred to Sheila Dikshit, again, as a 'broker of electricity companies'. He asked her to take three steps if she really wanted clean politics—decline tickets to candidates with a criminal background, reveal names of financial donors on the Congress website, and reject dynastic politics by not fielding two candidates from the same family. 'I am aware that if you announce this, then you will have to make a big sacrifice—either you or your son, Mr Sandeep Dikshit, will have to retire from politics. If you take the three above mentioned three steps, then people will believe that you really want to practice "clean politics".'

The letter challenged Sheila Dikshit to a public face-off. 'I invite you to a public debate in front of the citizens of Delhi. This debate can take place at Ramlila Maidan or any other large public venue. Date and time will be as per your convenience. I know that you will never accept this challenge. But I will still wait for it. If you agree to a public debate, it will lay a solid foundation for the start of "clean politics" in the country.' The letter concluded the way it started, with a subtle jibe: 'In future, if you need to say anything to me, please do not hesitate to write to me directly.'

Turning Point 8: November 2013, Jhaadu Chalao Yatra

If media coverage, people's contact and volunteer swell was any indication, the city's confidence in AAP was increasing. Opinion polls showed AAP would be a new factor in Delhi, an electoral battlefield that had historically seen a two-horse race between Congress and BJP. However, different opinion polls gave widely different estimates of how much of a factor it would be.

In the eleven opinion polls whose results were announced between 2 August 2013 and 4 November 2013 by various media companies, in partnership with various survey agencies, eight of them projected a return of between eight and eleven seats for AAP. The highest number projected for AAP was twenty-two seats, by CNN-IBN/Week. By comparison, AAP's own surveys were, as always, predicting a better showing, and suggested they were in the reckoning to assume power. One trend was common: AAP seemed to have momentum going. For example, ABP News-Nielsen came out with two polls, one on 4 August 2013 and another on 4 November 2013. The first one showed AAP winning eight seats, the second one eighteen seats.

If the party needed a push, it got one from its Jhaadu Chalao Yatra—a twenty-two-day roadshow AAP launched on 10 November 2013, aimed at registering a presence with as many people as possible. It was a play on its electoral symbol: the broom (jhaadu in Hindi). A notification dated 18 January 2013 from the Election Commission listed eighty-five symbols that were available to political parties, which included oddities like batsman, cake, carrom board, dish antenna and frock. AAP submitted 'broom', 'candle' and 'tap' as its three most preferred symbols in that order of priority. On 2 August 2013, the Election Commission allotted symbol number 14 in its alphabetical list, broom. AAP translated the word into Hindi, and went on to turn it into the stuff of legend. Announcing this choice, an AAP press release said: 'With the broom, which symbolises dignity of labour, the party hopes to clean the filth which has permeated our government and our legislature. The country needs a clean sweep of its corrupted mainstream political parties.'

The Jhaadu Chalao Yatra was essentially a small convoy of vehicles, with AAP leaders in an open jeep, passing through various neighbourhoods. Standing on the jeep, Arvind Kejriwal was a permanent fixture; his support cast of leaders kept changing from day to day, from area to area, the underlying idea being to carry a face representing the locality through which they were passing.

'Road shows will start every morning to ensure that the maximum number of people see and interact with Arvind Kejriwal and AAP's candidates,' an AAP press release announcing the roadshows stated. 'Routes for the yatra have been prepared keeping in mind that it travels more on inner main roads. AAP has also taken care to reach to maximum number of people and would be going to villages, resettlement colonies, unauthorised and authorised colonies. Each route has been prepared in consultation with candidates and local volunteers, with suggestions from local people also.'

After his victory, Arvind Kejriwal called the Jhaadu Yatra the 'biggest turning point' for AAP as it increased his reach exponentially. He regretted not having thought of this sooner because, he felt, had the party started this two months earlier, the impact on voters would have been much better. Before the Jhaadu Yatra, AAP was organising Jan Sabhas (small locality meetings), but those had their limitations. They could only organise the meetings in the evening when people were back from office. With the roadshow, Arvind Kejriwal truly reached out to people.

Turning Point 9: November 2013, The Sting

The Jhaadu Yatras added momentum to the AAP bandwagon. That said, speed breakers are never far away in the unpredictable landscape of politics, more so in this time of 24x7 media. On 21 November 2013, a media portal, Media Sarkar claimed to have done a sting operation on AAP's senior leaders, including Shazia Ilmi and Kumar Vishwas; it was alleged that they were taking cash donations for the party from people in lieu of getting land deals. For a party that had promised transparency in financing and insisted on above-board means for campaign finance, the allegations threatened to dislodge AAP from the high moral ground it had taken on the issue. 'This was the most testing time as it challenged the very foundation of honest politics for which AAP was formed,' says Yogendra Yadav.

AAP asked Media Sarkar for the raw footage. It refused and only shared the CD of the sting that had been given to other media companies. The next day, at a press conference, Yogendra Yadav said that the CD of the sting operation was 'doctored', and decided to file a criminal defamation suit against Media Sarkar and the media outfits that broadcast it without verifying its authenticity.

The party managed to get the raw footage of the sting operation from the Election Commission. According to Yogendra Yadav, party members and executive body members spent sixteen straight hours going through the raw footage. On 24 November 2013, it declared that the sting was doctored and none of its leaders were in the wrong. 'It brought joy, relief and conviction in what we had set out to do,' he says.

Two weeks before that, the Central government had said that it would initiate a probe into allegations of foreign funding of AAP. According to the Foreign Contribution Regulation Act (FCRA), the law that regulates funds received from nations abroad by Indian organisations, any financial contribution from any foreign source or company to a political party registered in India is a criminal offence. Union Home Minister Sushilkumar Shinde said the government had received several complaints that the funding coming to AAP violated the FCRA and had decided to probe the matter.

AAP's contention was that all the money it had received from outside India came only from non-resident Indians who held Indian passports. It clarified that it had a condition under which anyone holding a foreign passport, which technically makes this person a foreigner, could not contribute to AAP. The party saw the probe as a witch-hunt, another effort by the establishment to muzzle an outside force. The Centre's inquisition, announced on 11 November 2013, had an unintended effect—a day after the inquiry was announced, the volume of daily donations to AAP shot up four-fold, from seven lakh to thirty lakh rupees. On 17 November 2013, about two weeks before schedule, AAP met its twenty crore fund-raising target for Delhi, and it stopped taking donations. It had struck a chord with the people of Delhi. AAP had gone from skepticism to success.

Turning Point 10: 9 December 2013, Victory

It is forty-eight hours since the poll results in Delhi were declared. Mathematically, AAP is the second-largest party, winning twenty-eight of the seventy seats. Politically, it is the only one with any chance of forming a government—a stunning return for a party that arose from the streets less than thirteen months ago.

At 5.30 in the evening, Flat 403 of Girnar Apartments at Kaushambi in Ghaziabad is teeming with people. Kejriwal's two-bedroom home has become an open house—childhood friends, relatives, neighbours, strangers, just about any aam aadmi passing by. All congratulate him. They click pictures with him. One of them announces he is going to open 'a franchise AAP' in neighbouring Haryana. And then it's time to leave.

Arvind Kejriwal is scheduled to meet the other twenty-seven AAP MLAs—their first formal meeting as elected representatives of the people of Delhi—at the Constitution Club in Rafi Marg, in Lutyen's Delhi. It's a fourteen-kilometre, forty-minute car ride from a suburb that sees a convergence of people to a part of the capital that sees the convergence of power. Today, that ride is infused with deep symbolism, of an aam aadmi crossing over. But such symbolism will have to wait.

Outside Girnar Apartments, a bevy of television reporters and camerapersons wait for Arvind Kejriwal. They have been standing there for hours. The media is back on his side. Arvind Kerjiwal makes news again—he is the news. He waves to journalists, stops and has a word with each of them. At the end of the queue, the watchman in the society waits in attention. When Arvind Kejriwal reaches him, he offers a salute.

Arvind Kejriwal gets into his blue WagonR, which is on its way to becoming the most recognised car in the country. They stop at a petrol pump where he is a regular. An attendant greets him, and chats him up, delighted. 'Sir, thodi si kasar rah gayi. Bas aath seats aur miljate to baat ban jati…lekin fikar nahi, next chance par kar dikhayenge (we just missed out…if only we had eight more seats…but not to worry, we'll do it next time).'

Arvind Kejriwal shakes hands with the attendant while expressing regret for not making it. The WagonR is ready to leave. But the attendant forces Arvind Kejriwal to roll down the windows again. 'Par aapko sacchai par ladna hai aur sacche rahna hai (You have to wage the honest fight and you have to remain honest),' the attendant cautions before letting him drive away.

As evening falls in Delhi and the WagonR gathers speed, Arvind Kejriwal is silent for a minute. And then he speaks. 'The kind of responsibility we have now is huge. We can't afford to make any mistakes now. If we do, the electorate will not spare us,' he says, gazing at the long road ahead.

8

BROOM OF AMBITION

On a cold 11 January 2014 morning, Yogendra Yadav finds himself standing on a 4-inch wide brick wall of a government school building in Gharaunda village in Haryana, about a hundred kilometres from Delhi, holding a microphone that links into a megaphone held by an AAP volunteer, which crackles each time he speaks into it. A foot away from Yogendra Yadav, on that same four-inch weather-beaten pale yellow wall, sits his new-found driver, Vivek, a handsome man in his twenties and a strong contender for the most overqualified person in India in that job profile.

Vivek, who is also Yogendra Yadav's nephew, is a PhD student in political science at Columbia University, New York. This electoral season, though, he is gaining valuable field experience—logging in miles on the road, being a fly on the wall in electoral meetings, witnessing political churning and the extraordinary coming-of-age of a political start-up. When he is not driving, Vivek takes copious amounts of notes on his Apple MacBook, essentially transcribing what Yogendra Yadav says during his several public meetings in a day and firing it into cyberspace on a live blog. Today, he is struggling to find balance on the four-inch wide wall.

It doesn't help Vivek that Yogendra Yadav is in form, a bit removed from his usual mode of dignified articulation and measured restraint. Clearing his throat, Yogendra Yadav sings into the microphone, his pitch about five tones higher than usual. 'Dilli hui hamaari...ab Harryanna ki bari...' (We have won Delhi, next is Haryana), have says, breaking off into the distinctive Haryanvi dialect (with the double 'r' and 'n'). Like an orchestral symphony hitting a high note, his words and his posturing strike a chord with this small, hundred-odd strong audience. An old man, who would evoke the expression 'tau' (uncle) in these parts of India, stands up and, in a sing-song voice, says, 'yeh baat!' (loosely translated, well done).

It's the Delhi-effect impacting into the neighbouring state.

Just fourteen days earlier, AAP decided to take forward a popular mandate from the people of Delhi and, despite being only the second-largest party, it decided to form a government in the state, with outside support from bitter rival Congress that governs Haryana. Even as Arvind Kejriwal, Manish Sisodia and other AAP leaders prepared to embrace the present in Delhi, Yogendra Yadav moved out of the city and into the neighbouring state of Haryana to script the party's future.

For Yogendra Yadav, this moving out also meant a return to his past. 'For me, Haryana was a natural choice as I come from the state,' he says. 'I was born there, my village is there, my parents still live there.' But that morning, as Vivek pulled the car though Karnal district, Yogendra Yadav wasn't reacting to nostalgia. He was thinking numbers—many in AAP, starting with him, believed this fledgling party, powered by the ballast provided by Delhi, could wrest Haryana too when the state would go to polls in October 2014.

'If corruption was an issue in Delhi, it's ten times more in Haryana,' says Yogendra Yadav, adding that its stench exists in everything from land transactions to government jobs. 'This is one state where the movement against corruption got its biggest support, which still continues.' He reels off the many faces of that support—AAP organised itself here about a year ago, almost around the same time as Delhi; it is one of the states with the highest number of AAP volunteers; a number of Delhi constituencies were manned by volunteers from Haryana; after the Delhi election and formation of the government, this was one state where AAP received one of the strongest responses.

It's also ripe for picking, continues Yogendra Yadav. 'Look at it from the other end,' he says. 'Haryana is a state characterised by political vacuum. People are disgusted with the ruling party (Congress), the leader of the opposition (Om Prakash Chautala of Indian National Lok Dal) is cooling his heels in jail on charges of corruption. There is rampant corruption and simply no way out. I guess all these are reasons to believe the next political breakthrough the party would get is in Haryana.'

Even as the excitement in Delhi continued and the challenge of governance presented itself, Yogendra Yadav pulled himself away and made Haryana his base. With Vivek at the wheel, he started shuttling between Delhi, where the structure and spirit of AAP still resided, and its neighbouring state that needed a body support. That need to shuttle, often, meant early-morning starts. On this misty Saturday winter morning of 11 January 2014, at 7.00 a.m., four cars are ready to leave from Yogendra Yadav's modestly-done, book-lined, artefact-filled house in the East Delhi suburb of Madhu Vihar to make a 350-kilometre, day-long swing through eastern Haryana. Three of the cars carry journalists who are tagging along with Yogendra Yadav today, two of them from the two leading English dailies in the capital.

As Yogendra Yadav heads to his SUV in his apartment complex, a man approaches him and hands him an envelope. He had been waiting since 5.00 a.m., this man says, to meet Yogendra Yadav. He points to the long sedan of which he is the driver. He points to the envelope that his employer, the owner of the sedan, who is not there, has asked him to deliver. Taking the envelope and thanking the man, Yogendra Yadav gently makes a philosophical observation that is cutting without being condescending. 'It's amazing how much time and how much money people have in this country,' and gets into a Tata Safari Storme.

Also in the Tata Safari Storme, driven by Vivek, is Vijay Raman, a former CEO of a private company, who has now taken a new assignment; he is Yogendra Yadav's personal secretary. Among this former CEO's indelible contributions is setting up an interactive voice response (IVR) system on Yogendra Yadav's mobile. It has liberated him from the shackles of manning his phone; it has also given every citizen the opportunity to call him and granted him the space to revert to every caller. The IVR caller can use pre-programmed options to identify herself and state her reason for calling. It's a system that also recently made an appearance on a mobile number belonging to Congress leader Rahul Gandhi.

On Yogendra Yadav's phone, the IVR is set up in the AAP mould. It is not just for an aide or the connected journalist or a well-wisher, it is for the aam aadmi. 'Pankaj-ji' is the person who mans this IVR for media calls, and he too is in the SUV. A page in Pankaj-ji's notepad shows the shape of the day that lies ahead—meeting, road, meeting, road…it goes on.

In all, there are nine meetings planned, the first at 9.00 a.m. at Kundli border, about thirty-five kilometres away, and the last at 2.30 p.m. at Panipat. The first seven are roadside meetings, where Yogendra Yadav mingles with the people and makes conversation, at Murthal, Gannour, Samlakha and Gharaunda, among others. The last two are AAP volunteer meets, at Karnal and Panipat. These are relatively bigger, better organised and this is where Yogendra Yadav tries to fire up the troops and the electorate. AAP needs every supporter, every volunteer it can get.

Two staunch supporters join the cavalcade along the way, in their respective cars. One of them is Ashwant Gupta, who is also the convener of AAP in the state of Haryana. His story of political participation and nation-building is the archetypal AAP story. A businessman from Ambala, he is in the field of making speciality equipment used in medical surgeries. After many years in the US, he returned to India, and was pained by the contrast. 'I was taken in by the boards that were displayed when roads or highways were built in the US. They said this is being constructed by your tax dollars. It felt good to be a taxpayer,' he says. 'I came back to India with that spirit, but realised it is difficult to be an honest taxpayer here.'

But AAP gives him hope, and he thinks that will be the case for many others too. 'I have seen the change in the people and what this movement has done to voters,' says Ashwant Gupta. 'The last time Yogendra Yadavji was touring Haryana, we travelled from 9.00 in the morning till 9.00 in the evening, non-stop. In Mewat region, we found two hundred young people waiting for two hours in the cold to hear him and the AAP message. This is the clincher. This is what convinced me that we are on to something big.'

Modest signs of that sentiment are visible at the government school in Gharaunda. There are several cars parked there. Nearly all of them have a jhaadu (broom)—AAP's election symbol—tied on both sides of the vehicle towards the front. It acts as their red beacon, it is their calling card. The crowd is segregated by gender. On one side stand about twenty women in cheap, colourful, synthetic sarees, some with their heads covered in deference to the orthodox, male-dominated gender conventions in these areas; flanking them are young school-going girls, who seem to be there out of sheer curiosity.

The other side, and the more dominant one, comprises men of all age groups and stages of life. There is the old, greying 'tau' in a white pagri (turban) and a walking stick that seems taller than him. A twenty-something unemployed man lingers, busy cleaning his nose. A large part of this gathering is made up of AAP volunteers who have brought along generous provisions to this public meeting for their 'guests' from Delhi—tea to drink; biscuits to eat; moora (stool made of cane) and char pai (small bed made of rope) to sit on.

As Yogendra Yadav continues his address, he explains what the victory in Delhi—'Dilli hui hamaari'—means through the prism of how politics has changed in the last twelve months and how it has affected the life and choices of the ordinary citizen. 'I was going through Mewat a few days back and I met a gentleman,' he starts. 'He told me, "You have done something in ten days that the country couldn't do in sixty-five years". Maine kaha, "Yeh to Haryana hai, yahaan to mari sarkar nahi hai" (I told him, but this is Haryana, it's not an AAP government). He said, "No, my truck goes to Delhi every day. I have been working for thirty years and every day I pay the police official at the border. Those same policemen have stopped asking for it".'

Having given people the details of a situation they could relate to, Yogendra Yadav zooms out and draws for them the bigger picture. 'The phrase "Delhi hui hamaari" means there is a change in governance, in politics and in administration,' he says. 'We have begun changing the idiom of black money. For the first time ever, the aam aadmi, the common man, in Delhi has begun believing that he can compete with traditional and powerful politicians. A person like you and me can be a representative in the assembly and can win elections contested on white money, accounted-for money. People would warn us that candidates would be beaten up, and those same people defeated their opponents by tens of thousands of votes.' A loud applause ensues.

As Yogendra Yadav's thirty-minute address progresses, the applause grows louder, the slogans get shriller, each time with closed fists rising to the skies. The people declare allegiance to AAP and Yogendra Yadav, who, in this election run, is only on his second flying tour to the state. The previous weekend, he was in Mewat. The coming weekend, he plans to cover Karnal, Panipat and Chandigarh.

Except, barely ten days later, the best laid plans of AAP for Yogendra Yadav, their hopes that he would wrest Harayana in October and become the state's chief minister, were subsumed by a change that was spreading fast, wide and deep, faster than any of AAP's leaders could imagine or even keep pace with.

As AAP began governing Delhi, the groundswell of support from across the country kept growing. 'Post 8 December 2013, the kind of surge we have seen is unprecedented and unexpected,' says Pankaj Gupta, who handles fundraising for the party. 'Suddenly, we realised that all states were asking us how we managed the kind of surge we have seen in membership. People want to become part of the movement. In some way, in any way...they just want to get associated with it.'

Among these people were several accomplished Indians from diverse fields—Adarsh Shastri, the grandson of former Prime Minister Lal Bahudar Shastri, who left his job at Apple and is currently drafting the economic vision for the party in the largest electoral state of Uttar Pradesh; GR Gopinath, the man who introduced low-cost airlines to India; Meera Sanyal, former India head of Scottish bank RBS; classical dancer and activist Mallika Sarabhai; Gopalkrishna Gandhi, the former civil servant who is also the grandson of Mahatma Gandhi; V Balakrishnan, the former chief financial officer of Infosys, who joined the party a day after he left the company he had worked for, for the last twenty-two years.

'Coming from the corporate world I always learned to look at the big picture,' V Balakrishnan wrote in a 6 January 2014 NDTV blog. 'The big picture idea of AAP is to create a corruption-free polity in the country. Today, people in the country are fed up with our current political system and AAP, with its crusade against corruption, is a breath of fresh air and is providing the needed alternate in our current political system. Lot of youngsters I spoke to were craving for a change and there is a silent revolution happening in the country. I genuinely want to be part of such a change and revolution. I strongly believe that the real impact of AAP will be felt in the 2014 parliamentary elections.'

By now, AAP leaders had also begun to shift gears. The surge in membership, funding and interest emboldened the party's leadership into thinking bigger and they shifted the primary goalpost from the state to the national level. This meant becoming more ambitious about an election that was due, even before Haryana in October 2014—the national elections, scheduled in nine phases, from 7 April to 12 May 2014, the counting for which will begin on 16 May 2014. 'We have been pushed a bit into the Lok Sabha elections,' says Atishi Marlena, the policy coordinator in AAP. 'Not because a lot of senior leadership did not want to fight for national elections, but in some ways the churn that is happening in the country is not being led by us. And that is what needs to be recognised. People are coming out in such large numbers in our support. The decision to fight elections is because of the nature of the outpouring.'

But it's an enormous challenge to play catch-up with the imagination of a changed people, to live with the growing weight of its own expectations and capitalise on the space that is opening up for a third national force. 'There is a lot of energy and hope,' says AAP leader Gopal Rai. 'There is space for AAP on an all-India platform in the next five to six years.'

Claiming that space was easier said than done. Now that AAP had chosen to form a government in Delhi, Arvind Kejriwal, the party's most magnetic leader and the chief minister of the state for the next forty-nine days, would not be available for the national pitch initially. 'Arvind very clearly told us that he wants to concentrate on Delhi for the next two months,' says Pankaj Gupta. 'He has refused to participate in campaigning at this point.' All these permutations and combinations resulted in a change in brief for Yogendra Yadav—from 'win Haryana' he had to build the party across India and try and put a worthy foot forward in the 2014 general elections.

Those elections, simultaneously, present a challenge and pose a dilemma for AAP. The challenge is to scale up from a state to country, a situation, which by their own admission, AAP leaders never imagined. At one end of the spectrum is the danger of AAP stretching itself too thin and, in the process, ending up with nothing. At the other end of that spectrum lies the danger of AAP holding itself back, not fully harnessing the energies and expectations that have been unleashed, not using the party as a vehicle, and converting the general mood into political capital.

'Frankly, we do not know where we stand nationally,' says Yogendra Yadav. 'There is a double danger of taking media reports too seriously and beginning to believe that we are already there and of underestimating the surge and missing an opportunity. At the moment, we are trying to strike a balance and understand.' The question before AAP, therefore, is how much is too much and how much is too little? How much can it reasonably take on and do a good job with it?

The party needs to expand, and do so widely, deeply and quickly, to fight the Lok Sabha elections. 'There are problems in the party,' comes the candid assessment from senior AAP leader and one of its founders Prashant Bhushan, at his house in Noida. Such is the trouble-shooting he has been doing lately that he's missed two appointments in the last seven days and is running late even today. Six hours earlier, he was making a case that there was a problem elsewhere, in a multi-billion dollar natural gas contract between the Government of India and Reliance Industries Ltd.

Earlier in the day, at a press conference where Prashant Bhushan was also present, Arvind Kejriwal, acting on a representation made by four well-respected former bureaucrats, took the unprecedented step of asking the state's anti-corruption bureau to initiate an inquiry into the operations and contractual terms of an oil and gas field given by the Central government to the Mukesh Ambani Group. In thirty minutes, Prashant Bhushan will be talking more about that alleged problem. 'I have to be on the nine o'clock prime time,' he says apologetically, dressed in a red-cross checked sweater, a scarf around his neck. In his hand, he has some aam aadmi caps to be put on in front of the cameras. The caps are neatly folded and stacked.

A lack of order, even as the party grows, is a shortcoming, according to Prashant Bhushan's assessment of where his party stands today in terms of structures and staffing. 'We have neglected some of the party structures within AAP. We should have had more people who could take decisions and it should have had a much larger group of people,' he says. 'Unfortunately, very serious organisational thinking did not go behind the making of the party—what organs should be there, how many people, recruiting those people, the structures. We have not been able to tap all people. That's a great drawback in the party.'

That drawback becomes all the more glaring when juxtaposed against the promises made by the party; these promises will be tested in less than three months. The situation also seems daunting, given the additional complexities of managing a political party that now wants to spread its wings from a geographical unit that is India's sixth-smallest in area—roughly the size of Mauritius—to most of the twenty-eight states and seven union territories, if not all. 'Running a political party is virtually an intractable problem,' says Prashant Bhushan. 'It's a huge organisation, having all kinds of people. There is in-fighting, jealousy, the wrong kind of people try to get in and it's difficult to put systems in place so quickly.'

At the same time, there is an understanding among the party leadership that there is no going back. The opportunity is staring at them. The time is now. 'You handle them (the problems) as best as you can, but you can't handle them perfectly,' says Prashant Bhushan. 'You know that there will be problems, but there is no option.' What the party is able to do in the next three months will depend on how well it is able to balance speed with sensitivity, temerity with tact, even it confronts five challenges, specific to party organisation and electoral politics.

Surge of Members

The first step for the party was to gauge and then tap into the support it had among the people—one indicator of which lay in the number of members it had. 'The number of volunteers gives us an idea, a the sense of the support we enjoy in which part, and that should enable us to then take decisions about the contest and so on,' says Yogendra Yadav. While Haryana was a definite choice for AAP in terms of contesting all seats in the forthcoming assembly and general elections, the response from many other parts of India was also overwhelming.

'I was in Bengaluru a few days back and the volunteer

meet had thousands of people turning up,' he says. 'Something is happening in Karnataka. The response in Uttar Pradesh is amazingly good. Reports from Punjab too are good, though organisationally we don't have the kind of bandwidth we enjoy in Haryana. Gujarat, the response from this state says that we should be contesting all the twenty-six seats. Maharashtra, small towns and villages tell a similar story. Something is happening throughout the country. What we do not know is its extent, its depth, its spread throughout the country.'

What's happening is the creation of mutualism, a symbiotic relationship between AAP and aam aadmi. 'I would say that the aam aadmi is fuelling AAP and AAP is fuelling the aam aadmi to work for the party,' says Pankaj Gupta. 'Earlier, (they) were afraid to express their views. A lot of people were not ready to expose themselves. In our Delhi experience, people said, "We want to but we are afraid." Now that fear has gone. You might have seen that surge on the day of the swearing in—people moving in hordes, wearing caps, and shouting "Vande Mataram", "Bharat Mata ki Jai". My father was saying he has never seen this kind of thing. If he hasn't seen it in his seventy years then perhaps this is something new. And I think the simplicity of the party, the anti-corruption plank, and simple objectives is making ordinary people believe that they can achieve something.'

When AAP contested the Delhi elections, according to Yogendra Yadav, it had four lakh members. To become an AAP member, all a citizen had to do was fill a form and pay ten rupees. On 10 January 2014, basking in the glow of its Delhi showing, it launched a membership drive, called 'main bhi aam aadmi', whose target was to enroll one crore members—a twenty-five-fold increase in sixteen days—by 26 January 2014 and it waived the ten rupee joining fee. 'One of the things we hope this campaign will do is give us a map of AAP's support throughout the country,' says Yogendra Yadav.

The support shows up in the party's Hanuman Road office, in the heart of New Delhi, a microcosm of India itself. Within a span of an hour or so, a suite of religions and classes walked in to celebrate the future. A Sikh family of five sauntered into the courtyard and carefully filled up membership forms. A larger group of around a dozen or so Muslims, all men, skull caps proudly planted on their heads, their beards in various hues of black and white, hung around, talking animatedly, the forms in their hands. Another group of people, about twenty-five or so Christians, stood outside on the pavement talking to one another; one priest stood in his purple robes, another in white robes with a thick maroon strip racing around his neck, holding two crosses.

This old, wealthy but congested neighbourhood has become a venue of hectic activity, with cars, motorcycles, cycles and mostly pedestrians streaming through it, causing irritation to the residents around. A man walks out, carrying a dozen or so copies of Arvind Kejriwal's book and vision statement, *Swaraj*. Another man walks out with a carton-load of AAP caps. A man wearing an ill-fitting, out-of-fashion, pin-striped suit enters the courtyard and joins the line to collect forms. A BMW stops by and another man walks up to stand in line.

But it's not all rosy. The lack of organisational skills that Prashant Bhushan talked about is showing up too and some of the dreams are beginning to shatter. One man in a white, red and grey sweater is trying to convince a volunteer to allow him to go to the first floor of the office, where party functionaries sit, to meet an official.

'Why?' asks the volunteer.

'My local leader is not giving me membership forms,' replies the man in the sweater.

'The problem is that you don't get along and want to

complain, but there is no time for all that,' says the volunteer.

'Look, I have been with Arvind Kejriwal when there were just fifty people and now you want us to wait and tell us we can't meet anyone,' the man protests, showing more than a hint of agitation.

'Come on, how can they meet everybody?' the volunteer stands firm.

'This is not right,' the man walks off disappointed.

I ask the volunteer what the commotion was all about. 'His problem is that he does not get along with the local leader in Ghaziabad and wants to complain,' the volunteer says. 'But officials are busy with so many things. If he wants forms, why can't he just collect them from the counter there,' he points to the open office on the ground floor, where the membership line swells to the gate. 'We sent only fifty forms because we didn't know there were so many people wanting to become members.'

On 22 January 2014, Yogendra Yadav said AAP now had eighty lakh members. And more impressively, he added, about one-third were individuals who were not prompted by the party to become members—it was a bottom-up and not a top-down exercise. They did so of their own volition, using their own initiative, by sending an SMS or a missed call to a certain party number. At this point, the eighty lakh figure was unverified. This was the unfiltered number of people who had contacted AAP, either when prompted by an existing party member or on their own, with a desire to become a member.

In principle, therefore, this list could also contain fake names. Yogendra Yadav said that is possible but says it is unlikely to be the case as the benefits, in AAP as opposed to other parties, of being a member are very low. It is only a badge of support and allegiance, and it comes with no organisational privileges attached to it. The filtering, he said, would happen at the second level when AAP's state offices assessed who among this set wanted to volunteer for the party, and who was fit to do so.

On 28 January 2014, two days after AAP closed its 'main bhi aam aadmi' drive, the house-turned-office on Hanuman Road reflects the outcome of this campaign and the work it has initiated. This office is a working commune of sorts. A handful of young volunteers, all of them part-time, are hunched over their laptops, feeding the information on the physical forms and uploading it on to a central database.

Up on the first floor, Gopal Rai and a few other AAP functionaries are in a closed-door meeting. The main centre of activity is an open courtyard on the first floor. Heaps of vegetables—about twenty kilos each of cauliflowers and carrots—and twenty kilo sacks of wheat are stacked in one corner. In another corner, water is being heated in metal buckets with immersion rods.

About five to seven volunteers, some of whom have made the Hanuman Road office their home, are multi-tasking even as they help themselves to breakfast. They are all young, in their twenties. They possess an air of self-importance. They sport AAP caps or some other motif that identifies them with the party. Consumed in the present, they flit from activity to activity almost seamlessly. 'We have no plans for Ranchi just now, but please get in touch with our local representative there,' says a volunteer into a mobile phone, stuffing some roti and vegetable into his mouth, even as another mobile goes off in his pocket. He puts the first caller on hold, takes the second call, and sets up the time for a meeting with a party functionary.

Other volunteers are busy engaging with some of their own, who have returned with signed vouchers and donation slips from various centres where the membership drive is on. One checks the small books, almost like a cash receipt book, for the details of people who have signed up. Another is busy checking to see if addresses and contact details have been filled in. 'We have to get back to each one of them and verify, and so the details are very important,' he says.

A few minutes later, Gopal Rai says the party is close to one crore members. 'This is a first in India's democratic history,' he says. 'AAP has created a huge shift in mindset among people who are opposing Congress and BJP. The mindset is that alternative politics can exist and even win elections. Almost fifteen per cent of the people are against the options offered by the two national parties. A new space has been created.' He admits it also brings with it big challenges. 'This has also brought in a lot of opportunists into the party fold as the entry is open to one and all,' he remarks. 'We will need to sift through and get each one to be nominated and seconded before they are accepted as full members, something we can do only after the Lok Sabha elections.'

Creating a Cadre

As has happened in Delhi, AAP expects that from this army of one crore members will emerge many units of volunteers who will take charge of a state. These are the silent, faceless, nameless, industrious women and men, girls and boys. As in Delhi, they are the ones who will walk the streets, push the pamphlets, organise the meetings, conduct enrolment drives of all kinds, hold the banners, ambush social media and do all sorts of things to spread the name and message of AAP, so for still restricted to select urban pockets.

But if pre-elections polls are to be believed, these volunteers will not be able to go very far. The results of the first national poll, conducted by Times Now and C, were announced on 14

February 2014 and gave AAP all of eight seats in the 545-member house. Yogendra Yadav explains the work that needs to be done by AAP, especially by its volunteers, in the context of opinion polls, and why AAP will probably fare poorly in the early ones but gain with every subsequent one.

Here's why. The question that opinion polls ask a voter is an open-ended one: Who would you vote for if elections were held today? But if they were to ask a closed-end question—for instance, if AAP were to field a candidate, would you vote for him or her—the figure goes up. Yogendra Yadav says a lot of people, especially in semi-urban and rural areas, don't know about AAP and even less about its symbol, and that's the gap in minds that volunteers have to bridge.

Deepak Mayur, all of nineteen, bridged that gap in the 2013 Delhi campaign. A second-year student of political science in P.G.D.A.V. College in the capital, he became the go-to person for redress in Chilla Village, which lies next to the East Delhi locality of Mayur Vihar and houses about five thousand households, living in unplanned concrete houses, in an area of less than one square kilometre. His entire family—father, mother and three siblings—are AAP members, Deepak Mayur the most active among them. 'He has always been different,' says his mother Mukesh, who runs a beauty parlour. 'He used to teach younger children free of cost. He took responsibility from his young days.'

Deepak Mayur's initiation into party politics was spurred the way it often is in the case of the ordinary citizen burdened by corruption. Mayur's own family suffered such everyday grievances. Take, for example, the matter of the ration card that does not come and the ration shop that is an authority in itself; the licensing system that offers the Hobson's choice of either queuing five days for a driving licence or paying Rs 1,600 and getting one immediately; the police officer who demands money for a tenant verification; the community centre that is to be built for residents but is captured by the local hoodlum.

When the Anna Hazare anti-corruption movement erupted in Delhi, Deepak Mayur, then in school, gravitated towards it. 'Jan Lokpal appealed to me. I felt a lot of people were supporting it and I felt like supporting it. I went to see the gathering at the Ramlila Grounds out of curiosity,' he says. 'I found out about Jan Lokpal, asked my teachers and spoke to volunteers. I also realised during my discussions that while there are many laws against corruption, the problem lay in their implementation.'

He was also taken in by Arvind Kejriwal's personality. 'We feel he is one of us. He dresses like us and speaks in our language.' Seven days after AAP was formed, Deepak Mayur, five months out of school, went to its website, printed the membership form, attached a postal order of ten rupees, and posted it to the AAP office in Kaushambi in Ghaziabad. Four days later, he received a call from an AAP office bearer asking him to come to a meeting if he could spare some time to be a volunteer. 'That day I saw Kejriwal speak,' he says. 'Lots of leaders had come. We were a group of around five hundred volunteers, mostly young. Gopal Rai and (Manish) Sisodia spoke.'

In the following months, guided by a coordinator for volunteers, Deepak Mayur reached out to friends in college to form more groups ('most were sceptical') and distributed pamphlets in the intricate and dense localities of Old Delhi. When the Delhi campaign started, he was attached to Raju Dhingan, the AAP candidate for Trilokpuri who is now its MLA. Deepak Mayur would return from college at 2.30 p.m., head to the gym at 4.00 p.m., and hit the campaign trail by 5.00 p.m. 'I would go with him (Raju Dhingan) to houses in Trilokpuri. I would spend five to six hours every day,' he says. 'I also was involved in drives for membership, donations and volunteers. There are about fourteen to fifteen active volunteers in our locality and about fifty-odd volunteers who work part-time.'

For the Lok Sabha polls, party leader Ashish Talwar says, a member will be tracked for four months before being declared an active volunteer. Volunteers are undergoing training sessions at the Constitution Club, in New Delhi, in batches of three thousand, on the philosophy of the party and the issues it stands for. In three hundred districts, committees to oversee campaigning activity are being set up.

In Delhi, since the setup already exists, volunteers are taking another approach. According to Deepak Mayur, volunteers in Delhi have been assigned wards; and within wards, they have been divided into focus areas. 'In my locality, I am in charge of police, education and ration in ward number 212,' he says. 'This process has just begun as part of the national strategy. We will get a card for this and our numbers will be circulated. We will be given training. For police, we have training sessions with the SHO. For education, (Manish) Sisodia will hold training classes. Every volunteer has to go to the office at least two days a week. We can talk about problems in our locality and they brief us about the new messages.'

For now, Deepak Mayur can see himself doing only this. 'I do not have selfish ambitions for myself within the party,' he says. 'I will continue being a volunteer and work for the people. Do saal ya paanch saal baad main apne aapko aise hi dekta hoon (I see myself as a volunteer even five years down the line). I have put up a board outside our house to say that I can be reached on my number for any help. It is not important to be known as an AAP volunteer. I want to help people.'

Talking about the way in which AAP is changing, or could change, while scaling up, Yogendra Yadav worries about volunteers like Deepak Mayur and sees this as a major challenge for the party in the weeks, months and years ahead. 'As I travel all over the country and the state, I do feel among our volunteers a sense of anxiety—that newcomers will come and take over the party,' he says. 'This largely comes from the concern over probity within the party. The fear that, "I could be pushed aside in the organisation that I have played a role in." That worries me because we must enlarge our party in order to build this large organisation that is capable to respond to these huge opportunities. And this needs large-heartedness, which we may or may not have.'

Even as the party expands frenetically, it is trying to step back to organise itself and meet the aspirations of its supporters and volunteers better. For example, Prashant Bhushan's sister, Shalini, is now advising AAP on building the party organisation. 'She practised and specialised in organisational development in the US for years,' says Prashant Bhushan. 'She has left her job in the US, and now decided to work and volunteer to develop the party. She is trying to set up cells for grievance redress within the party. Many grievances are not being addressed. There are other people also. Now, we hope to address this systematically through a team.'

Candidates

One of the things that worked for AAP in Delhi was the early announcement of candidates. The party is working towards the same goal at the national level too, though the task of doing that is tougher than it was in Delhi. So far, gleaning from the many statements made by AAP leaders, a few points emerge on its candidate strategy. One, it will contest in as many seats as it is able to garner with public support; it will mobilise volunteers and put up good candidates. Two, it will apply the ambush strategy that Arvind Kejriwal used in Delhi by going into a straight fight against three-time chief minister Sheila Dikshit.

Three, as an extension of that, it will go for high-profile contests. A declaration to that effect came on 31 January 2014 from Arvind Kejriwal, when, at a meeting of the party's national executive, he released a 'list' of twenty-eight leaders from other parties whom he declared as 'corrupt' and said that fielding strong candidates against them would be a priority. The list included fourteen leaders from Congress (including Rahul Gandhi, P. Chidambaram and Kapil Sibal), four from BJP (including Nitin Gadkari and B.S. Yeddyurappa), two each from NCP (including Sharad Pawar) and DMK (A. Raja, Kanimozhi), and one each from SP (Mulayam Singh Yadav), BSP (Mayawati), NC, YSR Congress and JD(S).

A day later, even as Nitin Gadkari slapped Arvind Kejriwal with a defamation notice, AAP added the names of Sonia Gandhi and Narendra Modi to the list for leading, what it called, parties of tainted politicians. The party has since announced some match-ups: poet-turned-politician Kumar Vishwas will contest against Rahul Gandhi (Amethi), former banker Meera Sanyal against Milind Deora (South Mumbai) and Mayank Gandhi against Congress leader Gurudas Kamat (North-west Mumbai). This is where all the noise was.

Getting lost in this din is the disruption caused by AAP in the way it chose its candidates in Delhi, a process it intends to replicate at the national level. Unlike other parties, anyone can apply to be an AAP candidate. 'The whole idea is to search for good candidates,' says Atishi Marlena, a member of the selection committee. 'Unlike other parties, we cannot believe that all good candidates are already members of our party. So, we have to open ourselves to anybody who is interested.'

These applications are then posted on its website for a week for public comments. A screening committee in the party assesses candidates for probity, corruption and criminal records. Each candidate has to mention a constituency and obtain a certain number of signatures from that constituency. 'The stipulation is that you get a hundred signatures for every assembly segment that falls within that constituency,' explains Atishi Marlena. 'In Haryana, you would need nine hundred signatures for one constituency. And that is the biggest process. Nominations will be kept open till we take a decision for each constituency.'

Finally, a secret ballot is held in which volunteers vote and a final candidate is chosen. Atishi Marlena says, unlike Delhi, a secret ballot may be hard to replicate elsewhere. 'The organisational structure may not be quite in place,' she adds. 'If you try and hold elections without a clearly defined electorate, you run the risk of being captured by a small section of the electorate. So, while we may hold consultations with our volunteers, we may not go for a secret ballot.'

The selection process is currently on. And the rain of applications has turned into a torrent. So intense is the interest that on 8 February 2014, AAP announced it was shutting the application window for 238 constituencies, though it added a qualifier: 'Its political affairs committee reserved the right to consider more applications in special situations.' If an early closing of applications is any indicator of the party's popularity in these constituencies, the patterns make for interesting reading and a fascinating 2014 poll.

In the two Hindi-speaking heartland states, UP and Bihar, which account for a combined 120 of the 545 seats (or 22 per cent of all seats) in the Lok Sabha, AAP has closed applications in 103 constituencies (or 86 per cent)—75 out of 80 (or 94 per cent) in Uttar Pradesh, where Yogendra Yadav says AAP had put in place an organisational structure a year ago, and can gain from the three-way or four-way vote split and where it intends to focus its energies. There's also strong evidence of an urban dominance in this list. Three of the four constituencies in Bangalore are closed, the one open being Bangalore Rural; all six Mumbai constituencies are closed. All ten seats in Haryana are closed. Among other prominent states, the tally reads four out of forty-two in Andhra Pradesh, eleven of twenty-six in Gujarat, fifteen of twenty-nine in Madhya Pradesh, twenty-seven of forty-eight in Maharashtra, fourteen of twenty-five in Rajasthan and six of thirty-nine in Tamil Nadu.

All seven Lok Sabha seats in Delhi were also closed for applications. According to Ashish Talwar, who is involved in candidate selection, AAP received 1,100 applications for seven Lok Sabha seats, including from serving government officials, NGOs and volunteers, among others. He says the party has set up a state-level screening committee in about ten states, including Haryana, Punjab, Uttar Pradesh, Delhi, Madhya Pradesh, Karnataka, Tamil Nadu and Odisha.

Each committee has seven members. There's the AAP convenor for the state, four people nominated by the state convenor and one person nominated by the national executive. The seventh member, in what can be described as another of AAP's ways of disrupting the traditional rules of Indian politics, is what the party calls 'a fellow traveller'—an independent person of eminence. In states where there are not enough candidates, the national executive will handle the screening process. After the screening committee or the national executive decides, the final decision will be taken by its nine-member political affairs committee.

In its selection, as can be gleaned from its processes in Delhi, AAP is challenging old, set notions of candidate selection like giving primacy to a candidate who services the caste matrix in a constituency the best, even if the other credentials of the person are spotty. 'For any party that has a serious base in society, your candidate selection is bound to reflect the social chemistry of the place you go to,' says Yogendra Yadav. 'Unless you deliberately pick people who have nothing to do with the social composition of the place you go to, there is no huge mismatch between the social composition of the area and that of the candidate. When we think of caste politics, we normally talk of every other consideration being set aside and people being selected and voted purely on consideration of caste and community. That is a game we need not play because much of that politics is usually timid politics.'

Manifestos

Going national also means having a stand on every issue. 'As a party, we can't just keep saying anti-corruption over and over,' says AAP leader Praveen Singh, who has been involved with framing policy. 'People ask, "How can you be a national party if you do not have a view on foreign policy?" We are not embarrassed by the fact that we don't have the answers,' says Atishi Marlena. 'But we are going to find the answers. One or two leaders can sit together and form a policy on anything. But the idea is that it should be well-informed and that it should be thought through.'

In the 2013 Delhi elections, AAP tried to make its process of manifesto design a participative one. So, in January 2013, it set up thirty-one committees on various issues like power, water and women's safety. These committees had limited AAP representation and instead invited experts from various fields. 'Party members were more like observers who took notes,' says Praveen Singh. 'Most meetings of these committees took place virtually, through chats and Internet groups. Over a period of three to four months, we would have met three times physically, although we were exchanging notes every day.'

Between February and August 2013, all committees submitted their reports, and a position paper was made on thirty issues that were to be taken up for discussion. The work done by these committees 'will form the basis of our national policy framework', says Atishi Marlena. 'But then Delhi elections came upon us and we got down to bringing out a summarised version for Delhi (thirty-five-page document).' At the same time, AAP will do large policy consultations with, for example, farmers and farmer groups from across the country. 'We will be having consultations on what are the major issues facing the country at this time,' she says. 'All stakeholders would be involved. We want to make it as wide and deep as possible.'

AAP's moves on economic policy have not endeared it to industry, which generally likes it for its clean politics but sees a strident undertone that is inherently suspicious about business. 'They have to be very careful in their economic agenda, about the choice of words,' warns political scientist Ashutosh Varshney. 'For example, if they use the term "social democracy", it's better than socialism. Yogendra Yadav, in his recent interviews, has said the AAP does not believe in any "ism". That's a good step, it's a step in the right direction.'

Atishi Marlena admits that in its initial stage the party did not have enough market perspective in its economic policies, and that was for want of time—many people the party wanted to talk to were not available for giving inputs. 'Our intention was we don't want (the) doctrine of Leftists and we don't want (a) doctrine via Rightists either,' she says. 'But we want some people who can talk and evolve a new kind of economics, which is based on a pro-people kind of economics. (We need a doctrine that engages with) the aam aadmi, but let us look beyond complete free market and state control because neither has worked fully.'

In January 2014, AAP formed a seven-member committee to formulate its economic policy ahead of general elections. Headed by party leader Prithvi Reddy, it included Atishi Marlena, Dilip Pandey (who was a member of the screening committee during the Delhi assembly elections), former banker Meera Sanyal, environmental economist Aseem Srivastava, economist Laveesh Bhandari and Sanjeev Aga, former chief of Idea Cellular.

The other innovation AAP tried in Delhi was constituency-specific manifestos. Atishi Marlena admits that while that might not be possible for all constituencies in the national exercise, the party will try to make its output as representative as possible. 'In some places and in some constituencies, we will try and do it,' she says, adding that they are chasing time. 'We have to come out with the national manifesto by March. We are starting and doing it in parallel.'

Funding

Raising money for a small state election is one thing—challenging but when pushed, doable. But getting the funds for general elections is a whole new game. Given that AAP is a political toddler, cash generation will be an important factor in how much and how fast it is able to scale up. AAP contested in seventy seats in the Delhi elections with twenty crore rupees. To compete meaningfully, at the national level, the party has estimated it will need two hundred crores, at one crore rupees per seat.

Social media was the dominant medium of the Delhi funding campaign, followed by some focus group meetings held by Arvind Kejriwal, notably with non-resident Indians (NRIs). The emphasis was on individual donors. As of 9 February 2014, two months since the Delhi election results, AAP had collected an additional Rs 8.15 crore. Its pace of collections is not the same as on its best days, plummeting especially during the Rail Bhawan standoff, a situation that could lead it to chase big-ticket donations as well.

As it has done in the past, it is trying to encourage innovation. AAP is structuring new models of crowd-sourcing, especially in funding, and several ideas are being tossed around, says Atishi Marlena. For example, one idea is tie up with telecom companies to offer an option where a subscriber can agree to donate, say, twenty rupees every month, and this amount gets added to her bill or deducted from her talk time.

Another idea being discussed is to tap professionals who would be in the High Net Worth Individual (HNI) category and give a person from such a set the responsibility to reach out to peers and organise a certain amount. 'For example, you find groups of people who are professionals—IIT, IIM kind of professionals,' explains Atishi Marlena. 'To each, you give the responsibility (that) you have to get one lakh rupees each from friends and like-minded people. We have those kind of members in our outfit.'

Money and funding is an area of concern but the party will not compromise on its principles to get it. 'It has to come from people who believe in our politics,' she says. 'It cannot come from someone who would fund us in return for some favour. This would finish off our entire politics. We are not going to provide any favours because of the money we are getting.'

The man in charge of raising funds is Pankaj Gupta. And he has to negotiate this space that is coloured in many shades of grey in the traditional political construct. There is no space for a quid-pro-quo, no 'return on investment', no licences to be traded, no PPP deals to be offered, no privatisation details to be negotiated. Apart from being part of a change, the party offers nothing. Pankaj Gupta encounters the shades of grey in the ten foot by twelve foot room in AAP's Hanuman Road office from where he operates by a small table in one corner, a dirty window towards the right.

As you enter, a list of 'important email IDs' for the legal cell for the Lok Sabha elections greets you on a whiteboard to the left. Three young boys, barely out of college, sit at three small tables with their computers, tracking funds, people, meetings. Cheap plastic chairs are the only luxury in this Spartan room. Visitors enter, speak to the person concerned in a focussed manner and leave. A large fifty kilo plastic bag that once carried rice lies in the corner. It is now stuffed with papers and files. In this cold room, it is decided how AAP will fund the elections ahead. In this room, candidates are shortlisted for the forthcoming elections. In this room, one sees members coordinate with the fast-growing regional offices across the country.

'We have larger objectives and I don't know how it works with your organisation,' Pankaj Gupta tells a man wearing an orange cap with intelligent and intense eyes, as he leans over a grey table for two. 'And that is decentralisation of power.'

The orange cap says something that gets lost in the din.

'At this point we are not ready for any affiliation,' Pankaj Gupta tells him.

'Why?'

'You see, it gets difficult to manage.'

The orange cap says something about him representing a Tamil Nadu-based organisation that does philanthropy and engages in politics. 'We have a large network of party workers.'

'We will need a note on your group,' Pankaj Gupta says, softly but firmly. 'We need to know what is motivating you. You also need to know that our process is very rigorous. I also have a straight question, please don't mind.'

'Please ask.'

'Did he (the head of the group the orange cap is representing) use his government connections to get the contracts? If he has, he will be a misfit here.'

Around 3.35 p.m., a young volunteer, his moustache barely in its second flush, hurriedly stuffs morsels of his half-eaten lunch of rice, dal and vegetables into his mouth. Barely having managed two spoonfuls, he is dragged outside for another consultation. He leaves the plate on a window sill. He returns five minutes later and finishes the lunch, hardly noticing that it's cold, probably freezing. The flat expression on his face gives the impression that he has no tastebuds.

9
CURRENCIES OF CHANGE

Three men and their ideas will dominate the political discourse this election season, and they will continue to wrestle in the space of public policy and governance narratives even after. Even though the lines around the ideas are blurred, carved more by words than by deeds, more by packaging than by content, more by form than by subject, the brush of each narrative colours the landscape with unique strokes of possibilities. This may be a tug-of-war between faces, followers and philosophies. But to us, it represents the rainbow of India's democracy, rich in diversity, deep in offering choices, wide in its embrace. All three narratives talk about change. All speak of a glorious India. It is the routes to change where the narratives begin to clash.

And these are the currencies of a change foretold.

Heart, Soul and Politics of Future

The first of these narratives will be read out by the incumbent Congress and its vice-president Rahul Gandhi, who is expected to be the prime minister if the party returns to power. But chances of Congress getting a majority to run a third consecutive term are low. This is not because of an anti-incumbency wave playing out, charges of corruption and accusations of a policy drift that has hurt India's growth rate amid high prices. It is because Rahul Gandhi's priorities do not lie in winning the election.

'I'm here because I want to help use the energy of this country. I want to make this country powerful. I want to project the ideas of this country,' Rahul Gandhi said in his first interview to the TV channel Times Now, giving an impression of a man thinking about the long term but hesitant to take the first steps towards it, disengaged from the grime of politics. 'I don't go into an election thinking, if we lose it's the end of the world. We lose some elections, we win some elections. The real thing is that it's a heart thing. It's a soul thing. I'm sitting here because I feel with all my heart that we need to change the system.'

He's almost an aberration within the party, an outsider thrown into the thorny thicket of decision making, a rebel trying to change a large organisation from within, a serial dynast—he's the son of Congress president Sonia Gandhi, who is the widow of former Prime Minister Rajiv Gandhi, who was the son of former Prime Minister Indira Gandhi, who in turn was the daughter of former Prime Minister Jawaharlal Nehru—talking about ending dynastic politics. 'I am absolutely against the concept of dynasty,' he said. 'But you are not going to wish away dynasty in a closed system, you have to open the system. Dynasty or children of politicians becoming powerful happens in the BJP, it happens in the DMK, it happens in the SP, it happens in the Congress party, it happens everywhere.' He positions himself as an agent who will change this structure.

That change, he says, will happen by opening out the system, investing in processes. Rahul Gandhi's focus in the forthcoming elections seems to be on the fifteen seats where he has taken a leaf out of AAP's book and followed a merit-only approach to handing tickets, through US style primaries. He agrees that this humongous change in a large party like Congress is not going to be easy. 'It is going to take time, it is going to take effort and it is going to take structure.' Such a task can't be done in all 543 constituencies because 'the system would explode'. These fifteen seats, he said in the 27 January 2014 interview, will be a test case for future elections. But within a week, two of those fifteen merit seats, one of Kapil Sibal (Chandni Chowk in Delhi) and the other of Krishna Tirath (North West Delhi), were dropped from the list.

Governance, Leadership and Politics of Trust

The second narrative belongs to challenger Narendra Modi, the prime ministerial candidate of BJP who in sharp contrast to Rahul Gandhi, is the son of a tea vendor and served tea as a child. As a teenager, he would iron his shirt with a lota filled with hot water; the lota has gone, the ironed shirts and kurtas have remained. Apart from his humble background that resonates strongly in the political battlefield, he brings a formidable reputation for governance as chief minister of Gujarat. Narendra Modi is the face of what India's democracy can offer—a man from humble origins, belonging to a backward caste, holding the promise of good governance in a country yearning for it.

It is not only his stance or speech that distinguish Narendra Modi from Rahul Gandhi. His actions and promises too follow a different narrative. His recent speeches show an unmatchable skill at packaging strong political statements out of the state of governance. 'There is a need to shake off despair,' he told industry leaders on 15 January 2014 at a meeting in Gandhinagar, hinting at the failure of the UPA governing coalition at the Centre. 'An atmosphere of confidence and trust is very important in India now. India must be run by decision-makers.' His skill in merging the spirituality of ancient India with the aspirations of modern India are central to his discourse. From Satyameva Jayate to Ahimsa Parmo Dharma, his 'Idea of India' pulls at the catapult of culture to swing high with phrases like empowerment of women and redefining the poor.

As arguably India's most talked-about chief minister, he has a strong view on Centre-state relations. 'We dream of an India where development is the result of all chief ministers, the Prime Minister, state ministers, union ministers working together with even local body authorities as one team, a strong and united "Team India",' he said in his Republic Day speech in 2014. By wresting the moral control over Sardar Patel from Congress and building the 182-metre tall Statue of Unity, double the height of Statue of Liberty, he has highlighted Congress's obsession with the Nehru-Gandhi family at the cost of other leaders. 'For sixty years you gave chance to Shasaks (rulers), now I request you to give a Sevak (server) sixty months,' he said at his 30 January 2014 Vijay Shankhnad rally in Gorakhpur.

Narendra Modi's governance track record, however, has not gone unchallenged or unblemished. While political detractors from Congress or other parties that claim to be secular can still be dismissed at the altar of vested interests, what about independent critics, the most notable of them being Amartya Sen? 'As an Indian citizen I don't want Modi as my PM,' he told CNN-IBN in an interview. His main reason was Narendra Modi's rather tenuous relationship with minorities, particularly Muslims. But it is equally a criticism of Narendra Modi's track record of governance. Simply delivering growth is not enough, Amartya Sen feels. Narendra Modi's Gujarat is way behind Kerala and Tamil Nadu in human development indicators across health and education.

In the narratives of both Rahul Gandhi and Narendra Modi, the unifying theme is change. Narendra Modi wants to change the mode of governance and power through BJP's more market-friendly approach in contrast to Congress's left of centre stance.

But he forgets that BJP voted enthusiastically in favour of the Food Security Act, after initially criticising it. The differentiation hardly breaks the crusty surface. As an incumbent, Rahul Gandhi wants to change the way politics is done, by breaking down the power of incumbents and changing the way candidates are selected in political parties, by merit. The task before him could be termed as Mission Impossible.

Corruption, Devolution and Politics of Disruption

It is only in the third narrative, of Arvind Kejriwal's, that we begin to see the first signs of promises that carry no contradictions. That could simply be because there is no track record to dig out chunks of past from. The comfort of his uncompromising anti-corruption stance, the logic of his passionate pursuit of decentralisation and devolution, the succour of his schemes that border on the simplistic and the naïve, all add to the innocent and charming narrative that is still to be written. Not even a toddler yet in the rough and tumble of Indian politics, it almost seems as though the country is embracing a baby, helping it stand up, walk, talk, all the while nourishing this sole symbol of hope, a true aberration to the existing structures, an outsider who has challenged established parties and ideas of the past.

Beginning with his first speech, on 2 January 2014, in the Delhi Vidhan Sabha after winning the trust vote, his rhetoric has overtones of such obviousness that it made people wonder where such basics got lost in the current set-up. Right from the definition of the aam aadmi—that the middle class, the street food vendor, anyone who wants to banish corruption is one; while anyone who wants to promote corruption whether he is rich or poor is a khaas aadmi—Arvind Kejriwal made none of the usual class distinctions and instead united the rich and the poor as one victimised constituency. He highlighted his tool to fix corruption by showcasing the Jan Lokpal imagery. He ended the cycle of privileges, the VIP culture so to speak. No more lal battis, he announced. The opposition to FDI in retail enjoined him with BJP, seeking the best treatment for citizens in government hospitals and ending donations in private schools brought him close to the aam aadmi.

All through, Arvind Kejriwal's narrative has been of victimhood. Not the disempowered minorities or even highly empowered ones like the Jain community that Rahul Gandhi pandered to in his recent pre-elections largesse. Not the broader but fuzzier governance- and growth-seeking victims of Narendra Modi. Arvind Kejriwal has sounded out victims across class, caste, communities. His ideas are simple, closer to the immediate vicinity of citizens—water and power bills, the corporate as the new villain, user charges on infrastructure, the traditional politician as the protector of all evil, the gobbler of all privileges, the devourer of exchequer's money. They lack the governance articulation on foreign or economic policy for instance, that governance experience brings.

Above all, his most natural and dominant political narrative has been of ground protest and audacious disruption—though his dharna at Rail Bhawan took some of the sheen off his gleaming campaign. Detractors, political and independent, accused him of ushering in anarchy. Where is governance, they asked? You can't govern by dharnas, they said. President Pranab Mukherjee was particularly harsh: 'Elections do not give any person the licence to flirt with illusions,' he said in his address on the eve of Republic Day that Arvind Kejriwal had threatened to stall. 'Populist anarchy cannot be a substitute for governance. False promises lead to disillusionment, which gives birth to rage, and that rage has one legitimate target: those in power.'

Cry of the Enraged

The rage Pranab Mukherjee talks about is very real. It has been simmering for decades. With the proliferation of information through the booming electronic media and the active social media spaces of Twitter and Facebook, this rage has found new expression. It has broken boundaries and democratised the political discourse. In India, as in the rest of the world, there are four large forces creating and accentuating this rage. Because the timelines of these forces—globalisation, migration, demographics and inequality—have been compressed by technology, a perplexed nation now veers from one extreme to the other, seeking political, economic and social equilibrium.

From the brutal gang rape of a woman with twenty-first century aspirations in Delhi to brimming political expression binding the young through new political vehicles like AAP, a disturbing idea, a new rage is now simultaneously enveloping and driving an emerging India. This rage cuts across time, across labels such as prosperity and poverty. A young nation in a hurry, standing at the edge of an economic boom that could take millions of citizens out of poverty and catalyse its transition into the middle-income group of countries, seems frozen into submission before these four forces determining its destiny today. It is the rage around these determinants that Rahul Gandhi, Narendra Modi and Arvind Kejriwal have to address through their politics.

Globalisation. Many have attempted to define the phenomenon of globalisation. In a June 2006 paper, 'Definitions of Globalisation', Nayef R.F. and Gerald Stoudmann define it thus: 'Globalisation is a process that encompasses the causes, course, and consequences of transnational and transcultural integration of human and non-human activities.' While the word has become popular since the 1980s, the phenomenon dates back to prehistoric times, in fact, right from the point that the first man was born, says Nayan Chanda in his insightful 2007 book, *Bound Together*.

In recent history, globalisation has not merely brought about an information revolution, providing communication access to millions, it has also brought disruptive ideas with it. Along with empowerment that has come from using technology as its entry point, a much-needed cultural invasion is disturbing traditional living rooms, raising long-buried issues such as women's rights and individual freedom. The platform of trade in goods and services that has generated employment and opportunities is also creating new desires for a good life that don't always materialise in the face of global business cycles.

Commodity prices, particularly of energy and food, are creating dissonance as households try and balance the instabilities they bring. The lack of adequate experience of dealing with capitalism is turning its economic benefits into pressing social issues. These problems are common to governments across the world and the new reality is that the power of sovereigns to deliver local governance in the face of acute globalisation is falling. The India experience is no different. Long used to being protected against rising prices by a government that fed itself on welfare schemes, for instance, the sudden each-household-for-itself mode of life is carrying a burning rage in Indian kitchens.

Migration. Expand the footprint of globalisation as a search for a better geography, more opportunities and less risk, and we reach the second force. According to International Organisation for Migration, this force is defined as the movement of people, either across an international border or within a state. It encompasses any kind of movement of people, whatever its length, composition and causes and includes migration of refugees, displaced persons, economic migrants, and persons moving for other purposes, including family reunification.

Apart from being home to migrants from Bangladesh, India's intra-country migration from rural to urban areas is creating tensions of space, between those aspiring for a life of dignity and others trying to preserve the differences. Over the next two decades, India is going to see the largest-ever migration on the planet. If estimates turn out to be accurate, 250 million people will migrate to urban centres by 2030, which is half the time such massive numbers took in the previous forty years, according to an April 2010 McKinsey report, 'India's Urban Awakening: Building Inclusive Cities, Sustaining Economic Growth'. According to Census of India 2011, the biggest reason why men migrate is work—37.6 per cent of all migrating men do so because of jobs or opportunities. This is not surprising: seven out of ten new jobs created in 2030 will be in cities, quadrupling India's per capita income. For women, marriage is the biggest factor in migration (64.9 per cent of migrants).

But along with these opportunities come related issues of inadequate housing and poor infrastructure, as prosperity rashly drives them up the concrete wall; infrastructural burdens on power, water and sewage; and urban slums, crime and anomie. The unskilled hands invest scarce resources to buy into skills—driving, building or as cooking for households—and endure a poor quality of life in urban slums so that their worse-off kin in villages receive a balm in the form of a money order economy. An unconscious sense of stress is taking a toll on city dwellers' bodies and minds, leading to rage on roads, in queues, over parking, water, much of which leads to violence and deaths.

'One of the most important reasons (for disruption) is the erratic increase in urbanisation and the state's inability to cope with the expectations and requirements of infrastructure,' says sociologist Dipankar Gupta. 'The rapid growth in urbanisation has taken place without the accompanying growth in social services. Because a large number of people are now turning urban, they are demanding the state to deliver on many of these counts.'

Demographics. With a quarter of the Indian population under the age of twenty-five and two-thirds below the age of thirty-five, India is as young a nation as can be. Such a demographic has the potential to change the destiny of nations. This young demographic is transforming India with strong hands and feet that can, on the one hand, sweat their way to a good life and, on the other, disrupt social structures. This demographic is amplifying the expression of rage that globalisation and migration have founded.

For such a demographic to be productively employed, the politics will have to transform. Governments will have to look beyond designing unfunded welfare schemes and provide opportunities where small private entrepreneurs—the job engines of any economy—can put their money, minds and enterprise, and create jobs and wealth. They will have to beef up infrastructure and urban amenities, particularly low-cost housing, power, water supply, sewerage systems and drains, and mass transport. For this to happen through the private sector, the services provided will have to be economically viable and the regime of fair user charges will have to be enforced.

To presume that a nation of 1.2 billion will be fed and housed by doles is living in a dream that has already been punctured by the global economic crisis and India's inability to undertake structural reforms to stem the tide of economic contraction. Broken promises of prosperity could break the nation itself, as masses of unemployed young men express the angst of shattered aspirations through crime. A skewed sex ratio that is showing no sign of balance carries a risk, over the next generation, of turning India into a place where crime against women will increase, putting a never-before-experienced pressure on law and order services.

Inequality. Gone are the days when the wealthy could enjoy their wealth in peace—the information revolution has democratised the flow of news. Despite this, even today, in India, the ostentatious display of wealth exists alongside acute poverty. Added to this is the pain of dealing with unfairness. Daniel Kahneman et al questioned the traditional assumption that fairness is irrelevant to economic analysis as far back as 1986. Fairness ties up with the idea of corruption too. 'When there is corruption, we may have a complementarity between past and current policies for two reasons: either because more corruption in the past means more inequality in the present, or because more corruption in the past means more unfairness in the present,' write Alberto Alesina et al in 'Corruption, Inequality and Fairness'.

With 850 million citizens living on less than two dollars a day, the poverty in India is depressing. But what compounds this dismal number is the inequality—India has the second-fastest growing number of millionaires after Hong Kong, according to World Wealth Report 2013; it has 152,750 millionaires, up 22 per cent over the previous year. And we are not even showcasing the biggest beneficiaries of reforms, the sixty-one Indian billionaires. When we see such acute concentration of wealth, democracy's sense of fairness gets diminished. The resentment that follows erodes the legitimacy of democracy and can, if stretched to an extreme, result in political instability.

Inequality showcases political bias in favour of the wealthy. 'All statistics show that the conditions of the poor are improving,' then Chief Economic Advisor and now Chief Economist of World

Bank Kaushik Basu told me in an earlier interview. 'But the top end income is increasing so much more rapidly that inequality is rising. I wish there were less inequality in India and the world.' The stream of welfare schemes that governments dole out could perhaps act as first-aid for its deep wounds. This inequality, largely of incomes and wealth but equally of social groups and gender, is creating chasms between segregated communities, rifts that risk becoming permanent.

When inequality is viewed through the prism of justice, the poor are not getting their 'fair share' of the benefits of globalisation and capitalism. Being a young nation, this sense of injustice leads to seething resentment, or finds expression through bursts of violence. Take the example of the security guard at the gates of malls that sport the best goods from across the world; he is often seen with contempt. Invisible to the affluent trooping in and out, after two shifts in wonderland, the guard returns to a weather-abused five foot by eight foot room, if lucky.

The excesses of the 2008 economic crisis, that still has nations reeling, have made people question the basis of capitalism itself. Though not articulated through these words in India, the blatant abuse of markets by the wealthy and the powerful has led to agitations across the country. Some examples are the farmers' agitation around Noida where large builders got farmland to be developed into swanky apartments in 2012; or the seething rage in the eight states with a strong Maoist presence. At some level, this reduces the legitimacy of capitalism as a tool for economic development and we return to what we know best—state control.

Juxtaposed against an enraged India is the putrefying politics of excessive state control, extreme corruption and dying public efficiency. These are now at war with the hopes of 1.2 billion people. A new politics of aspiration is clashing with the visible frustration of a governance that relies on buying votes rather than empowering citizens. This dissonance is breaking down traditional ideas of not only economics and justice but also family and society. A transformation is needed and that's going to come only through a shake-up in politics.

Challenge Before the Troika

As an incumbent there is very little Rahul Gandhi can do to address this rage; incumbency has its own dynamics, and current conversations put the blame on Congress. No amount of welfare schemes, increased subsidised gas cylinders just before elections or talking about change will convince the electorate that Rahul Gandhi is the man of the season. His track record for fighting corruption—arguably the biggest political issue today—has been patchy and impulsive at best and self-destructive at worst.

Narendra Modi has the brightest chance of harnessing this rage into votes. Since 13 September 2013, when he was declared the prime ministerial candidate of BJP, Narendra Modi has been speaking to the young and the alienated. His 'chai pe charcha' (chat over tea) is a brilliant way to speak to the poor on political issues. The risks: he is seen to be an individual player, a non-secular, minority- and gender-alienating force who will find it difficult to make political alliances. What that force will do after coming to power is an open-ended debate.

That leaves Arvind Kejriwal. While the possibility of AAP getting hold of a majority in Parliament is close to zero, there is a rising probability that the surprise that the Delhi elections gave could get repeated nationally on a smaller scale. A huge number of voters, who were tired of Congress's party-executive arrangements that leave accountability in the prime minister's office and authority in 10 Janpath, had veered towards Narendra Modi. He offered a decisive change, had rich governance experience, and talked about growth that the middle class would benefit from. Despite the apparent fumbling with governance in Delhi, Arvind Kejriwal is building political equity in Haryana, Uttar Pradesh and Bihar at Mach speed. All told, at the time of writing, the party is expected to stand for three hundred seats, seventy-three of them against candidates of other parties that have criminal records.

The change that Narendra Modi offers is one that simply replaces. Partly because it has been in the political space for years and partly because while India's spirit is willing its flesh is weak, BJP does not offer an alternative to the establishment. BJP replacing Congress is seen to be more of the same state of affairs—both talk about how more roads were built in their tenures, both highlight economic growth, both talk about change. Both are targets of Arvind Kejriwal, who calls them corrupt.

Arvind Kejriwal shatters this paradigm of governance through the tool of disruption. The currency of change he uses to transact power involves breaking down old structures and rebuilding them all over again. Having been in power for just forty-nine days before relinquishing it, gives him the luxury to go to voters with a mandate for transformation, not merely change. 'Given a choice (between Rahul Gandhi and Narendra Modi), people would prefer an alternative in Arvind Kejriwal,' says Yogendra Yadav. 'The significant thing in the Vidhan Sabha elections in Delhi was that people wanted change but in places like Rajasthan, voters had no alternative; they only had a substitute within the establishment.'

In Delhi, he emphasises, voters had a choice—they could either go for a substitute or for the alternative. 'So when they voted for an alternative it sent a message throughout the country. Every ordinary person felt empowered. It felt as if someone had breached something that was considered impregnable before.

There was a hope that ordinary people can stand in elections, that a party that fights on issues can actually become viable and that you can use white money in politics. It gave hope to the people and this has led to the national upsurge. We do not know frankly where we stand nationally. The alternative story comes from a work in progress at AAP.'

The tributaries of rage that voters harbour can easily join the river of protest that Arvind Kejriwal's politics offers. Even as his protest at Rail Bhawan was being termed as 'anarchy', voters remained sympathetic. The groundswell of support for a chief minister who slept on a freezing Delhi road in order to deliver law and order was captured in the image the newspapers carried the next day. But whether this support has summarily passed to other states as well remains an open-ended question.

Of course, the rage of voters aligns strongly with Narendra Modi, as well. BJP left no stone unturned in directing the same rage towards Congress in session after session of Parliament. Polls show a clear traction towards BJP. According to a poll by CNN-IBN and CSDS-Lokniti, Narendra Modi is the most preferred prime ministerial candidate in eighteen states, with the support of 34 per cent of voters; Rahul Gandhi comes a distant second with 15 per cent; and Arvind Kejriwal stands way behind with 3 per cent. Even together, Rahul Gandhi and Arvind Kejriwal do not match up to the mighty juggernaut of Narendra Modi.

Even as pre-election polls show AAP barely making it to Parliament, with less than ten seats, most analysts give AAP anything between twenty and forty seats in Parliament in this election. While that may not be adequate to take them to power, it would be enough to create a headache for the governing coalition in Parliament. And, as has happened in Delhi, it could set the stage for Congress supporting AAP in the Centre in order to keep Narendra Modi out, the seeds of which are being sowed every time the party uses the word 'secular'.

'It would be disastrous for the country to have Narendra Modi as the next prime minister,' Prime Minister Manmohan Singh said in his 3 January 2014 press conference. He defended the allegation that he was a weak prime minister by saying, 'If by a strong prime minister they mean you preside over the massacre of innocent citizens on the streets of Ahmedabad, if that is the measure of strength, I do not believe that is the sort of strength this country needs, least of all from its prime minister.' But such tactics can backfire—and they did, in less than a month.

In a ninety-minute grilling interview, Arnab Goswami of *Times Now* asked Rahul Gandhi why Narendra Modi should apologise for the Gujarat riots. 'People died,' Rahul Gandhi said, 'Mr Narendra Modi was in charge of Gujarat at that point.' But Congress was in charge of Delhi when the 1984 Sikh riots took place. 'The difference was that the government in 1984 was trying to stop the riots, trying to stop the killing whereas the government in Gujarat was allowing the riots to happen,' Rahul Gandhi said, adding that there was a legal process. But the courts cleared Narendra Modi, so why should he apologise? Rahul Gandhi was evasive, defensive, incoherent.

Arvind Kejriwal has nothing holding him back—not riots, not corruption, not misgovernance, not slowdown. He has no stakes—not in the Centre, not in states (barring Delhi, where he is supported by Congress), not in municipal bodies, not in panchayats. As an outsider, the playground is not levelled—he has a distinct advantage, he can break old systems down, he can promise new ones, he can pretty much offer the world, speak as he pleases, make unsubstantiated allegations against political rivals, large companies, media.

The slate he has to chalk his politics on is clean, but it's not this slate that he will use. It's not this slate he will use. He will break the slate and build a new one; going by early indications, he may not even build a new slate. Arvind Kejriwal is most likely to be the craftsman who will get the eight hundred million voters to chalk out their own problems and aspirations. These he will collate and convert into action.

Since Arvind Kejriwal transacts in the currency of disruption, whatever he gets from the people will have to play out, possibly at once—it will sound like a political cacophony to some but could make sense to slivers of voters. If disruption is Arvind Kejriwal's currency, simple solutions define his trade. One month into governing Delhi and he was convinced about results. 'I have received reports that government servants are by and large not taking bribes from the aam aadmi in the state government now,' he said in a 31 January 2014 press conference of AAP executive meet's Day 2, driving the knife into the previous Congress government. 'What could not be accomplished in sixty-five years, we did in one month.'

He then turned the knife. 'We have not come to play politics, we have come to remove corruption,' he said in the fifteen-minute speech at Constitution Club, his trademark black muffler around his neck and an itch in his throat. 'Our aim should be that not a single corrupt person exists in Parliament. We need to change all this. We are providing an option to the people of the country and the country has to work to make sure that not one corrupt person is elected to the parliament.' He then listed out fifteen names of what he called corrupt politicians.

Arvind Kejriwal then urged the people to add to the list. 'Let us get together to make sure that not one corrupt person wins a seat this year.' If there is an honest politician among these, he asked the people to let him know. There was a smugness he carried, knowing fully well that nobody could raise any finger of accusation about corruption against anyone in AAP.

To that effect, he is setting the political stage of disruption to his convenience. But a wrong decision does not always mean a corrupt decision, as finance minister P. Chidambaram pointed out—and which is the correct position. Will Arvind Kejriwal be able to shoot the same arrows a decade from now, when in the grime of governance he has some wrong decisions in his quiver?

Further, making such wild allegations, without any substantiation, is the mark of an outsider, a disrupter. For others, the stakes are too high—for hidden in the crevices and the folds are corrupt practices, contracts, tenders, obligations, money trails, file notings that can backfire. Only an Arvind Kejriwal and his motley crew of zero-track-record leaders can shoot from the hip on the eve of one of the most closely-watched elections in history. If some of those whom he has alleged to be corrupt drag him to court, for say defamation, it opens up the possibility of long years with the threat of investigations looming over such complainants. Such actions will also make him some sort of victim, strengthening his identity as an aam aadmi fighting for the aam aadmi—a political hero.

Arvind Kejriwal's articulation of solutions sounds fuzzy because it seems he's learning on the job. On the issue of Delhi riots in which around three thousand Sikhs were killed, he said it's been twenty-eight years since the riots and Sikhs have been asking for a special investigation; BJP and Congress have also been asking for it. Both have been in power in Delhi and at the Centre, and despite that AAP has had to ask for it themselves. 'I met the lieutenant governor yesterday and asked for an investigation and he agreed. On Monday's cabinet meeting we will ask for this investigation.' There are problems in the country, he said, 'but slowly I'm understanding that solutions can be provided.'

It's not that the rhetoric is missing. 'We are not here to take power. We're not here to do the politics of power. We are not here to fight for three hundred seats, four hundred seats. We are not here to become chief ministers. We are not here to become ministers. We are not here to become prime ministers,' he says to an engaged audience. 'We are here to remove corruption from this country. Our aim is to have not even a single corrupt member of Parliament or a member with a criminal record. We want freedom from families and dynasties in Parliament. We will not fight elections. People of this country will fight elections. We are offering an alternative to Congress and BJP. We will try and make Elections 2014 not another election; we will make it a revolution in politics.'

Howsoever fuzzy, Arvind Kejriwal's political rhetoric feeds India's rage—and draws the aam aadmi towards him. Irrespective of whether this rage of the aam aadmi translates into votes for AAP in this election or next, the awakening to possibilities has happened. This is the biggest disruption Arvind Kejriwal has brought into the expectations, the hopes, the dreams of the aam aadmi. This is his currency of change. Whether voters transact with it, however, remains to be seen.

10

HAND OF GOD

The journey of Arvind Kejriwal from an atheist to a believer needs to be seen in wider perspective than merely the touch of a miracle. An overwhelming sense of emotion can capture the sharpest of minds, the strongest of hearts. A sudden success in Delhi, seemingly impossible—and short-lived—no doubt, cannot merely be attributed to the equally sudden blessings of gods. Besides, to measure blessings based on something so fleeting, so on-the-surface, so tiny in the larger scheme of things, makes faith vulnerable. What if the party fails in the general elections in May or in the assembly elections in Haryana in October or other assembly elections thereafter? Will Arvind Kejriwal return to being an atheist? In which case, we need to ask if his celebration of and gratitude to the gods is a mere transaction, a petty give-and-take.

'I have begun believing in God and I have admitted this in many interviews,' Arvind Kejriwal says, his breath short from the intense morning walk. 'Whatever is happening is not because of us. Something very powerful and divine is happening. This entire big thing…' he trails off, only to pick it up again, '…a common man like me becomes a chief minister…the strike call by Anna got thousands of people to the streets…' But isn't this what is known as the power of the people? Where does the intervention of the divine enter this conversation? Arvind Kejriwal is silent for moments that stretch, creating a vacuum in the conversation.

'Power of people could have happened earlier too but why is it all happening now? Several forces and some divine intervention alone can make this happen. And this, despite the biggest of conspiracies against us. There is something divine. I am not an atheist and this is a core change in me. I think it is divine.'

The hand of god in the victory of AAP is a motif that now peppers Arvind Kejriwal's speeches. 'I wish to thank Parampitah Parmeshwar, Ishwar, Allah, Waheguru for this victory that looks like a miracle of nature,' he said at his oath-taking speech on 28 December 2013, his sincerity ringing deep. 'Barely two years ago, we couldn't have thought that in our country there could be such a revolution, when we would be able to overthrow corrupt parties and establish the rule of the people,' he paused to punctuate his speech with a trademark cough. 'This did not happen because of us. This is definitely a miracle of nature. And for this I thank Bhagwan, Ishwar, Allah.'

So deep is this sense of the miracle that it has percolated down into the party. 'When we started in the first week of August 2012, I met Arvind and he said, "Humne keh to diya, ab karenge kaise yeh nahin maloom (we've formed the party but how we will deliver I have no idea)." The enormity of it was so strange that to think we could achieve it was not easy,' says Pankaj Gupta, the party's treasurer, sitting behind a table for two that's seating six, in a ten foot by twelve foot room for eight but one that's crammed with bodies. 'But as we started taking steps, one step at a time, started discussing what could be done, and things started falling in place, it seemed that there was some divine power, that whatever we were doing was proving to be correct,' he paused to articulate the 'miracle' into words. 'I would say that results are forcing us to start believing that there is a divine (force) taking care of us.'

Unlike Arvind Kejriwal, who was an atheist until success

showered its blessings of belief, Pankaj Gupta seems to be an agnostic. 'I don't know if I am a believer or not. It is very difficult to say. Because I never go to the mandir specifically to pray. But if someone there is doing something I have no problem.' How is it that the atheist and the agnostic were overwhelmed by the sense and touch of the divine at the same time, in the same space, working on the same purpose? Neither of them look like they play, or even need to play, the faith card in their politics; they have nothing to gain from aligning with either religion or with secularism. And yet, both speak with a conviction that goes beyond words. On the other hand, if it is indeed a transactional relationship—success creates faith, failure destroys it—it is a foolish statement to make.

What is the truth?

To figure that out, we need to look beyond individuals. An invisible force is pushing not merely Arvind Kejriwal and his politics towards change, it has also equally gripped the thought processes of Rahul Gandhi and Narendra Modi. Each of these three faces, as well as the ideas behind them, have their set of followers blinded by faith in their leaders' prowess, detractors rubbishing any and every statement the other two make. Any idea that they pronounce, finds commentators who are willing to lead all three to the gallows, tossing words like democracy and liberalism that don't belong to India but that have left their imprint here.

Each of them is experimenting with the idea of a new India. Each is being driven by this force. Each is articulating it to whatever degree possible. Each is fighting battles to capture what is no longer the mind of the voter; it's her soul they want. The status quo, represented by Rahul Gandhi, may seem to clash with the change the high-decibel, fifty-six-inch-chested Narendra Modi brings. Both, in turn, are being influenced by this new kid on the block, Arvind Kejriwal, whose idea of change is disruption, even as the end product—the promise of better governance—remains the same.

Incumbent Rahul Gandhi wants to harness and propel the voices of his party workers into the governing landscape. His first experiment of trying out a concept he has borrowed from the US style of elections, the 'primaries', will see results in thirteen Lok Sabha seats in the general elections, three months away. The aam aadmi's political aspirations are disturbing the status quo fostered by a dynastic regime. And ironically, it is India's primary dynast that is leading the change.

For all the criticism he gets for being born in India's most powerful family, it is heartening to see Rahul Gandhi listen to the voices of change that have gripped the nation. He may not succeed yet. But the fact that he is sensitive to it and is attempting a makeover despite having no reason to do so—a party of retainers, sycophants and bootlickers, continues to slaver for power under the 'Gandhi' brand—shows a push that goes beyond his pale of understanding or articulation. It is the force of the aam aadmi's aspirations, reaching out through modes beyond communication technologies, that is driving Rahul Gandhi.

The focus of challenger Narendra Modi is in offering a strong leadership that he alleges has been missing for the past nine years. In strength of action lies growth, he feels. The future of a young India can be ushered in decisive strokes, he extols. And as the BJP cadre converges towards him, speaking about a glorious 'Congress-free' India in one, concentrated voice, that convergence too can be seen to be a ground-up phenomenon, only more organised. Narendra Modi is the face of what Rahul Gandhi says he hopes to do—listen to voices of party workers to help choose a leader.

Unlike Rahul Gandhi, the deification of Narendra Modi by

BJP is unique. While Rahul Gandhi's is a fall from the graces of dynasty, in Narendra Modi we see the creation of a larger-than-life poster boy of a future, not unlike the sky-high scaffoldings that dot the Tamil Nadu political landscape. Narendra Modi's articulation of the decentralisation of power, with states as administrative entities, is in deep harmony with the soul of India. Again, it is the force of the aam aadmi's expression for change that's driving Narendra Modi.

With Arvind Kejriwal, the sense of change is wider, more profound and definitely more tangible and palpable. With no cadre to back him, no workers to organise, no history to lean on or take a leap forward from—a distinct advantage in these disruptive times—his is an entrepreneurial endeavour that draws intellectual strength from the freedom movement, Mahatma Gandhi's brand of self-denial and the conviction that disruptive politics will bring him closer to the aam aadmi. There is no doubt that breaking institutions down is easier than creating them, and if a positive politics—in this case, an anti-corruption stance—is wound around that imploding narrative of disruption, it may work, as witnessed during Kejriwal's forty-nine day stint as chief minister.

The ideas of Arvind Kejriwal—anti-corruption, decentralisation of decision making, devolution of power to gram sabhas and mohalla sabhas, discarding VIP privileges and so on—capture the angst of the aam aadmi like neither of the other faces have or can. The primaries Rahul Gandhi is trying to execute in thirteen Lok Sabha seats is inspired not just by US politics but by Arvind Kejriwal, for whom ground-up democracy is a political statement. His devolution of power to the smallest political entity goes farther than Narendra Modi's sketch of decentralisation. As a disrupter, he is setting the standards here; as a political entrepreneur, he has the luxury to do so.

Despite these differences in outer manifestations, there is something deeper that's binding all three politicians. The glue binding them is a question India's aam aadmi is asking: with the rights, privileges that exist for those in power, where are the outcomes? The call for change through various media like TV, internet, newspapers, protest marches, rallies and so on, is merely the outer expression of a far wider change that's strumming in the hearts of the Indian people. It is in the air, electrifying the atmosphere with hope for greater equality, justice, truer freedom, with the promise of a vaster, deeper democracy, a democracy that goes beyond rights and privileges, a democracy that serves all citizens, not the few with power.

Future historians might call this 'a spiritual tipping point'.

What we're talking about is a spiritual transformation of Indian politics, without the fuss of religion, morality, rituals, ceremony—spirituality has no religion and the religious are hardly ever spiritual. We are probably sitting on the cusp of a major shift in consciousness that all nations go through every few centuries. The Renaissance in Europe, the destruction and subsequent rise of Germany after World War I, the Celtic revival of Ireland in the twentieth century, the ongoing Islamic revival since the 1970s and its current broadening through the Arab Spring, are all examples of moments in time that changed destinies of nations.

'The lifeless attempt of the last generation to imitate and reproduce with a servile fidelity the ideals and forms of the West has been no true indication of the political mind and genius of the Indian people,' wrote Sri Aurobindo two generations ago in his 1921 essay, 'A Defence of Indian Culture'. 'But again amid all the mist of confusion there is still the possibility of a new twilight, not of an evening but a morning Yuga-sandhya. India of the ages is not dead nor has she spoken her last creative word; she lives and has still something to do for herself and the human peoples. And that which must seek now to awake is not an anglicised oriental people, docile pupil of the West and doomed to repeat the cycle of the Occident's success and failure, but still the ancient immemorable Shakti recovering her deepest self, lifting her head higher towards the supreme source of light and strength and turning to discover the complete meaning and a vaster form of her Dharma.'

What is this 'Shakti' he refers to? 'What is a nation,' he asked in a 1905 pamphlet, 'Bhawani Mandir', arguably the most inspiring call to stand up for the country, ever. 'What is our mother-country? It is not a piece of earth, nor a figure of speech, nor a fiction of the mind. It is a mighty Shakti, composed of the Shaktis of all the millions of units that make up the nation, just as Bhawani Mahisha-Mardini sprang into being from the Shaktis of all the millions of gods assembled in one mass of force and welded into unity. The Shakti we call India, Bhawani Bharati, is the living unity of the Shaktis of three hundred millions of people; but she is inactive, imprisoned in the magic circle of tamas, the self-indulgent inertia and ignorance of her sons. To get rid of tamas we have but to wake the Brahma within.'

'What is the meaning of spiritualising the political life of the country,' Mahatma Gandhi asked in a 1915 speech. 'What is the meaning of spiritualising myself? That question has come before me often and to you it may seem one thing, to me it may seem another thing; it may mean different things to the different members of the Servants of India Society itself. It shows much difficulty and it shows the difficulties of all those who want to love their country, who want to serve their country and who want to honour their country. I think the political life must be an echo of private life and that there cannot be any divorce between the two.'

Rahul Gandhi, Narendra Modi and Arvind Kejriwal are probably listening—or being forced to listen—to the inner urgings of India. From the outside, this change is in the same direction as other such collations pushing for change. The freedom movement that climaxed in 1947 captured the aspirations of an enslaved India. Reservations, for scheduled castes and tribes right away and for other backward castes in 1989, took charge of the aspirations of a vast majority of India's voiceless. Regional aspirations followed, with 1996 being the tipping point with vote share of regional parties exceeding the 50 per cent mark for the first time. Each of these painted India's vibrancy in new colours, captured the aspirations of millions of Indians, and consolidated India's democracy like never before.

Now, the same phenomenon is repeating itself, with the aspirations of another section of people called the aam aadmi being acknowledged. This section, despite being unencumbered by histories of prejudice, feels disenfranchised—it is free; it is casteless and there is no high or low differential; it can be from any region of India; it can belong to any religion. Yet it is powerless. Probably for the first time, the hopes of the rich and the poor alike are being captured. The change being ushered in blurs the gender divide. It sweeps over the age gap. It binds people across all educational backgrounds. The aam aadmi phenomenon is really the united aspirations of millions of Indians, who for the first time, have come together to drive change. The vehicle for this change is not just Arvind Kejriwal and AAP; this change is coming from traditional parties, as well. The advantage AAP has is a clean slate; the advantage Congress and BJP have is organisation power and governance experience. All three have to harness the power of the people and ensure their aspirations and expectations are met.

Perhaps the sense of a nation we lost, after long years of

slavery and colonisation, is now returning with new vigour, greater creativity—and most importantly, in the midst of acute disruption—forcing all of us to introspect. This collective cry of 1.2 billion Indians (minus, of course, the five thousand-or-so hyper-privileged) is leading Rahul Gandhi to change the 'system'; it is pushing Narendra Modi to offer a new 'leadership'; and is impelling Arvind Kejriwal towards, to borrow from Austrian economist Joseph Schumpeter, creative destruction in India's politics.

India today is the collective voice of a nation in agony and this voice now commands power. It is sending a strong message to Rahul Gandhi, Narendra Modi and Arvind Kejriwal, the three faces and ideas that hope to govern it going forward. The brutalised body of India is there for all to see—even sub-Saharan Africa has better human development indicators than India. Its mind, conquered and in the process of being consolidated by a grammar that doesn't belong to it, waits for a fierce and urgent resurgence. Its soul, long smothered, awaits an incarnation. It hopes to wrench the ideal of politics from the clutches of trade and profession and place it back where it belongs—to serve, and find salvation in the process of that service.

Much of political discourse is about the tangible, the material, the vital. But real change revolves around national swadharma, around India attaining selfhood. When the cry of 'Vande Mataram' echoes at the rallies of Narendra Modi and Arvind Kejriwal, the surface trawlers might see it as a repackaging of an old and even irrelevant freedom movement. But when you hear the cry in context of a change that's coming towards us at an unbelievable speed, it sings a different song. Leaders would do well to follow the aspirations of the aam aadmi and envision the swadharma of India as the collective swadharma of all its citizens.

We need a change of laws and rules that have been blindly

borrowed from our colonial past—laws that were designed to keep India enslaved. We need a change in leadership, and not merely leaders—politicians who listen to and engage with aam aadmi. We need a change in the mode of social engagement, that brings back what Rahul Gandhi calls empowerment, Narendra Modi labels as trust and Arvind Kejriwal terms as swaraj. We need a change in relationship between the governors and the governed, using tools that Rahul Gandhi calls primaries, Narendra Modi labels as governance and Arvind Kejriwal terms as devolution.

In fact, the aam aadmi phenomenon goes beyond the boundaries of India. From the Arab Spring in West Asia and North Africa to the Occupy and the 99 Per Cent movements in Europe, the US and the West, the spirit of transformation is upon us across the world. The aam aadmi that Congress labelled and which AAP politicised is not exclusively an Indian phenomenon anymore; it is a global unification. Almost like the fraternity Jean-Jacques Rousseau referred to—it follows liberty and equality—a new brotherhood is beginning to bind races and peoples across the world, without their conscious knowledge.

It is this spirit that Rahul Gandhi, Narendra Modi and Arvind Kejriwal have to acknowledge, when they make their promises, organise plans and offer change. Irrespective of who gets to govern India, these transformative forces can no longer be smothered; they are here to stay. The unified soul of the aam aadmi is now cutting through and severely disrupting traditional modes of governance and politics. The common man is rising in a spiritual storm; leaders must bend and serve or else be blown over. The hand of god is really the soul of the aam aadmi, blessing all parties with agnostic detachment and cornering them into delivering a new, dynamic and audacious tomorrow.

EPILOGUE: CONSOLIDATION OF AUDACITY

The cold winter wind tugs at our jackets as we walk on the main road connecting Greater Kailash II to Alaknanda. It's a wide road with palatial homes of the super-rich looking down at us. This is perhaps one of the widest intra-neighbourhood roads in the city of Delhi. This road, and several such, have been taken over by residents, who have illegally extended their large homes on to the road and turned them into private and fenced gardens. Beyond these gardens are parked their BMWs, Mercedes, Land Rovers and other symbols of luxury, making the wide road that much narrower. Once upon a time, the pavement across the road was meant for pedestrians to walk on. Today, it is smothered by cars.

'This is our next fight,' Ashutosh Dikshit says as we walk on the road, fast cars now sweeping cold air into our faces as they scream past. 'We want our pavements back.' As members of Citizens' Alliance trail around cars and vendors blocking pedestrian traffic, we come across a large site, where million-dollar plus homes are under construction. 'This will make matters worse for walkers.' A group of drivers and security guards, who ensure that the space encroached upon by their wealthy employers outside the large homes is not taken away, look at us with disdain.

'This fight for pavements is going to be a tougher fight than the fight for the removal of the mega mall,' Ashutosh Dikshit says. 'Here, we have to bring a change within the community. On the other hand, it may not be so difficult. I think once change is in the air, people begin to respond. It will be a different kind of fight. It might not even be fair to call it a fight. It is more about engaging the community in a discussion and bringing about a debate around freeing the pavements for people to walk on. This is both legal and justifiable.'

And even before the setting up of a mega mall has been permanently stalled and pavements handed over, the aam aadmi of Citizens' Alliance is readying to tackle other issues. 'We have a library that doesn't function. We wanted to adopt a government school and try and take care of it. In a large group of people there are various drives and not necessarily everything gets taken up because we don't have the bandwidth. So we have to focus on one thing at a time. Also remember that none of these are projects that can happen overnight.'

You can sense rebellion, audacity in the air. For too long too many citizens have been taken for granted—by governments, by vested interests driving those governments, and, in a race to the bottom, by fellow citizens themselves. The fact that professionals from the middle class, who are beneficiaries of all that's good in India, from jobs to consumption, are out on the roads trying to save their neighbourhoods, shows the groundswell of angst that citizens carry and which AAP is harnessing into a political voice. The atmosphere of an audacious citizenry is growing, one issue, one neighbourhood, one right at a time.

While Citizens' Alliance was expanding its audacity in the neighbourhood, Arvind Kejriwal was scaling up with the same audacity, on a grander canvass. He announced a new short-term goal, a target to get one crore members by 26 January. In a national membership drive called 'mein bhi aam aadmi' (I too am a common man), he gave five venues for those seeking to become members, including a phone and a web option, and waived off the ten rupee membership fee. 'But our membership drive will continue after that as well,' he said. All of sixty thousand people joined on day one.

The audacious rise of the aam aadmi, seen through the actions of Citizens' Alliance in New Delhi's Alaknanda, is not going to come to a halt. The phenomenon is national, with a sudden surge of energy now flashing like lightening across the country. From 1,453 Dongria Kondh tribals on an isolated mountain in Niyamgiri (Odisha) fighting the government and a company seeking to extract bauxite from their beloved mountain, to the eleven thousand people, largely fishermen, living in Koodankulam, Tamil Nadu, protesting against the setting up of a nuclear plant—the rise of the aam aadmi is sending a message to the political leadership—listen to us, involve us in decisions regarding our environment, our neighbourhoods.

Or else, step aside.

From aam aadmi struggles to AAP, the leap has been smooth so far. But will the grime of governance taint Arvind Kejriwal and his well-meaning but inexperienced hands? Will citizens who voted for him in Delhi, but saw him walk away in forty-nine days, give him another chance? If he gets another chance, will he indulge in serial resignations? Or will he learn to accommodate the opposing voices India's democracy throws up and sing his freedom song, despite being out of beat with the other parties? Will those people who have been able to bring, organise and steer change in their communities—from stalling mega malls to reclaiming pavements—stop? Will Arvind Kejriwal be able to channel these energies, organise those who are challenging what is traditionally known as 'development', and yank them into the mainstream?

That is a story still to play out. And while we wait for data to get created and trends to emerge, the only thing we can say with some degree of conviction is that this is an irreversible phenomenon. It is not restricted to neighbourhoods or cities or states or even countries. The audacious rise of the aam aadmi is an international phenomenon. It is going to change the landscape of global discourse. And in places, it already has. It is going to redefine and refine politics in no less revolutionary a manner than the birth of democracy itself.

In a few years, Citizens' Alliance may be forgotten. Over time, we will know whether AAP was another flash in the political pan or if it will have a lasting presence. We will also see whether other parties get subsumed by this storm or quell it. 'Parties will come and go,' says Baijayant Jay Panda. 'I think the empowerment of the citizen is an ongoing story. It's been going on gradually for the last sixty-seven years. Today, we've reached a tipping point. This is not the end of the story. In many ways this is only the beginning of the story. And for many decades we will continue to witness the empowerment of the citizen in a democracy.'

But of three things we are sure. One, the audacious aam aadmi is here to stay and his ranks will grow—deal with it. Two, the disruption he causes will cut across politics, economics, society, culture—embrace it. And three, the political landscape, as a result, will change—adapt to it. Welcome to the new world of the audacious aam aadmi.

Made in the USA
Monee, IL
03 May 2026

49438692R00152